Ichinen Sanzen - 84,000 Dhammakkhanda

Scientology of Happiness, Peace, and Enlightenment

Suddhadhamma

Dr. Vinod D. Rangari

D. Litt.

First Edition: 2025
Copyright © Dr. Vinod D. Rangari 2025
All Rights Reserved.

ISBN

Hardcase 979-8-89610-995-2
Paperback 979-8-89556-963-4

Dedicated to Triple Gems

The Buddha, Dhamma, and Sangha

&

All Diligent Seekers of

Truth, Happiness, Peace, & Wisdom

Contents

Preface

In the ever-evolving landscape of spiritual and scientific inquiry, the quest to understand the nature of human consciousness and the path to enlightenment remains timeless and urgent. It is within this dynamic framework that I present my work, "Ichinen Sanzen: 84,000 Dhammakkhandha-Scientology of Happiness, Peace, and Enlightenment." This book attempts to navigate the intricate convergence of Buddhist meditative practices and modern scientific perspectives, offering a comprehensive exploration of how these two realms of knowledge can inform and enrich one another.

At the outset, I would like to clarify my perspective on the title of this book, "Ichinen Sanzen-84,000 Dhammakkhandha: Scientology of Happiness, Peace, and Enlightenment." The first part of this title integrates two traditional Buddhist practices: Mahayana's 'Ichinen Sanzen' and Theravada's '84,000 Dhammakkhandha'. Although literal meaning of Ichinen Sanzen, '3,000 Realms in a single thought' resonated with me, it was too lengthy for the title. Regarding the second part, 'Scientology of Happiness, Peace and Enlightenment,' my intention is clear. I have utilized the word 'Scientology' to convey total scientific relativity, leveraging its Latin root 'scintia,' shared with 'science.' While Hubbard's Scientology focuses on spiritual knowledge and self-discovery, I partially align with this view, ensuring empirical scientific enquiry remains within scope. In essence, this title harmoniously blends the Buddha's Dhamma with scientific enquiry towards seeking happiness, peace, and liberation from suffering through an integrated approach.

The genesis of this book can be traced back to my previous research, *"Encounter with Satipaṭṭhānā: 84,000 Dhammakkhandhā of Buddhism,"* which delved into the Buddhist framework of 84,000

Dhammakkhandha. This initial exploration laid the groundwork for a deeper investigation into the relationship between this framework and the Nichiren Buddhist concept of the 3,000 Realms. It is evident that both frameworks, while rooted in different traditions, share a common goal: the attainment of enlightenment and the cultivation of inner peace and happiness.

The objective of this book is to present a systematic and respectful analysis of how the Buddhist teachings on 3,000 Realms and 84,000 Dhammakkhandha intersect with contemporary scientific understanding. This endeavor was not undertaken lightly; it involved a careful and nuanced approach to ensure that the spiritual significance of these teachings was preserved while exploring their compatibility with modern scientific insights.

The journey begins with an exploration of the historical perspectives of Buddhism and its meditative practices. Chapter one provides an overview of various Buddhist traditions, including Theravada, Mahayana, Zen, Sarvastivada, Tibetan Vajrayana, and Nichiren Buddhism. This broad overview establishes a foundation for understanding the diverse approaches within Buddhism towards achieving spiritual goals.

In Chapter two, I delve into the concept of Ichinen Sanzen, or "3,000 Realms in a Single Moment of Life." This chapter examines how this profound idea can be experienced within a single thought moment and discusses the Lotus Sutra and its recitation mantra, "Nam Myoho Renge Kyo." The exploration of Nichiren Buddhism and its interpretation of Ichinen Sanzen provides a crucial context for understanding this concept.

The subsequent chapters offer a critical analysis of both the 3,000 Realms and the Theravada philosophy of 84,000 Dhammakkhandha. Chapter three explores the Buddhist viewpoint of causal genesis, detailing the relativity and validity of the ten Worlds, extended ten Worlds, ten Factors, and three Realms of Existence. It also addresses the perceptibility, limitations, and practical obstacles encountered in the practice of 3,000 Realms.

Chapter four investigates the hypothesis that Satipaṭṭhānā meditation serves as a foundation for the clear perception of reality. It elaborates on the "Ekayano Maggo" presented by the Buddha in the Mahāsatipaṭṭhānā Sutta and explores the mind as a base for all sensory streams. This chapter critically examines the five hindrances (nivaranā), five aggregates (khandhā), and sensory bases (āyatana), proposing a framework for integrating modern scientific insights with Buddhist practices.

Chapter five builds on this foundation by detailing the framework of 84,000 Dhammakkhandha, including the interplay of seven factors of enlightenment and the Four Noble Truths. This chapter aims to establish the interconnectivity of these elements as a psycho-cosmic map for understanding happiness, peace, wisdom, and enlightenment.

In Chapter six, the focus shifts to the relativity of 3,000 Realms and 84,000 Dhammakkhandha in cultivating insight. This chapter correlates various Buddhist practices, including the 84,000 hooks of Zen Buddhism, the Dhammakkhandha of Sarvastivada, and the concept of 84,000 dhamma aggregates envisioned in the legend of King Asoka, to present a comprehensive view of the Buddha's complete teachings.

Chapter seven explores the cognitive scientology of happiness, peace, and enlightenment, examining how these concepts relate to modern neurological science. I propose a hypothesis on the "Ten-step mindfulness" as a mode for establishing mindfulness and understanding reality, highlighting the role of meditative practices in achieving spiritual well-being.

The final chapter addresses the conditions that either support or obstruct the journey of meditators on the path to happiness, peace, and wisdom. It provides practical insights into the background support systems available within the frameworks of Ichinen sanzen and Dhammakkhandha, offering guidance for those seeking to cultivate insight and wisdom.

This book represents a sincere effort to bridge the ancient teachings of Buddhism with contemporary scientific perspectives. While I am aware that my analysis may provoke diverse reactions, my intention is not to challenge or undermine established traditions but to contribute to a broader understanding that harmonizes spiritual and scientific viewpoints.

I extend my deepest gratitude to Most Ven. Bhikku Aryawangso Guruji, Chief Buddhist Monk of the Sangha Supreme Council of Thailand, for his invaluable blessings. My association with him over the past fifteen years-through various Dhamma activities and meditation retreats-has enriched me with profound insights. I am heartily grateful to Dr. Mahesh Deokar, Professor and Head, Department of Pali and Buddhist Studies, Savitribai Phule Pune University, Pune for his comprehensive foreword which offers a clear and thoughtful outline of this book. I extend my heartfelt gratitude to Prof. Asanga Tilakaratne, Emeritus Professor of Buddhist Studies, University of Colombo, Sri Lanka for his insightful blurb for this book. I offer my sincere gratitude to Dr. A. H. Salunkhe, a distinguished thinker and writer, for his constructive criticism and kind words of appreciation which greatly inspired and fueled my enthusiasm to continue writing this book. I am thankful to Dr. Alok Kumar Chakrawal, Vice Chancellor, Guru Ghasidas University, Bilaspur, for his encouragement and support during a challenging period. His interactions were indeed a blessing in disguise which instilled in me the confidence to pursue this endeavour with renewed vigour. Special thanks to my dear friend Ayus. Ashok Wathore, whose selfless encouragement and support made all the difference in the final stretch of this publication journey.

My father had always been in my thoughts during my good and deep meditation practice and even after 40 years, I feel as if he is shining my path in the darkness like a beacon with a smile on his face. My mother has always showered her blessings upon me. I heartily wish their wellbeing and progress on the path of Dhamma in their future life. My brother

Ayus J. D. Rangari has always been a continuous source of motivation and encouragement. I am thankful to all my brothers, sisters, friends and well-wishers for their company and help in shaping and constructing my personality to be able to perceive, clearly understand and write my revelations on Ichinen sanzen and 84,000 Dhammakkhandha. Back home, all my family members my wife Dr. Varsha, son Vivarta and daughter Varshika, filled me with motivation at all times. They had shown their patience and forbearance towards me.

I offer my sincere appreciation to my nephew Ayus. Vivek Khobragade, whose tireless dedication and expertise were invaluable in checking and refining the manuscript during its development and publication. I am thankful to Facit Printers, Nagpur for graphic design of the book. I acknowledge with deep appreciation the professionalism and expertise of Notion Publication, Chennai, and the guidance of Ms. Nidhi Setty, Senior Publishing Manager, in making this book a reality. May they all be happy, peaceful and on clear and progressive path of Dhamma. I invite readers to engage with the concepts presented in this book with an open mind and a contemplative spirit. The insights and conclusions offered here are meant to stimulate further reflection and discussion, ultimately enriching our collective journey on the right path of happiness, peace and enlightenment.

Date: October 17, 2024   With deep respect and gratitude,
        Ashwin Purnima

Dr. Vinod D. Rangari
Professor,
Guru Ghasidas University,
Bilaspur (C.G), India

Foreword

Ichinen Sanzen-84,000 *Dhammakkhandhā* is the second book by Dr. Vinod D. Rangari on the topic of *Dhammakkhandhā*. The first book entitled 'The 84,000 *Dhammakkhandha* of Buddhism' was published in 2019. It is indeed amazing that Dr. Rangari who is a scholar of Pharmaceutical Sciences has not only developed a keen interest in Buddhism but has thoroughly studied Buddhism specially from the perspective of a practitioner in the search of truth. In his first book Dr. Rangari has tried to unravel the mystery behind the figure 84,000 associated with the word Dhamma and *Dhammakkhandhā*. He has approached the problem of the exact significance of the number 84,000 from a historical point of view. Since, the textual evidence regarding the number 84,000 is scanty and inconclusive, Dr. Rangari had tried to approach the problem based on his meditative experience and intuitive knowledge. In his first book Dr. Rangari had connected the number 84,000 with the practice of *Dhammānupassanā*, which forms a part of the four *satipaṭṭhāna* practices taught by the Buddha. Although the solution provided by the author was speculative in nature and could not be verified with the help of textual evidences, it encourages us to approach the question of 84,000 *Dhammakkhandha*s from a totally new point of view. Dr. Rangari was awarded with the Degree of D. Litt. for this book by the Kavikulaguru Kalidas Sanskrit Vishwavidyalaya, Nagpur.

Dr. Rangari has now come up with the new book 'Ichinen Sanzen-84,000 Dhammakkhanda: Scientology of Happiness, Peace and Enlightenment,' which can be seen as a sequel to his earlier book. In this new book, Dr. Rangari has elaborated on his thesis that the number 84,000 refers to the entire world of *Dhammānupassanā* practice comprising its five major components, namely, *nīvaraṇa*s (hindrances), *khandha*s (aggregates), *āyatana*s (internal and external sensory and mental spheres), *bojjhaṅga*s (factors of enlightenment) and *sacca*s (four noble truths).

The book attracts its readers right from its title. It clearly indicates author's intention to discuss the two important concepts in Buddhism. The first is Ichinen Sanzen, which is a Japanese term and the second is *Dhammakkhandha* which is a Pali term. The concept of Ichinen Sanzen is found in the Nichiren sect of the Japanese Buddhism, which is based on the Saddharmapuṇḍarīkasūtra popularly known as the Lotus Sūtra of the Mahayana school. In the second chapter of this book the author has elaborated upon the concept of Ichinen sanzen of experiencing 3,000 realms in a single moment. Although Nichiren sect is gradually becoming popular in India, its authentic and scientific knowledge is still wanting in the Indian society. The present book fills that gap to a certain extent by providing an outline of the Nichiren sect and detailed exposition of the Ichinen sanzen. Dhammakkhandha is an important philosophical concept in early Buddhism. The author has differentiated the concept of *Dhammakkhandha* from the concept of mere *dhamma*. He argues that in the textual tradition the word *dhamma*, especially in connection with the number 84,000, is related to the teaching given by the Buddha and his disciples, whereas the Buddha's use of the word *Dhammakkhanda* appears to be peculiar. It does not seem to be connected with teaching but rather to the mental contents of an individual. A detailed exposition of the word *Dhammakkhandha* in the context of *Dhammānupassanā* practice of *Satipaṭṭhāna* can be found in chapters 4 and 5 of this book. Although there are a number of books and articles written on the *Satipaṭṭhāna* meditation, the explanation of its *Dhammānupassanā* factor from the point of view of the concept of *Dhammakkhandha* is a unique contribution of Dr. Rangari.

The second part of the title 'Scientology of Happiness, Peace and Enlightenment' brings forth the purpose and methodology of the book. The ultimate aim of writing this book is to provide its readers a key to happiness, peace, and enlightenment. As observed by the author, this key is not a magical spell or a matter of superstition or speculation. Being a scientist himself, Dr. Rangari has applied a test of scientific enquiry to the practice of *Satipaṭṭhāna* meditation which, according to him, is the key to achieve the desired goal. In this context, the author has discussed Buddha's charter of free enquiry given in the *Kālāma sutta* of the *Aṅguttaranikāya*. He has applied this method of scientific enquiry to the practice of Ichinen Sanzen and the chanting of the mantras "*Nam Myoho Renge Kyo*" and "*Om Mani Padme Hum*". Since the experience of Ichinen Sanzen does not fall within the normal limits of human mind, the author has showed his inclination to the *Satipaṭṭhāna* practice that stands to the test of scientific free enquiry. This is well explained by the author in the third chapter of this book. His scientific approach is well reflected in the word scientology used in the title. The term was first coined by an American science fiction writer L. Ron Hubbard in 1955. It means a religious system based on the seeking of self-knowledge and spiritual fulfilments through graded courses of study and training. In the opinion of Dr. Rangari, the *Satipaṭṭhāna* meditation is a scientific training that helps a practitioner to achieve the goal of happiness, peace, and enlightenment.

Thus, the title of the book fulfils all the traditional requirements of a good title. According to the Indian commentarial tradition, a good title clearly states the subject matter of the book along with its purpose and the nature. The title of this book fulfils all these three criteria and hence can be called as an appropriate title.

Dr. Rangari has discussed the scientology of Ichinen Sanzen and 84,000 *Dhammakkhandha*s in this over 300 pages long book divided into ten chapters. In the first chapter the author has taken a brief historical overview of different Buddhist traditions and their meditation practices. These includes Theravada, Mahayana, Zen, Sarvastivada, Tibetan Buddhism, and Nichiren Buddhism. The terms Theravada and Sarvastivada are often used keeping in mind the philosophical position adopted by their followers. They have no direct bearing on the mode of practice or its goal. In other words, a Thervadin can very well aspire for Buddhahood and hence can be called as Mahayanist, whereas a follower of Mādhyamaka philosophy aspiring for mere *Arahathood* can be declared to be a *Śrāvakayānist*. It is observed that common people and sometimes even scholars use the word Theravadin as alternative to Hinayānists and the word Mādhyamaka and Yogācārin as equivalents of Mahayanists. Boundaries between different *yāna*s and *darśanprasthāna*s need to be understood clearly to have the correct grasp of Buddhism.

While explaining the concept of Ichinen sanzen (the 3,000 realms) the author has equated it with the expression *trisāhasra-mahāsāhasra-lokadhātu,* the expression commonly used in many Mahayana *sūtra*s. In fact, according to the commentarial tradition the latter does not mean 3,000 world elements (*lokadhātu*). Whether the 3,000 realms of Ichinen Sanzen can be equated with the idea of *trisāhasra-mahāsāhasra-lokadhātu* is a question that needs to be investigated further. Similarly, in chapter two, the author has speculated the connection between the word *Nam* in the mantra *Nam Myo ho Renge Kyo* with the word *nāma* in the expression *nāma-rūpa*. Since the word *Nam* in the mantra is commonly understood as salutation, and therefore equivalent to the Sanskrit word *namaḥ* or Pali *namo*, connecting it with the word *nāma* representing mental aspect of our personality as against the material, appears to be a bit farfetched. Another interesting point to be noted is the list of ten worlds given by the author in the third chapter in accordance with the tradition of Ichinen Sanzen. Here we find a slight deviation as compared to the sequence of *gati*s (realms) found in other Buddhist traditions. In Ichinen Sanzen the animal world is listed after the world of hungry spirits and before the world of *asura*s. In most of the Buddhist texts that list six *gati*s, the world of animals is placed higher than *asura*s and below the humans. The actual reason for this deviation is unclear and needs some justification. In the same list after the world of Gods there are world of Voice hearers, world of Cause-awakened One, world of Bodhisattvas, and world of Buddhas. If one just reads the English names, one might be puzzled as to what the world of Voice hearers and world of Cause-awakened One mean. However, someone who is acquainted with the Mahayana terminology can immediately spot that the world of Voice hearers is an awkward English translation of the Sanskrit word *Śrāvaka* representing the world of *Arahats*, and Cause-awakened One is that of the Sanskrit word *pratyekabuddha* referring to the world of solitary Buddhas. Such connections with the Theravada or Mahayana scriptures often come to our mind while reading this book.

Dr. Rangari has explained that although the ten worlds of Ichinen sanzen are beyond our normal perception, one can experience them at the emotional or psychological level. The ten worlds represent ten psychological stages associated with the whole range of emotions from most impure to the purest. One can therefore experience these ten worlds within oneself through the experience of these varied emotions. In this sense we can not only experience the ten worlds within ourselves in a single moment, but can also produce these worlds in the form of our emotional responses to different situations. This psychological interpretation of Ichinen sanzen's ten worlds can easily appeal to even a most rational thinker.

One more striking feature of this book is its author's open approach to many spiritual and metaphysical ideas. He does not impose these ideas on his readers but allows them a free choice. He acknowledges that many of these concepts are culturally bound and are acceptable to only those who follow that belief system. Being a scientist himself, Dr. Rangari appears to be more inclined to the empirical approach to the knowledge. Although he does not clearly reject some of the metaphysical ideas or beliefs prevalent in the Nichiren sect, his approach to them is that of a cautious investigator.

At the end of the third chapter the author presents his hypothesis by connecting the idea of 3000 realms with the concept of

Dhammakkhandha. He proposes that just as Nichiren has taught the practice of experiencing 3000 realms in a single thought moment within oneself through the meditation on the mantra, *Nam Myoho Renge Kyo,* it is possible to establish a connection between the experience of 84,000 *Dhammakkhandha*s and the *Dhammānupassanā* practice of the *Mahāsatipaṭṭhānasutta.* The remaining chapters of this book present a detailed investigation of this hypothesis. He starts his investigation with an overview of the fundamental Buddhist doctrines of four noble truths and dependent origination, and a discussion on the *Vipassanā* and *Satipaṭṭhāna* meditation.

In chapter four the author has presented a detailed exposition of *Satipaṭṭhānasutta* with Pali text and English translation. The main focus of his discussion is on *Dhammānupassanā* section of this *sutta.* As the first part of *Dhammānupassanā* practice he discusses sections on *nīvaraṇa* (hindrances), *khandha* (aggregates) and *āyatana* (sense spheres). The author links this part of *Dhammānupassanā* with the Ichinen Sanzen of Nichiren and draws parallels between them particularly with respect to the experience of sensory world. This chapter is very informative as it provides detailed charts of *nīvaraṇa*s, *khandha*s, and *āyatana*s.

The author continues the discussion on the second part of the *Dhammānupassanā* in the fifth chapter of the book. He presents a detailed analysis of seven factors of enlightenment and four noble truths, and demonstrates how the five subsections of *Dhammānupassanā* can account for the number 84,000. According to Dr. Rangari, all these elements of *Dhammānupassanā* can alone be called *Dhammakkhandha.* When interpreted in this manner, we get the magical figure 84,000 *dhammakkhandha*s. This indeed is an innovative thought. Although we do not find textual support for this understanding in the commentarial tradition of Pali and though the author's claim may appear a bit speculative, it is worth a close scrutiny and investigation by scholars and practitioners of the *satipaṭṭhāna* meditation. It is quite clear that Dr. Rangari had his inspiration from the practice of *satipaṭṭhāna* meditation and he applies that principle to his current investigation of the *Dhammānupassanā* practice. This raises several questions as to the understanding of the words *dhamma* and *Dhammakkhandha,* and the application of principles of one tradition to another. The word *dhamma* in Pali is multifaceted. Its most relevant meaning in the current context is however 'all constituents of the world of experience, physical and mental, external and internal'. The word *Dhammakkhandha* simply means the mass of such *dhamma*s. Although the author tries to distinguish the two words categorically, the line of distinction between them is unclear and warrants thorough investigation. The application of the principles of Ichinen sanzen to the practice of *Dhammānupassanā* is certainly innovative. However, whether it was originally intended by the Buddha is a million-dollar question. The Theravada Buddhist tradition, both textual as well as the one reflected in practice, is completely silent about it. Therefore, this new proposal of Dr. Rangari needs to be examined with utmost care and sincerity. Despite this, one cannot take away from Dr. Rangari the credit of initiating a new discussion and exploration of this topic. As declared by the Buddha, his *dhamma* is open to investigation. It is *ehipassiko*. The author whole-heartedly appreciates this characteristic of *dhamma* and expects the same approach to his new find. This book is an open invitation to scholars and practitioners to come and investigate his proposal.

In the sixth chapter the author has examined the idea of 84,000 *Dhammakkhandha*s from different perspectives. In his opinion the practice of *Dhammānupassanā* is a most elaborate scheme of meditation that can bring the practitioner face to face with the reality. He assures the readers 'Overall, the practice of jhana can help individuals to develop a more direct and immediate perception of reality, which can lead to a greater sense of inner peace, happiness, and well-being'. This is the scientology that can lead us to our ultimate goal as a human being.

The seventh chapter of the book provides a direct initiation into this scientology of happiness, peace, and enlightenment. Dr. Rangari first explains this scientology from the point of modern psychology and neuroscience. He then turns to the scientific explanation of meditation and its impact on our mind and body. In the latter half of this chapter the author has detailed different aspects of Buddhist meditation in a comprehensive manner. It is a good guide for someone trying to understand Buddhist meditation.

In the eighth chapter Dr. Rangari has unfolded the whole inventory of Buddhist practice. Just like the model of destructive and constructive emotions, the author here works with the scheme of promoters and adversaries of happiness, peace, and enlightenment. Such a psychological presentation of the Buddhist path is very educative not only for a practitioner but also for a student of Buddhism. The author has touched upon all the major areas of Buddhist practice and has provided an important guidance to his readers taking a scientific approach.

In the last chapter Dr. Rangari concludes his discussion by summarizing earlier chapters. He makes it quite clear that although the practices of Ichinen Sanzen and *Dhammānupassanā* differ in their practical details, they have the common goal of leading a practitioner to happiness, peace, and enlightenment. When one applies the lens of scientific scrutiny as presented in the *Kālāmasutta*, one finds that the practice of *satipaṭṭhāna* and particularly that of *Dhammānupassanā* helps the practitioner to get a direct and clear experience of the reality, which is necessary for the attainment of the goal of these practices. Learning how to attain happiness, peace, and enlightenment is a prime objective of this book. How to accomplish that learning in a most scientific way is the core question discussed in this book. Is the happiness, peace and freedom from suffering an elusive dream or an achievable reality? Exploring this fundamental question may hold the key to transforming our lives. I feel that Dr. Rangari has tried his best to set out that roadmap for us through his own experience of Buddhist meditation and scientific temperament in accordance with the Buddhist spirit of *ehipassika*. I hope that this book will inspire its readers to undertake the Buddhist meditation in the most sincere and scientific manner to be happy, peaceful, and enlightened living beings.

Date: 29.8.2024

Dr. Mahesh A. Deokar
Professor and Head,
Department of Pali and Buddhist Studies,
Savitribai Phule Pune University,
Pune, India.

Chapter 1

Introduction

Historical Perspectives of Buddhism and Buddhist
Meditative Practices

---

*"The affairs of the world will go on forever. Do not delay the
practice of meditation"*

– Milarepa

Buddhism is a major world religion with a rich history spanning over two and a half millennia. Here is a historical perspective of Buddhism and Buddhist meditative practices, highlighting key developments and milestones:

Origins (6th Century BC): Buddhism traces its origins to Siddhartha Gautama, who later became known as the Buddha, "the Awakened One". He was born in Lumbini, in present-day Nepal, around 563 BCE. Siddhartha's enlightenment, which occurred around the age of 35, at Bodhgaya, in present-day India, marked the beginning of his teaching career. He began spreading his insights into the nature of suffering, the four Noble truths, and the Eightfold path. After his enlightenment, the Buddha attracted followers and established a monastic community (Sangha). His teachings were initially transmitted orally.

The First Buddhist Council was convened shortly after the Buddha's passing to compile and recite his teachings. This marked the beginning of the preservation of Buddhist scriptures, known as the Tripitaka.

King Ashoka, played a crucial role in spreading Buddhism throughout India and beyond. He sent Buddhist missionaries to various parts of Asia. Buddhism spread to Sri Lanka, Southeast Asia, Central Asia, and eventually to East Asia (China, Korea, Japan) and Tibet. Each region adopted and adapted Buddhist teachings to its own culture. Over time, Buddhism diversified into different schools or sects, each with its own interpretations and emphasis on specific aspects of the Buddha's teachings and Buddhist practices. The two main early branches were Theravada and Mahayana Buddhism.

1.1 Applied Buddhism

Applied Buddhism is the practical application of Buddhist teachings of Dhamma in everyday life. It involves using the teachings and practices of Buddhism to cultivate a positive and compassionate outlook on life, transform negative habits and emotions, and develop a greater understanding of the nature of reality.

The core teachings of Buddhism, such as the four Noble truths and the Eightfold path, provide a foundation for applied Buddhism. These teachings emphasize the importance of cultivating ethical behavior, mindfulness, compassion and wisdom. Practitioners of jhana seek to integrate these teachings into their daily lives, using them as a guide for how to live and interact with others in a skillful and beneficial way.

Meditation is considered the heart of applied Buddhism. It is one of the primary practices which is a way of training the mind to be more aware and focused, and to develop greater insight into the nature of reality. Through regular meditation practice, one can cultivate mindfulness, concentration, and insight, which can then be applied to transform one's thoughts, emotions, and actions.

Another important aspect of the meditative practices is the cultivation of compassion and kindness towards others. This involves developing an awareness of the interconnectedness of all beings and recognizing that all beings desire happiness and freedom from suffering. By cultivating compassion and kindness towards others, one can develop a greater sense of empathy and understanding, and work towards creating a more peaceful and harmonious world. These meditative practices also emphasize the importance of ethical behavior, such as refraining from harmful actions and cultivating positive virtues like generosity, patience, and honesty. By cultivating ethical behaviours, one can develop a strong sense of integrity and cultivate positive habits that benefit oneself and others.

1.2 Meditative Practices in Buddhism

Meditation is a central practice in Buddhism. Meditative practices are viewed as indispensable tools for personal and spiritual development. It is a means of self-transformation that is integrated into daily life and is a cornerstone of Buddhist monastic life as well as lay Buddhist practice that allows individuals to gradually let go of attachments, desires, and the ego-self, moving towards a state of selflessness and liberation. The specific techniques and practices may vary among Buddhist traditions, such as Theravada, Mahayana, and Vajrayana, but the fundamental role of meditation remains a common thread throughout Buddhism.

Analyzing the historical perspectives of various sects of Buddhism and their meditative practices is important for several reasons:

1. Understanding the Evolution of Buddhist Thoughts: Buddhism is a dynamic tradition that has evolved over time. By studying the historical development of different Buddhist sects, one can gain insight into how Buddhist thought and practice have changed and adapted to various cultural, social, and historical contexts. This understanding helps us appreciate the diversity within Buddhism and how it has responded to different challenges and influences.

2. Preservation of Traditions: Some Buddhist sects and their unique meditative practices may be at risk of being lost or diluted over

time. By studying and documenting these traditions, scholars and practitioners can help ensure their preservation for future generations.

3. Comparative Study: Analyzing different Buddhist sects and their meditative practices allows for comparative study. This can lead to a deeper understanding of the commonalities and differences between various forms of Buddhism and how they approach meditation and spiritual development.

4. Identification of Universal Principals: While each sect may have its own specific practices, there are often universal principles and insights that can be extracted from the various approaches to meditation. These insights can be valuable for individuals seeking to deepen their own practice or to develop more inclusive and adaptable approaches to meditation.

5. Historical Context and Influences: Understanding the historical context in which different sects and practices developed can shed light on the social, political, and cultural factors that shaped them. This historical context can help us appreciate why certain practices or teachings emerged at specific times and how they were influenced by the prevailing conditions.

6. Impact on Contemporary Practice: Many contemporary meditation practices in Buddhism and beyond have been influenced by historical developments within Buddhist sects. Analyzing the historical perspectives of these practices can provide valuable insights for modern practitioners and teachers, helping them adapt and refine meditation techniques.

7. Interfaith and Cross-Cultural Dialogue: Buddhism has had a significant impact on the spiritual and philosophical landscape of Asia and beyond. Understanding the historical perspectives of different Buddhist sects and their meditative practices can facilitate meaningful dialogue and exchanges with other

religious and philosophical traditions, promoting greater mutual understanding and tolerance.

8. Personal and Spiritual Growth: For individuals on a spiritual journey, an understanding of the historical development of meditation practices within Buddhism can provide a broader context for their own practice. It can also offer inspiration and guidance for those seeking to deepen their meditation practice. Critical analysis of the historical perspectives of various Buddhist sects and their meditative practices is essential for understanding the richness and diversity of Buddhism, preserving valuable traditions, fostering cross-cultural dialogue, and deepening one's own spiritual journey. It allows us to appreciate the historical context in which these practices developed and to draw valuable insights for contemporary meditation and mindfulness practices.

The Buddha set a criterion for sound logical reasoning to help navigate the ideological maze of truth, falsehood and dogma-driven manipulation. The Kalama sutta, popularly known as the Buddha's 'Charter of free inquiry,' discourage blind faith, encourages a continual critical assessment of all claims for the clear perception of the reality defying dogmatism. The most heartening part of the Kalama sutta is that implicit to, it is a timeless measure of integrity. It is the mark of the noble and secure intellect to encourage questioning even to the Buddha's own convictions [1]. With this conviction, the author has undertaken this scrutiny of the framework of the major Buddhist practices. The analysis of the historical perspectives and the development of the meditative practices of various major sects of Buddhism follows in the foregoing part of introduction.

1.3 Theravada Buddhism

Theravada Buddhism, also known as the School of the Elders, is one of the oldest and most traditional branches of Buddhism. It is often associated with the preservation of the earliest Buddhist teachings and is primarily practiced in Sri Lanka, Myanmar (Burma), Thailand, Cambodia, and Laos. Here are the historical perspectives of Theravada Buddhism:

Origin and Early Development (3rd Century BC): Theravada Buddhism traces its origins to the First Buddhist Council, which was convened shortly after the passing of the Buddha in the 5th century BCE. At this council, the Buddhist monastic community (sangha) gathered to recite and codify the Buddha's teachings, known as the Tripitaka (Three Baskets), which includes the Vinaya (monastic rules), Sutta (discourses), and Abhidhamma (philosophical and psychological analysis). Theravada, meaning "Doctrine of the Elders," is named after its claim to follow the original and authoritative teachings of the Buddha.

Spread to Sri Lanka (3rd Century BC): Theravada Buddhism was introduced to Sri Lanka by the missionary monk Mahinda, the son of Emperor Ashoka of India, around the 3rd century BC. Sri Lanka became a stronghold of Theravada Buddhism, preserving the Pali Canon and providing a foundation for its later spread to Southeast Asia.

Theravada in Southeast Asia (1st Century CE): Theravada Buddhism gradually spread to Southeast Asian countries, including Myanmar, Thailand, Cambodia, and Laos. Over time, Theravada Buddhism became the dominant form of Buddhism in these regions, influencing local culture, society, and religious practices.

Scholastic and Monastic Traditions (1st Century CE -Present): Theravada Buddhism places a strong emphasis on monastic discipline and scholarship. Monastic communities play a central role in preserving and transmitting the Buddha's teachings. In addition to the Pali Canon, Theravada Buddhism developed a rich tradition of commentaries and sub-commentaries to elaborate on and explain the canonical texts.

Cultural and Artistic Influence: Theravada Buddhism has had a significant impact on the art, culture, and architecture of the regions where it is practiced. This influence is particularly evident in the temples, stupas, and religious art of Southeast Asia and Sri Lanka.

Challenges and Revival (19th Century CE-Present): In the 19th and 20th centuries, Theravada Buddhism faced challenges such as colonialism and political changes, which led to the erosion of monastic institutions and practices in some regions. Mainland of India remained largely devoid of Buddhism from around the 12th to the 20th century, roughly 800 years due to Islamic invasions and Hindu revivalism. Revival of Buddhism in India began in the 19th and 20th century with the foundation of Maha Bodhi Society, Calcutta by a Sri Lankan Buddhist Monk Ven. Anagarika Dhammapala in 1891 and Dr. B. R. Ambedkar's mass conversion to Buddhism at Deeksha Bhumi, Nagpur on 14th October, 1956. Theravada Buddhism has experienced a revival in recent decades, with renewed interest in meditation practices and the establishment of monastic centers worldwide.

Globalization (20th Century-Present): In the modern era, Theravada Buddhism has expanded beyond its traditional homelands. It has gained followers and practitioners in Western countries, particularly through the spread of mindfulness meditation and insight practices.

Interactions with Other Buddhist Traditions: Theravada Buddhism maintains its distinct identity but has also engaged in dialogue and exchange with other Buddhist traditions, including Mahayana and Vajrayana Buddhism. Today, Theravada Buddhism continues to be a vibrant and influential form of Buddhism with a rich historical tradition that emphasizes the importance of monastic discipline, meditation, and the study of early Buddhist texts [2, 3].

Meditative Practices in Theravada Buddhism: The Buddha is constantly seen encouraging his disciples to practice and develop jhana. The Buddha points to the bliss of the jhanas as his alternative to sense pleasures. Overall, applied Buddhism is a way of integrating Buddhist teachings and practices into everyday life in order to cultivate greater awareness, compassion, and wisdom. It emphasizes the practical application of these teachings in order to transform oneself and benefit others, and can be practiced by anyone, regardless of their religious or cultural background.

Vipassana Meditation: Vipassana meditation stem from the Buddhist tradition, refers to the broader practice of insight meditation taught by the Buddha. Vipassana, which translates to "insight" or "clear seeing," involves cultivating a deep awareness of the present moment and gaining insight into the true nature of reality. It aims to develop insight into the impermanent, unsatisfactory, and selfless nature of phenomena. S. N. Goenka, a prominent teacher of Vipassana meditation, initiated a global movement to preserve and spread the teachings of Vipassana through the establishment of the Vipassana International Academy (Dhamma Giri) in 1976, located in Igatpuri, Maharashtra, India. Under his guidance, a network of meditation centers was set up worldwide, fostering the growth of Vipassana as an accessible method for mental purification and self-awareness.

Vipassana meditation often involves observing bodily sensations, thoughts, emotions, and mental states without judgment or attachment. It advances further into the practice of satipaṭṭhānā meditation. The Satipaṭṭhānā practice involves systematically observing and exploring the different aspects of one's body and mind, in order to develop a deep and clear understanding of the nature of experience. The practice is divided into four main categories or foundations of mindfulness of the body, feelings, mind and Dhamma [4].

Satipaṭṭhānā Meditation: Satipaṭṭhānā, meaning "establishment of mindfulness," is a specific framework outlined in the Satipaṭṭhānā Sutta, a foundational Buddhist text. It provides a systematic approach to developing mindfulness in four key areas briefed as follows:

Mindfulness of the Body: In this foundation of mindfulness of the body (kayānupassanā), the practitioner cultivates awareness of the physical sensations and processes of the body, such as breathing, movement, and posture. The aim is to observe these sensations without judgment or attachment, in order to develop a deeper understanding of the impermanent and impersonal nature of the body.

Mindfulness of Feelings: In this foundation of the mindfulness of the feelings (vedanānupassanā), the practitioner observes and investigates the various feelings and emotions that arise in the mind, such as joy, sadness, anger, or boredom. The aim is to observe these feelings without getting caught up in them or identifying with them, in order to develop a deeper understanding of the nature of emotions and the causes and conditions that give rise to them.

Mindfulness of Mind: In this foundation of the mindfulness of the mind (cittānupassanā), the practitioner observes the different mental states and qualities that arise in the mind, such as clarity, dullness, restlessness, or calmness. The aim is to observe these mental states without judgment or attachment, in order to develop a deeper understanding of the nature of the mind and the causes and conditions that influence its functioning.

Mindfulness of Mind contents (Dhamma): In this foundation of the mindfulness of mental contents (dhammānupassanā), the practitioner observes and investigates the different mental objects and phenomena that arise in the mind, such as thoughts, perceptions, and concepts. The aim is to observe these phenomena without getting caught up in them or identifying with them, in order to develop a deeper understanding of the nature of mental processes and the ways in which they shape our experience of the world.

The Satipaṭṭhānā practice is typically undertaken in a structured and systematic way, with the practitioner dedicating time for each of the four foundations. Through regular practice, one can develop greater awareness, concentration, and insight into the nature of reality, leading to a greater sense of peace, clarity, and wisdom. The Satipatthānā practice can be challenging at times, as it involves facing and investigating aspects of the body and mind that may be uncomfortable or unfamiliar. However, with patience, persistence, and guidance from a qualified teacher, one can develop a deep and transformative practice of mindfulness and insight.

1.4 Mahayana Buddhism

Mahayana Buddhism is one of the major branches of Buddhism and has a rich and complex historical development. It emerged as a distinct form of Buddhism around the 1st century CE and has since evolved and diversified. Here is an overview of the historical developments of Mahayana Buddhism:

Early Mahayana Origin (1st Century CE): The term "Mahayana" translates to "Great Vehicle" and reflects the idea that this form of Buddhism is more inclusive and accessible to a broader range of people than earlier forms. Early Mahayana texts, such as the Perfection of Wisdom (Prajnaparamita) sutras, began to appear during this period. These texts emphasized the concept of "emptiness" (shunyata) and the bodhisattva ideal.

Spread to Central Asia and Beyond (2nd to 5th Century CE): Mahayana Buddhism spread along the Silk Road to Central Asia, where it merged with various indigenous traditions and influenced the development of new schools, such as the Madhyamaka and Yogacara. During this time, key Mahayana texts were translated into Central Asian languages and made their way to China and other regions.

Mahayana in China (2nd to 6th Century): Mahayana Buddhism was introduced to China around the 2nd century CE. It underwent significant adaptations to Chinese culture and thought, giving rise to Chinese Mahayana schools like Tiantai (Tendai in Japan) and Huayan (Hua-yen in China). The translation of Buddhist scriptures into Chinese was a major undertaking, leading to the formation of a Chinese Buddhist canon.

Flourishing in India (4th to 7th Century): India saw the flourishing of Mahayana Buddhism during the Gupta period. Nalanda and Vikramashila universities became centers for the study of Mahayana philosophy and practice. Figures like Nagarjuna, Asanga and Vasubandhu made significant contributions to Mahayana thought, with Nagarjuna being a key proponent of the Madhyamaka school. Transmission to East Asia (5th Century): Mahayana Buddhism spread to East Asia, particularly to Korea, Japan, and Vietnam. In each of these regions, Mahayana Buddhism adapted to local cultures and gave rise to various schools and sects. In Japan, for example, Zen and Pure Land Buddhism are two prominent forms of Mahayana Buddhism.

Tibetan Buddhism (7th Century CE): Mahayana Buddhism arrived in Tibet in the 7th century CE and evolved into what is known as Tibetan Buddhism or Vajrayana Buddhism. Tibetan Buddhism incorporates elements of Mahayana philosophy and practice, along with unique tantric rituals and teachings.

Modern Developments (20th Century CE): Mahayana Buddhism has continued to evolve and adapt in the modern era, especially in response to globalization and the challenges of the contemporary world. Mahayana teachings have spread to the West, with various Mahayana schools and traditions having a presence in North America, Europe, and other parts of the world.

Throughout its history, Mahayana Buddhism has produced a vast body of literature, diverse philosophical schools, and a wide range of practices, including meditation, devotion, and rituals. It remains a vibrant and influential form of Buddhism with a global following. The ideology of the 84,000 hooks of Zen meditation or 3,000 realms of Nichiren Buddhism seems to have been evolved from the Chinese form of Mahayana traditions [5, 6].

1.5   Zen Buddhism

The historical development of Zen Buddhism is a complex and fascinating journey that spans centuries and involves the transmission of teachings and practices from India to China and later to Japan. Here is a simplified overview of the historical development of Zen Buddhism.

Origin in India (6th Century CE): Zen Buddhism, like all forms of Buddhism, has its roots in the teachings of, the Buddha. His teachings on meditation and enlightenment form the basis of Zen practice.

In India, meditation practices evolved over time, with various schools emphasizing different approaches to meditation and insight.

Transmission to China (5th Century CE): Zen Buddhism began to take shape in China as Chan Buddhism around the 5th century CE. The term "Chan" is derived from the Sanskrit word "Dhyana," which means meditation. Bodhidharma, a legendary figure, is often credited with bringing Chan Buddhism to China from India. He is said to have arrived in China in the early 6th century and transmitted the practice of "zazen" (seated meditation).

Chan Buddhism in China developed its own unique character, blending elements of Indian Buddhism with Chinese Taoist and Confucian influences. It emphasized direct experience and meditation, as well as the use of enigmatic sayings and stories to convey teachings.

Tang Dynasty and Development of Chan (7th to 10th Cencury): The Tang Dynasty (618-907 CE) was a significant period for the development of Chan Buddhism. Several important Chan masters emerged during this time, and the tradition gained recognition and support from the Chinese imperial court. Key figures in this era include Huineng, the Sixth Patriarch of Chan, and Mazu Daoyi, known for his "just ordinary mind" teaching.

Song Dynasty and the spread of Chan (10th to 13th Centuries CE): The Song Dynasty (960-1279 CE) saw the further development and institutionalization of Chan Buddhism. Chan monasteries and communities flourished during this time. The Five Houses of Chan, a system of classification for Chan schools, emerged during this period. The Linji (Rinzai in Japanese) and Caodong (Soto in Japanese) schools are two of the most prominent.

Transmission to Japan (12th Century-present): Chan Buddhism was introduced to Japan by monks like Eisai and Dogen in the 12th century. Eisai brought the Rinzai Zen tradition to Japan, while Dogen founded the Soto Zen school.

Zen Buddhism, as it came to be known in Japan, had a profound impact on Japanese culture, including art, tea ceremony, and martial arts. The practice of Zen meditation, or "zazen," became a central focus in Japanese Zen monasteries.

Modern Zen (20th Century-Present): Zen Buddhism continued to evolve in Japan and spread to other parts of the world in the 20th century. Zen teachers like Shunryu Suzuki and D.T. Suzuki played significant roles in introducing Zen to the West and influencing Western philosophy, psychology, and the arts. Today, Zen Buddhism has a global presence, with practitioners and Zen centres worldwide. Throughout its history, Zen has undergone various schools, lineages, and adaptations, but its core principles of direct experience, meditation, and enlightenment have remained central to its teachings and practices. Zen continues to be a prominent and influential form of Buddhism in the contemporary world [7, 8].

Zen Meditation: Zen meditation, also known as Zazen, is a form of seated meditation that is central to Zen Buddhism. It is characterized by its simplicity, focus on breath and posture, and the aim of attaining deep insight into the nature of reality and the self. Here are the details on Zen meditation:

Posture: Zen meditation begins with the proper posture. Sit on a cushion (zafu) on the floor or on a chair with your back straight but not stiff. Your hands are placed in a specific mudra (hand position): left hand on top of the right, with thumbs lightly touching, forming an oval.

Breathing: The breath is a central focus in Zen meditation. Breathe naturally through your nose, with your mouth closed. Pay attention to your breath without trying to control it. Some practitioners count their breaths to help maintain concentration.

Eyes: In Zen, there are different instructions regarding eye position during meditation. Some practitioners keep their eyes open with a soft gaze focused on the floor in front of them. Others prefer to close their eyes. The choice often depends on the tradition and the teacher's guidance.

Focus and Mindfulness: In Zazen, the emphasis is on mindfulness (sati) and awareness of the present moment. This involves simply observing thoughts, sensations, and emotions as they arise without attachment or aversion.

There is no specific object of meditation in Zen, as in some other forms of meditation. Instead, the mind is open and receptive, allowing whatever arises to come and go.

Duration: Zazen sessions typically range from 20 minutes to an hour or more, depending on the practitioner's experience and the tradition. Beginners often start with shorter sessions and gradually extend the duration as they become more comfortable with the practice.

Silence: Zazen is generally practiced in silence. It is a solitary endeavor, and practitioners sit in stillness without chanting or guided instructions. The focus is on direct experience.

Direct Experience: Zen places a strong emphasis on direct, experiential understanding over reliance on scriptures or intellectual knowledge. Zen teachings often involve pointing directly to one's own mind and immediate experience as the path to enlightenment. Non-attachment: Zen teaches the importance of non-attachment to material possessions, desires, and even to ideas and concepts. Letting go of attachments is seen as a way to free oneself from suffering and delusion.

Impermanence: Zen recognizes the impermanent and ever-changing nature of reality. Understanding and accepting impermanence is considered essential to achieving enlightenment. This principle is often expressed in the saying, "The only constant is change."

No-Self (Anatta): Zen, like other Buddhist traditions, teaches the concept of anatta, or "no-self." This means that there is no permanent, unchanging self or soul. The self is seen as a construct of the mind, and realizing its emptiness is a central aspect of Zen practice.

Kinhin (Walking Meditation): In some Zen traditions, Zazen is alternated with Kinhin, or walking meditation. During Kinhin, practitioners walk slowly in a circle while maintaining mindfulness of each step and breath.

Dokusan (Teacher-Student Interviews): In traditional Zen practice, students have regular one-on-one interviews with their Zen teacher (roshi) to discuss their experiences, ask questions, and receive guidance. These interviews are called Dokusan and are an integral part of Zen training.

Koens: Some Zen traditions use koans, paradoxical questions or statements, as a tool for meditation. Koans are designed to challenge the rational mind and encourage insight. For example, "What is the sound of one hand clapping?" or "What was your original face before you were born?"

Sesshin (Intensive Retreats): Zen practitioners often participate in intensive meditation retreats called sesshin, which can last for several days. During sesshin, practitioners engage in long periods of Zazen, Kinhin, and Dokusan, with minimal sleep and conversation.

Goals: The primary goal of Zen meditation is to attain direct insight (kensho or satori) into the nature of reality and the self. This insight is not reached through intellectual analysis but through direct experience [7, 9].

Everyday Mindfulness: Zen meditation is not limited to the cushion. Practitioners aim to carry mindfulness and presence into their daily lives, bringing the insights gained in meditation to their interactions, work, and daily activities.

Simplicity and Minimalism: Zen monastic life is characterized by simplicity and minimalism. Monks and nuns live with few possessions and focus on the essentials of life, aligning with the principle of non-attachment.

Embracing Paradox: Zen often uses paradoxical language and concepts to challenge dualistic thinking and encourage a direct experience of reality beyond ordinary distinctions.

Zen Buddhism can vary in its interpretation and practice across different schools and lineages, but these basic principles are fundamental to the Zen tradition as a whole. Ultimately, Zen aims to help individuals transcend suffering and delusion and awaken to their true nature through direct experience and realization.

Zen Meditation sometimes describe it as a mind of 84,000 sharp hooks, walking through a very tight corridor (your present consciousness field) of an impermeable, buoyant material or prime- subset that best could be described as soft and stick-friendly bark tissue.

Upon its surface, your hooks, all in number more than you can ever keep count of, at any given moment, and all created by your every desire since beginning less time of countless births you cannot recall in your ordinary state of mind-numbness.

Every such hook was and still is born out of ignorance through your mind's constant division of itself into form (to some), sensation (to others), thought and memory (to most), makes you become stuck on that bark tissue-like wall of samsara, causing an experience of interdependent origin to your mind and hence a spiritual friction, which is anything but true Dharma and the blissful completeness of noble wisdom and perfect freedom found in the latter.

In other more radical sects, like the Zen Buddhist sect especially by the Chan Masters of the Tang and Sung Era, it was strongly advised to cut off all hooks in one swift cut hence allowing the freed mind, to ascend to its true level of being self aware as mind only, instantly curing the illusion of being the lower reflection of itself, or the no- self, which Mara had tricked it into hooking on.

There are of course many other sects in Buddhism that through the millennia have approached the dilemma of the mind of 84,000 hooks, but that is for you to find out if you desire to explore those options, of finding a way to completely unhook yourself from the body consciousness of ignorance and suffering [10].

Overall, Zen meditation can have a positive impact on many aspects of one's life, from mental and emotional well-being to physical health and spiritual growth.

1.6 Sarvastivada Buddhism

Sarvastivada Buddhism was one of the major early Buddhist schools that existed in ancient India. It had a significant impact on the development of Buddhist thought and practice. Here is a historical perspective on Sarvastivada Buddhism:

Early Development (3rd Century BC): The Sarvastivada school emerged as one of the early Buddhist schools around the 3rd century BCE, shortly after the passing of the Buddha. The name "Sarvastivada" can be translated as "Doctrine that All Exists," reflecting its doctrinal emphasis.

Abhidharma Tradition: The Sarvastivadins were known for their rigorous study of the Abhidharma, a systematic analysis of Buddhist teachings. They developed their own Abhidharma texts, which included detailed classifications of phenomena, elements of mind, and dharmas (individual mental and physical factors). The Sarvastivada Abhidharma is often considered one of the most comprehensive and systematic of all Abhidharma traditions within Buddhism.

Spread and Influence (2nd Century BC- 1st Century CE): The Sarvastivada school had a significant presence in various parts of India, with monastic centers in regions such as Kashmir and Gandhara (modern-day northern Pakistan and eastern Afghanistan). It played a prominent role in the preservation and propagation of Buddhist teachings and monastic discipline.

Schisms and Sub-schools: Like many early Buddhist schools, the Sarvastivada tradition experienced internal divisions and schisms. One of the most significant schisms led to the formation of the Mulasarvastivada school, which later played a central role in the development of Buddhism in Central Asia and Tibet.

Central Asian and Tibetan Transmission (2nd Century CE-7th Century CE): The Mulasarvastivada school, a branch of Sarvastivada, played a crucial role in the spread of Buddhism along the Silk Road, particularly in regions like Central Asia and Tibet.

Sarvastivada texts, including Abhidharma texts, were translated into various Central Asian languages and served as foundational texts for Buddhist study and practice in these regions.

Decline and Disappearance in India (7th Century CE-12th Century CE): Sarvastivada Buddhism, like other early Buddhist schools, gradually declined in India due to factors such as the rise of Hinduism and the Muslim conquests. By the 12th century CE, the Sarvastivada tradition had largely disappeared from the Indian subcontinent.

Survival in East and Southeast Asia: Some elements of Sarvastivada thought were incorporated into later Buddhist traditions in East and Southeast Asia, particularly in Theravada Buddhism and some Mahayana schools.

Historical Significance: The Sarvastivada school had a lasting impact on the development of Buddhist philosophy, particularly through its Abhidharma literature. Its emphasis on the idea that "all exists" influenced later Buddhist thought and debates, including those found in Tibetan Buddhism.

The Dharmaskandha philosophy is also an important concept in the teachings of the Sarvastivada sect of Buddhism, which was one of the early schools of Buddhism that emerged in India. According to the Sarvastivada tradition, the universe is composed of a complex network of dharmas, which are the ultimate constituents of reality. Dharmas are understood to be the building blocks of all things, including physical objects, mental states, and abstract concepts. Each dharma is considered to be momentary and impermanent, arising and passing away in an instant. If we set out Dharmaskandha into 84,000 fragments of reality, meditative practices followed by Sarvastivada sect would have been very effective for clear understanding of reality. However, no information is available about the meditative practices followed by the Sarvastivada tradition [11, 12].

1.7 Tibetan Buddhism-Vajrayana

Vajrayana Buddhism, also known as Tantric or Esoteric Buddhism, is a distinct branch of Buddhism that emerged in India and later spread to Tibet and other Himalayan regions. It is characterized by its use of tantra (sacred texts and rituals) and the belief in the transformative power of mantra, mudra (hand gestures), and mandala (symbolic diagrams). Here are the historical developments of Vajrayana Buddhism:

Origin and Early Development (7th Century CE): Vajrayana Buddhism emerged in India as an evolution of Mahayana Buddhism during the 7th century CE. The earliest texts associated with Vajrayana are the tantras, which are believed to have been composed during this period. These texts contain esoteric teachings and practices aimed at achieving spiritual realization more rapidly.

Padmasambhava and the Spread to Tibet (8th Century CE): One of the pivotal figures in the transmission of Vajrayana Buddhism to Tibet was the Indian tantric master Padmasambhava (Guru Rinpoche). He is credited with subduing local deities and spirits and establishing Buddhism in Tibet. Padmasambhava's teachings, along with those of other Indian masters, laid the foundation for Tibetan Buddhism, including its Vajrayana tradition.

Growth of Different Tibetan School (9th Century CE-preset): Tibetan Buddhism diversified into various schools and traditions, each with its own interpretations and practices. The Nyingma, Kagyu, Sakya, and Gelug are among the most prominent Tibetan Buddhist schools. Each school has its unique lineages of transmission, emphasis on specific tantric practices, and approaches to meditation.

Great Tibetan Masters and Scholars (10th Century CE-Present): Throughout its history, Tibetan Buddhism has produced numerous great masters and scholars who have made significant contributions to the tradition. Examples include Tilopa, Naropa, Marpa, Milarepa, Tsongkhapa, and Longchenpa, among others.

Integration of Bon and Indigenous Beliefs (11th Century CE-Present): Tibetan Buddhism integrated elements of the indigenous Bon religion and other local beliefs and practices, making it syncretic in nature. This integration helped solidify the unique character of Tibetan Buddhism, with its emphasis on deity yoga, empowerments (initiations), and complex ritual systems.

Spread to the West (20th Century CE-Present): Tibetan Buddhism, including its Vajrayana practices, gained popularity in the West during the 20th century. Figures like the Dalai Lama and other Tibetan Buddhist teachers have played a significant role in introducing Vajrayana teachings to Western audiences. Western students and practitioners have embraced meditation practices, deity yoga, and the study of Vajrayana texts.

Modern Challenges and Preservation Efforts (20th Century CE- Present): Tibetan Buddhism faced significant challenges in the 20th century, including the Chinese occupation of Tibet, which led to the exile of many Tibetan lamas and monks. Efforts to preserve and promote Vajrayana teachings and practices continue through monastic institutions and Tibetan Buddhist centers around the world [13, 14].

Tibetan and Vajrayana Meditative Practices: Vajrayana Buddhism is known for its complex rituals and esoteric practices, and it places a strong emphasis on the guidance of a qualified teacher or guru. It continues to thrive and evolve, both in its traditional homeland of Tibet and in the global context as it adapts to contemporary settings and new generations of practitioners. Here are some key aspects of Vajrayana and Tibetan meditative practices. Vajrayana practices often begin with empowerments (also known as initiations) conferred by a qualified teacher (lama or guru). These empowerments are rituals that establish a spiritual connection between the practitioner and a particular deity, mandala, or practice.

Deity yoga: Deity yoga (Yidam Practice) is a central feature of Vajrayana meditation. Practitioners visualize themselves as a chosen deity, such as Tara, Avalokiteshvara, or Manjushri, to embody the qualities and enlightened attributes of that deity. Deity yoga involves mantra recitation, mudras (hand gestures), and visualization. It is a powerful method for transforming ordinary consciousness into enlightened awareness.

Mandala: Mandalas, intricate geometric patterns and diagrams, are used as aids in meditation. Mandalas represent the microcosm which serve as sacred spaces for deity yoga and other practices. Mandalas are used both as external representations (painted or constructed) and internal visualizations during meditation.

Mantra Recitation: Mantra recitation is a fundamental practice in Vajrayana. Mantras are sacred syllables or phrases associated with specific deities or enlightened qualities.

Repetition of mantras is believed to purify the mind, remove obstacles, and generate spiritual power. The most famous mantra in Tibetan Buddhism is "Om Mani Padme Hum," associated with Avalokiteshvara, the bodhisattva of compassion.

Guru Yoga: Guru yoga is a practice that involves devotion to one's spiritual teacher (guru) and recognizing the guru as the embodiment of enlightened qualities.

This practice fosters a close spiritual connection with the guru and is considered essential for the transmission of Vajrayana teachings and blessings.

Clear Light Meditation: Clear Light meditation is an advanced practice that aims to experience the luminous, unobstructed nature of the mind. It is associated with the subtlest level of consciousness. This practice is often part of the death and dying process in Vajrayana, as it is believed to facilitate the transition of consciousness at the time of death.

Dream Yoga: Dream yoga is a form of meditation that focuses on recognizing the dream state as illusory and using it as a platform for spiritual practice. Practitioners train to become aware of their dreams, understand the dreamlike nature of reality, and even gain insights and realizations in the dream state.

Great Perfection and Mahamudra: Great Perfection (Dzogchen) and Great Seal (Mahamudra) are advanced meditation practices in Vajrayana. They emphasize direct, non-conceptual realization of the nature of mind and reality. These practices are often considered the pinnacle of Vajrayana meditation, offering a direct path to enlightenment [15].

Tibetan Buddhism and Vajrayana seems to be much deviated from the traditional Buddhism. The meditative practices followed by them cannot be directly supported with the notion of physical aggregates, mental states, and abstract concepts of Buddhist practices.

1.8 Nichiren Buddhism

Nichiren Buddhism is a Japanese Buddhist tradition that traces its roots to the teachings and life of Ven. Nichiren Daishonin, a 13th-century

Buddhist reformer and scholar. It is characterized by its focus on the Lotus Sutra and the belief that the chanting of the mantra "Nam-myoho-renge-kyo" can lead to enlightenment. Here's an overview of the historical developments of Nichiren Buddhism:

Life and Teachings of Nichiren (1222-1282 CE): Ven. Nichiren Daishonin was born in Japan in 1222 CE. He studied various forms of Buddhism and concluded that the Lotus Sutra (Saddharma-pundarika Sutra) was the highest and most profound teaching of the Buddha. Ven. Nichiren believed that the key to enlightenment was found in the recitation and devotion to the Lotus Sutra, particularly through the chanting of the mantra "Nam-myoho-renge-kyo." He faced persecution for his teachings, was exiled, and endured numerous hardships throughout his life.

Formation of Nichiren Schools (13th Century): After Nichiren's death in 1282 CE, his followers continued to propagate his teachings and established various Nichiren Buddhist schools and sects. The most prominent Nichiren schools include Nichiren Shoshu (True Nichiren School), Nichiren Shu, and Soka Gakkai. Each of these schools interprets Nichiren's teachings differently.

Nichiren Shoshu (13th Century CE-Present): Nichiren Shoshu is one of the earliest and most traditional Nichiren Buddhist schools. It maintains a strong connection to the Taiseki-ji Temple on Mount Fuji, which Nichiren himself founded. The sect places great importance on the Dai-Gohonzon, a sacred object of devotion believed to have been inscribed by Nichiren. The High Priest of Nichiren Shoshu plays a central role in the tradition.

Nichiren Shu (13th Century CE-Present): Nichiren Shu, also known as the Nichiren School, is another major branch of Nichiren Buddhism. It follows a more flexible and inclusive approach compared to Nichiren Shoshu. The school has temples and centers in Japan and various parts of the world. It emphasizes the teachings of Nichiren but is open to diverse interpretations.

Soka Gakkai (20th Century CE-Present): Soka Gakkai is a lay Buddhist organization that emerged in Japan in the 20th century. It was founded by Tsunesaburo Makiguchi and later led by Daisaku Ikeda. Soka Gakkai follows the teachings of Nichiren and places a strong emphasis on faith, practice, and community building. It is known for its extensive global outreach and activism.

Global Spread (20th Century CE-Present): Nichiren Buddhism, particularly through Soka Gakkai, has expanded its presence worldwide. Soka Gakkai International (SGI) is an international network of Nichiren Buddhists with millions of members in various countries. SGI promotes peace, education, and cultural exchange and has a strong focus on the practical application of Nichiren's teachings in daily life. Nichiren Buddhism, with its emphasis on the Lotus Sutra and the chant "*Nam myoho renge kyo*," has attracted a significant following in Japan and beyond. Its various schools and sects continue to adapt to modern times while preserving the teachings of Nichiren Daishonin [16, 17].

Ichinen Sanzen: Ichinen sanzen is a Japanese Buddhist concept that translates to "three thousand realms in a single moment of life." It is a fundamental principle in the Nichiren school of Buddhism and is based on the Lotus Sutra, which teaches that all beings have the potential to achieve enlightenment in their current lifetime. The meditative practices of Ichinen sanzen are based on this principle and aim to help practitioners realize their inherent Buddha-nature. The basis of the meditative practices in Ichinen sanzen is the concept of '*Nam myoho renge kyo*', which is a chant used in Nichiren Buddhism. The practice involves chanting the phrase while focusing on a specific goal or desire. Through consistent practice, it is believed that the individual's life force, or ki, can be awakened and directed towards achieving the desired goal.

The application of Ichinen sanzen meditative practices involves a three-fold process of observing the mind, controlling the mind, and purifying the mind. Through observation, practitioners become aware of their thoughts, feelings, and desires, and learn to detach from them. By controlling the mind, practitioners learn to focus their attention and direct their life force towards their desired goal. Through purification, practitioners learn to eliminate negative thoughts and emotions, and cultivate positive qualities such as compassion and wisdom.

The practice of Ichinen sanzen also includes daily recitation of the Lotus sutra, reading of Ven. Nichiren's writings, and participating in Buddhist study and discussion groups. These practices aim to deepen the practitioner's understanding of Buddhist teachings and help them develop a strong spiritual foundation. Similarly, the 3000 Realms refer to the various realms or levels of existence that one can experience through Buddhist practice. These realms are often depicted in Buddhist cosmology as different planes of existence, ranging from the lowest realms of suffering to the highest realms of enlightenment. Again, the number 3,000 is not meant to be taken literally but rather symbolizes the vastness and complexity of existence [16, 18].

The ultimate goal of the meditative practices in Ichinen sanzen is to help practitioners realize their true nature as the Buddhas and to manifest their inherent potential for enlightenment in their daily lives. By cultivating a strong connection to their Buddha-nature, practitioners can lead fulfilling and meaningful lives, while also contributing to the happiness and well-being of others.

Now that we have been introduced to the fascinating world of Buddhism and Buddhist meditative practices, let's delve deeper into the purpose of this book.

The author would like to clearly state the primary purpose of writing this book. In the past over 2,550 years of Buddhism, a question had often been raised about the magic figure 84,000 associated with the extent of the Buddha's teachings. The author has explored the details about this notion in his book, "Encounter with Satipaṭṭhānā: 84,000 Dhammakkhandha of Buddhism." In this book, the author would like to correlate various Buddhist meditative practices with special emphasis on the 3,000 Reams and 84,000 Dhammakkhandha. For genuine reasons, the author would like to provide his critical analysis about the framework of Ichinen sanzen and 84,000 Dhammakkhandha with reference to their objectives of cultivation of wisdom and enlightenment. The author would like to explore the scientology with which the Dhamma works and the role of various promoters and adversaries in the journey of the seeker of truth on the path of liberation from suffering.

The readers of this book would really require enthusiasm and commitment during this journey on the path of wisdom. The author offers an invitation to readers to join his endeavor on this exploration of Buddhism for the cultivation of wisdom and enlightenment.

Chapter 2

Ichinen Sanzen

3,000 Realms in a Single Moment

*A person of wisdom is not one who practices Buddhism apart
from the worldly affairs but, rather, one who thoroughly
understands the principles by which the world is governed.*

– Nichiren

Soka Gakkai organizations and members throughout the world believes that the essence of Buddhism is the conviction that we have within us at each moment the ability to overcome any problem or difficulty that we may encounter in life; a capacity to transform any suffering. Our lives possess this power because they are inseparable from the fundamental law that underlies the workings of all life and the universe.

Ven. Nichiren, upon whose teachings the Soka Gakkai is based, awakened to this law, or principle, and named it "Nam-myoho-renge-kyo." Through the Buddhist practice he developed and provided a way for all people to activate it within their own lives and experience the joy that comes from being able to liberate oneself from suffering at the most fundamental level [16].

2.1 Lotus Sutra

The Lotus Sutra, also known as the Saddharma Pundarika sutra in Sanskrit or the Miao-fa Lien-hua Ching in Chinese, is a Mahayana

Buddhist scripture that is considered one of the most important and influential sutras in Buddhism. The record of the Buddha's teachings to awaken others was compiled in the Tipitaka. It is believed that some suttas, which culminate in the Lotus Sutra, are considered very important in Mahayana Buddhism.

The Lotus sutra begins, "Thus I have heard, at one time Buddha was at Rajgriha, staying at mount Gridhakuta." This is a nod to the way Ven. Ananda who recited all his master, The Buddha's sermons at the first Buddhist Council and was said to have begun each recitation this way. The sutra is divided into 28 chapters in the translation of Ven. Kumarjiva.

This sermon given by the Buddha is said to have been attended by an unimaginable number of beings both human and nonhuman heavenly beings, dragons, garudas and many others including bodhisattvas and Arahats.

In early passages, the Buddha tells the assembly that his earlier teachings were provisional. People were not ready for his highest teachings. In particular, the Buddha addressed the doctrine of three vehicles for the attainment of Nibbana. The three vehicles namely, Shravaka vehicle, Pacchek-Buddha vehicle and Bodhisattva vehicle which describe people who realize enlightenment by hearing the Buddha's sermons, people who realize enlightenment for themselves through their own efforts, and the path of the Bodhisattva. But the Lotus sutra proclaims that the three vehicles are one vehicle, the Buddha vehicle, through which all beings become Buddhas.

The Buddha is presented in the Lotus sutra as Dharmakaya-the unity of all things and beings, unmanifested, beyond existence and nonexistence, unbound by time and space. As the dharmakaya is constituted by all beings, all beings have the potential to awaken to their true nature and attain Buddhahood [18, 19].

Over a thousand years after the Buddha, Ven. Nichiren Daishonin similarly began a quest to recover the essence of Buddhism for the sake of the suffering masses. Awakening to the law of life himself, Ven. Nichiren was able to discern that this fundamental law is contained within Shakyamuni's Lotus sutra and that it is encapsulated and concisely expressed in the sutra's title *Nam myoho renge kyo*. Ven. Nichiren designated the title of the sutra as the name of the law and established the practice of reciting Nam-myoho-renge- kyo as a practical way for all people to focus their hearts and minds upon this law and manifest its transformative power in reality. *Nam* comes from the Sanskrit *namas*, meaning to devote or dedicate oneself.

The Lotus sutra was likely composed in India between the first and third centuries CE. It was later translated into Chinese and other languages and became widely known and revered throughout East Asia. The Sutra contains many teachings and parables that are intended to help practitioners develop wisdom and cultivate enlightenment. One of the most famous teachings in the sutra is the concept of the "three thousand realms in a single moment of life," which describes the idea that within each moment of our lives, there are three thousand different potential states of existence, ranging from the lowest realms of suffering and delusion to the highest realms of enlightenment and Buddhahood.

The Lotus Sutra also emphasizes the importance of faith, perseverance, and compassion in the Buddhist path, and teaches that true enlightenment is not simply a matter of intellectual understanding, but also requires a deep and profound transformation of the self.

According to the Lotus sutra, the concept of the "three thousand realms in a single moment of life" arises from the interdependence and interconnectedness of all things. The sutra teaches that all phenomena in the universe, including living beings and inanimate objects, are intimately connected and mutually dependent on each other. The three thousand realms are said to be generated by the interactions between the ten Worlds and the three realms of existence. The Ten Worlds are ten different states of existence that living beings experience, ranging from the lowest realms of hell and hunger to the highest realms of

Buddhahood. The three realms of existence, on the other hand, are the realm of desire, the realm of form, and the realm of formlessness. Further, each of the ten Worlds can manifest in each of the three realms of existence, resulting in a total of 30 potential states of existence. However, each of these states is also constantly changing and evolving, leading to a total of 3,000 potential realms or states of existence in each moment of our lives. The Lotus sutra emphasizes that all of these realms are present within each moment of our lives and are accessible to us through our practice. By cultivating wisdom, compassion, and faith, we can learn to navigate and transcend these realms, ultimately realizing our own Buddha nature and attaining enlightenment.

Overall, the concept of the three thousand realms in a single moment of life is a profound teaching in the Lotus sutra that emphasizes the interdependence and interconnectedness of all things and provides a framework for understanding the Buddhist path towards enlightenment. The Lotus Sutra asserts that all paths to enlightenment ultimately lead to the same goal, referred to as the "One Vehicle" (Ekayana). This signifies the unity of different teachings and practices within Buddhism. Both the Lotus sutta and the Satipaṭṭhānā sutta (Ekayano maggo) present valuable perspectives on the path to enlightenment, with the former focusing on the inclusivity of teachings and the latter emphasizing practical mindfulness. Together, they illustrate the diverse approaches within Buddhism, enriching the understanding of the spiritual journey.

In any event, in the expansion of the 100 worlds into 1,000 factors and 3,000 realms, it is clear that sentient beings and their insentient environments constitute one great entity of life. But, does this principle of Ichinen sanzen as clarified in "the Juryo" chapter of Sakyamuni's Lotus sutra have meaning for the people of the Latter Day of the Law, who are profoundly attached to the self and riddled with the three poisons of greed, hatred and delusion? The Latter Day of the Law refers to the age when the teachings of the Sakyamuni Buddha lose their power to lead people to enlightenment. It was generally regarded to mean the period starting two thousand years after the Buddha's Mahaparinibbana. In Japan, it was believed that this age began in the year 1052 CE.

Ichinen sanzen of both the theoretical and essential teachings of Sakyamuni's Lotus sutra are theoretical, and only the reality of Ichinen sanzen hidden in the depths of the Juryo chapter- the Ichinen sanzen established by Ven. Nichiren in the Latter Day of the Law, can lead us to enlightenment. In his Gosho, the Ten Factors of Life, Ven. Nichiren states, "The 100 worlds correspond to the truth of temporary existence (ketai), the 1,000 factors correspond to the truth of non-substantiality (kutai), and the 3,000 realms correspond to the truth of the Middle way." In the depths of Ichinen sanzen of the Juryo chapter of Sakyamuni's Buddhism, which fully clarifies all 3,000 realms of life, lies the one, fundamental law that is the single truth of the Middle Way.

2.2 Nam Myoho Renge Kyo

"*Nam Myoho Renge Kyo*" meaning, "Devotion to the Mystic Law of the Lotus Sutra", is a vow, an expression of determination, to embrace and manifest our Buddha nature. It is a pledge to oneself to never yield to difficulties and to win over one's suffering. At the same time, it is a vow to help others reveal this law in their own lives and achieve happiness.

The individual characters that make up *Nam myoho renge kyo* express key characteristics of this law. *Nam* comes from the Sanskrit namas, meaning to devote or dedicate oneself and this meaning is generally taken by the believers of Nichiren Buddhism. However, the author has a different view in this regard. In Buddhism, "*Nam*" term is widely used for the formless mental aggregates along with the term "rūpa" for the aggregate of the physical form. Compositely, mental and physical aggregates together are referred to as the "Nam-Rūpa," The formless mental aggregates are divided in four categories namely feeling (vedanā), perception (saññā), mental formation (saṅkhārā) and consciousness (viññāṇa). Hence the consideration of the "Nam", the very first word of the *Nam myoho renge kyo*, as the formless mental aggregate goes in agreement with the scientology of Buddhism. It is meaningful within the context of 3,000 realms in a single moment as all perceptible phenomena are constituted from the physical and mental aggregates in this world.

Myo can be translated as mystic or wonderful, and *Ho* means law. This law is called mystic because it is difficult to comprehend. What exactly is it that is difficult to comprehend? It is the wonder of ordinary people, beset by delusion and suffering, awakening to the fundamental law in their own lives, bringing forth wisdom and compassion and realizing that they are inherently Buddhas able to solve their own problems and those of others. The mystic law transforms the life of anyone, even the unhappiest person, at any time and in any circumstances into a life of supreme happiness.

Renge, meaning Lotus blossom, is a metaphor that offers further insight into the qualities of this mystic law. The lotus flower is pure and fragrant, unsullied by the muddy water in which it grows. Similarly, the beauty and dignity of our humanity is brought forth amidst the sufferings of daily reality.

Further, unlike other plants, the Lotus puts forth flowers and fruit at the same time. In most plants, the fruit develops after the flower has bloomed and the petals of the flower have fallen away. The fruit of the lotus plant, however, develops simultaneously with the flower, and when the flower opens, the fruit is there within it. This illustrates the principle of the simultaneity of cause and effect; we do not have to wait to become someone perfect in the future, we can bring forth the power of the mystic law from within our lives at any time.

The principle of the simultaneity of cause and effect clarifies that our lives are fundamentally equipped with the great life state of the Buddha and that the attainment of the Buddhahood is possible by simply opening up and bringing forth this state. Sutras other than the

Lotus sutra taught that people could attain the Buddhahood only by carrying out Buddhist practice over several lifetimes, acquiring the traits of the Buddha one by one. The Lotus sutra overturns this idea, teaching that all the traits of the Buddha are present within our lives from the beginning.

Kyo literally means sutra and here indicates the mystic law likened to a lotus flower, the fundamental law that permeates life and the universe, the eternal truth. The Chinese character *Kyo* also implies the idea of a "thread." When a fabric is woven, first, the vertical threads are put in place. These represent the basic reality of life. They are the stable framework through which the horizontal threads are woven. These horizontal threads, representing the varied activities of our daily lives, make up the pattern of the fabric, imparting color and variation. The fabric of our lives is comprised of both a fundamental and enduring truth as well as the busy reality of our daily existence with its uniqueness and variety. A life that is only horizontal threads quickly unravels.

These are some of the ways in which the name "*Nam myoho renge kyo*" describes the mystic law, of which our lives are an expression. To chant *Nam myoho renge kyo* is an act of faith in the mystic law and in the magnitude of life's inherent possibilities. Throughout his writings, Ven. Nichiren emphasizes the primacy of faith. He writes, for instance: "The Lotus sutra says that one can 'gain entrance through faith alone.' Thus, faith is the basic requirement for entering the way of the Buddha." The mystic law is the unlimited strength inherent in one's life. To believe in the mystic law and chant *Nam myoho renge kyo* is to have faith in one's unlimited potential. It is not a mystical phrase that brings forth supernatural power, nor is Nam myoho renge kyo an entity transcending ourselves that we rely upon. It is the principle that those who live normal lives and make consistent efforts will reach their goals. Members of Soka Gakkai organizations believe that the teachings of Nichiren Buddhism offer a means for each of us to manifest within the realities of daily life the unlimited capacity for wisdom, courage and compassion we all possess.

From day to day, moment to moment, our state of life is susceptible to change. Quite often these changes create a type of attraction or aversion depending upon the situations that makes an individual happy or unhappy. Buddhism categorizes this seemingly infinite ranges of life situations into inner and outer "worlds." But these outer and inner worlds have been mostly misunderstood by the human mind not being able to perceive the real nature of the worlds and worldly conditions. This concept of the "Worlds" offers a useful framework for understanding both the changeable nature of our moods and the basic nature or tendencies of our character. More significantly, it provides us with a sense of the great possibility inherent in life at each moment.

2.3   Nichiren Buddhism and Ichinen Sanzen

The Lotus sutta is one of the most popular in all Mahayana literature, and two schools, the Tendai (T'ien t'ai) of China and Nichiren of Japan are build round it. The exposition of Ven. Vimalkirti is a favorite with laymen, for it stresses that not only the monks and nuns but also the householders may live the Bodhisattva life [20].

Nichiren Buddhism and Ichinen sanzen of Japan observe the principle of the Ten worlds, forms the foundation of the Buddhist view of life. These worlds have been categorized, in ascending order on the basis of the degree of free will, compassion and happiness one feels, the worlds of: (1) hell, (2) hungry spirits, (3) animals, (4) asuras, (5) human beings (6) heavenly beings, (7) voice-hearers, (8) cause-awakened ones, (9) bodhisattvas, and (10) Buddhas.

Buddhism developed in this context as a practice offering the possibility of transcending and freeing oneself from the sufferings of life. Among the teachings of Buddhism, the Lotus sutra further revolutionized this paradigm, teaching that the Ten Worlds are ten states of life equally inherent within each living being at each moment.

The pre-Lotus sutra teachings taught that it is possible to be born in a higher or more enlightened life state depending on one's actions, specifically by carrying out acts of good and practicing the Buddha way. By accumulating good acts, one offsets the balance of evil acts one may have accumulated.

The Lotus sutra, by contrast, teaches that the life states of all of the Ten worlds, including that of Buddhahood, are inherently present in one's life. Life at each moment manifests one of the ten Worlds. And each of these worlds possesses the potential for all ten within it (the principle of "the mutual possession of the ten Worlds"). Therefore, it is possible to open up any of these life states, including Buddhahood, at any moment through contact with an external stimulus that enables one to do so.

The stimulus that opens the world of Buddhahood is the teaching that expounds the truth of the Buddha's enlightenment, namely that it is possible to immediately open this world within oneself. Ven. Nichiren embodied this teaching and principle in the physical object of the Gohonzon-a scroll inscribed with Chinese characters. He taught that by chanting *Nam myoho renge kyo* to the Gohonzon with faith in our inherent Buddhahood, we are able to open the world of Buddhahood within us and harness the Buddha virtues such as wisdom, compassion and courage.

"Ichinen sanzen" is a doctrine of transformation that shows the principle for ordinary people to attain Buddhahood. "Ichinen" is the moment-to-moment life of each and every one of us. "Sanzen" meaning "Three Thousand" refers to "all laws," that is, all things, all phenomena and functions. The principle of Ichinen sanzen preaches that every moment contains 3,000 different dharmas, and that Ichinen sanzen dharma spreads universally throughout the 3,000 dharmas.

2.4 3,000 Realms

3,000 Realms or worlds is a combination of 10 worlds, 10 worlds, and 3 worlds (100 worlds x 10 factors x 3 worlds = 3,000 worlds). It may be equated with the expression trisāhasra-mahāsāhasra-lokadhātu, the expression commonly used in many Mahayana sūtras refering to 3,000 world elements (lokadhātu). The Buddha describes 18 dhatu's - the six sense bases, their six sense objects, and the six sense consciousnesses, all function through the five aggregates. As these 18 dhatu's functions through the six sensory bases through their ten step sensory phenomena (Loka), therefore they are also be reffered to as 'lokadhātu'.

Ichinen sanzen is a holistic view of our life and the world by synthesizing the laws of life and its cause and effect from different angles, such as the ten worlds, the ten Nyoze, and the three worlds.

Ichinen sanzen is the principle of hope and change, that "infinite possibilities" are hidden in your life from moment to moment, and if you change your thoughts, the environment surrounding you will change, and eventually you will be able to change the world.

When "Three thousand" is correlated with all the phenomena and all dharmas, we must try to understand the meaning of the phenomena and dharmas. Obviously all the dharmas are phenomena that we perceive through our sense organs and develop the attraction or aversion towards it. Ichinen sanzen shall be critically observed from the angle of the cause and effect of the worldly phenomena in the process of cultivation of wisdom and enlightenment [20].

2.5 Calculation of 3,000 Realms

The Great Teacher Ven. T'ien-t'ai in the sixth century developed the principle of three thousand realms in a single moment of life as a way to explain the truth revealed in the Lotus sutra: that the tremendous potential called Buddhahood resides in each person's life.

"Three thousand realms" points to all aspects of life and their varied functions, while "a single moment of life" refers to life at any moment. The number 3,000 combines three Buddhist concepts that approach life and the law of causality from different perspectives. It derives from multiplying the number 100 - from the mutual possession of the ten Worlds (10 worlds × 10 worlds = 100) - by the "ten factors of life" and then by the "three realms of existence" (100 × 10 × 3 = 3,000). This connectivity has been illustrated in fig. 2.1 and 2.2.

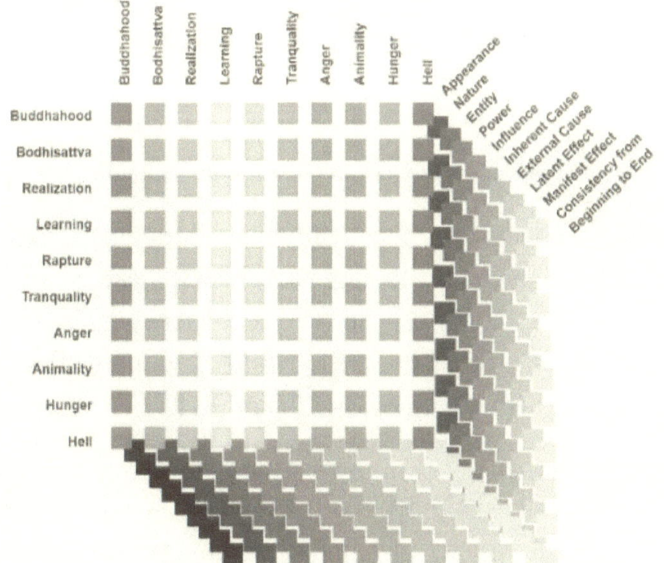

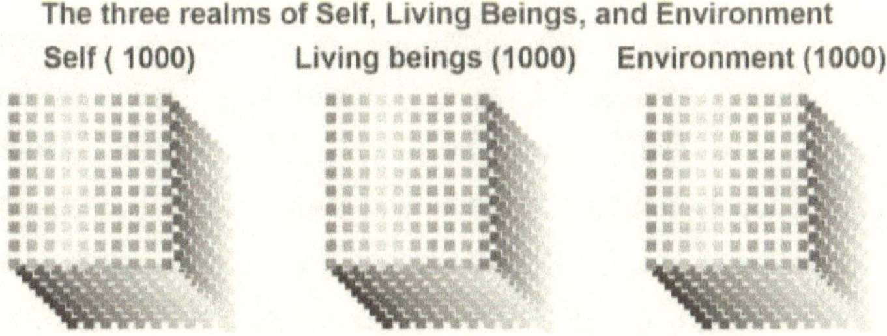

Fig. 2.1: 3,000 realms in a single moment of life

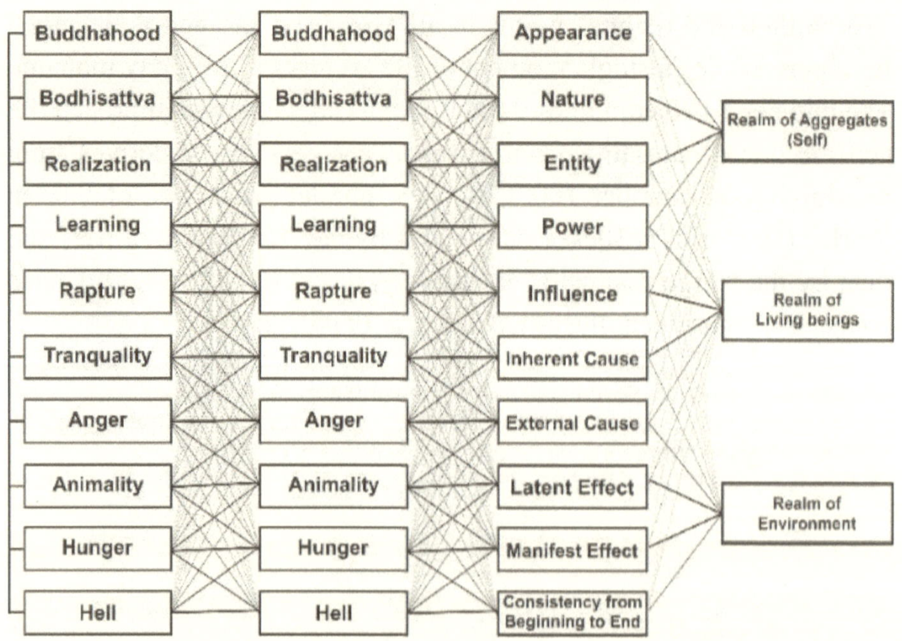

Fig. 2.2: Connectivity of 3,000 realms in a single moment of life

Nichiren Buddhism encourages the belief that, through its faith and practices, spiritual and material blessings and benefits can be available to everyone in this life. Needs can be met, and success achieved, not merely for oneself but for others (and the world) through dedication to the Lotus sutra, a central teaching of Buddhism [21].

New Religious Movements (NRMs) have always been and will always be with us. So will their study. Offering an assessment of the state-of-the-field of the study of NRMs, *Visioning New and Minority Religions* begins by considering the analytical tools for the study of new or minority religions, drawing on the perspectives of diverse academic disciplines. The Church of Jesus Christ of Latter-day Saints and the Christian Scientists, and groups with comparatively shorter histories, such as various forms of contemporary Paganism, Soka Gakkai, and the Diamond Way Buddhist group is of interest to scholars from across religious studies and sociology, as well as members of new and minority religious groups and those in "cult watching" groups [22].

In 2010 Daisaku Ikeda discussed the relationship between religion and science in a dialogue with the Japanese neuroscientist Kenichiro Mogi. In this dialogue Ikeda took the firm position that religion and science should not be treated as separate from each other, nor should they remain in a conflict relationship. Instead, they should complement and mutually benefit each other. We would like to follow Ikeda's constructive and value-creating approach by presenting in this book our attempt to build a bridge between the wisdom of Nichiren Buddhism, contemprary Theravada and the knowledge of modern science.

2.6 Nichiren Buddhism and Daimoku

The concepts and principles of the Nichiren Buddhism (Nichiren Buddhism 3), in "Change Your Energy, Change Your Life", the effects of Daimoku have been explored in details mainly in terms of "energy". Measures of the positive effects of daimoku on human body and energy centers (chakras) and also its energetic effects on individual's energy field. The studies have also been done on measurement of the energy in the room where the chanting is done. In the further practical exploration, (Nichiren Buddhism 3.1), a closer look at the effects of Daimoku in terms of "consciousness" have been checked. Consciousness can be regarded as one type of energy because it is related to our brain activity, which can be measured in the form of vibration and frequency. The results of our brain wave measurements taken whilst chanting Daimoku has been studies which indicates that our consciousness is related to our changing bodily and mental activities. This mechanism has been explained using the Buddhist deep psychology of the subconscious nature of karma. The specific effects can be seen from the results of the brainwave measurements taken whilst chanting Daimoku. One can explore out the neuroscientific principles of what makes the practice of Daimoku so powerful, including new research into brain synchronization, and how it can affect your wellbeing and success. In "Change your brainwaves, change your karma", explanations on how and why a person is strongly influenced from our own self and family karma, stored in the subconscious mind and even in the body. With such types of studies Nichiren Buddhism explains, how and why Daimoku can break through the persistent patterns of our karma in neuroscientific terms. How and why the positive neuro- physiological effects of Daimoku can dramatically improve our physical, mental and emotional wellbeing. How Daimoku is linked to your success in life and helps you to achieve your desired goals? Getting answers to these questions enables one to deeply understand the practical meaning of Daimoku and to chant with more conviction than ever before. This new approach to the practice of Nichiren Buddhism allows its practitioners to open up a new dimension in all areas of their life [23,24].

2.7 Gohonzon

The Gohonzon and the Clear Mirror are two important concepts in the practice of Nichiren Buddhism. The Gohonzon which literally means Devotion, is a sacred scroll or mandala containing the essence of the Buddha's teachings and is believed to be a tool for observing and transforming one's own mind. It is believed to contain the essence of the teachings of the Buddha and is considered to be an object of devotion and inspiration for practitioners. In the practice of Nichiren Buddhism, the Gohonzon is believed to be a tool for observing and transforming one's own mind. This process is known as "shōdai" or "the arising of the life-condition." The idea is that through the repeated contemplation and recitation of the Gohonzon, one can uncover and understand the deeper causes of one's suffering and negative tendencies, and ultimately transform them into positive, enlightened qualities.

To observe one's mind with the Gohonzon, practitioners typically recite the mantra *"Nam myoho renge kyo"* in front of the scroll, focusing on the meaning of the words and the accompanying visualization. This process is known as "daimoku" or "the title of the Lotus sutra." The repetition of the mantra is believed to help practitioners connect with the enlightened state of mind represented by the Gohonzon and to align their own lives with the principles of the Lotus sutra.

Overall, the process of observing one's mind with the Gohonzon is an ongoing and lifelong practice, with the goal of cultivating a more enlightened and compassionate way of being in the world.

2.8   Clear Mirror

The Clear mirror, on the other hand, is a metaphor for the enlightened mind, which is said to be free from delusion and able to reflect the true nature of reality. In the practice of Nichiren Buddhism, the Gohonzon and the Clear mirror are closely related, as the former is believed to be a means for cultivating the latter. Through the repeated contemplation and recitation of the Gohonzon, practitioners seek to uncover and understand the deeper causes of their suffering and negative tendencies and to transform them into positive, enlightened qualities. This process is known as "shōdai" or "the arising of the life- condition."

One way in which the Gohonzon is believed to help practitioners cultivate the clear mirror is through the repetition of the mantra *"Nam myoho renge kyo."* This mantra is believed to represent the enlightened state of mind represented by the Gohonzon, and its repetition is thought to help practitioners align their own lives with the principles of the Lotus sutra. By focusing on the meaning of the words and the accompanying visualization, practitioners are able to connect with the Gohonzon and the enlightened state it represents, thereby helping to purify and transform their own minds.

In addition to reciting the mantra, practitioners may also engage in various other forms of devotional practice, such as chanting, reading scriptures, and participating in group discussions and study sessions. These activities are believed to help deepen one's understanding of the teachings and to cultivate a sense of connection with the Gohonzon and the broader community of believers.

By cultivating the Clear mirror, practitioners are able to see the true nature of reality more clearly, and to live their lives in accordance with the principles of the Lotus sutra.

But the question remained: How does one awaken to or manifest this innate Buddhahood? The great teacher Ven. T'ien-t'ai emphasized the practice of "observing the mind" as a form of meditation focused on perceiving the true nature of the mind. But his system of meditation was extremely demanding and beyond the reach of anyone involved in the realities and responsibilities of daily life and society. Even among the monks who dedicated themselves fully to it, few were able to achieve its ultimate objective of enlightenment.

Ven. Nichiren pointed out that of the ten worlds, the nine worlds-except for the world of Buddhahood-are readily observable within the lives of people. The Buddha nature within us, however, is not so easy to see. Believing that one's life or mind contains the Buddha nature is a requirement for one's absolute happiness. Therefore, a practice that enables one to see and manifest this truth is essential.

Ven. Nichiren defined the principle of "embracing the Gohonzon is itself observing one's mind" (Jpn *juji soku kanjin*) as follows: "The observation of the mind means to observe one's own mind and to find the Ten Worlds within it [25, 26]". He concludes that the true meaning of observing the mind and perceiving the Ten Worlds lies not just in observing but also in manifesting the world of Buddhahood within one's life.

Here, the word embracing means "to accept and uphold," which is the first of the "five practices" described in "The Teacher of the Law," the 10th chapter of the Lotus sutra. The five practices are to: 1) embrace (accept and uphold), 2) read, 3) recite, 4) expound (explain or preach) and 5) to transcribe (transmit to others or to propagate).

The Ven. Nichiren taught that, when it comes to the practice of the Mystic Law, to embrace-the first of the five practices-is the direct way to attain

Buddhahood and includes all five practices. As such, Ven. Nichiren teaches that we need a "Clear mirror" (WND-1, 356) to carry out the practice of observing the mind, and he inscribed his life in the form of the Gohonzon for that purpose [27]. Simply having the Gohonzon and chanting to it, though, does not fully constitute embracing the Gohonzon. If we face the clear mirror of the Gohonzon, for example, passively begging it for benefit or depending on it for protection, then no matter how much time we spend chanting before it, we ourselves will not manifest our inherent and limitless potential.

In "Letter to Gijo-bo," which Ven. Nichiren wrote just one month after writing "The object of devotion for observing the mind," he explains in terms of his own life the principle of "embracing the Gohonzon is itself observing the mind."

Ven. Nichiren declares: "As a result of this passage, I have revealed the Buddhahood in my life" (WND-1, 389). And he says he has "attained the fruit of Buddhahood, the eternally inherent three bodies" (WND-1, 390). He urges his disciples to follow his lead and practice with the same spirit, saying, "This is what I mean when I emphatically urge you to give up even your body, and never begrudge even your life for the sake of the Lotus sutra" (WND-1, 390).

Ven. Nichiren taught that chanting Nam-myoho-renge-kyo to the Gohonzon with the spirit of single-minded devotion constitutes "observing the mind." Further, when one chants, the Buddha nature inherent in one's life can be manifested. Ultimately then, the practice that he expounded for the sake of humanity is expressed in the principle that "embracing the Gohonzon is attaining Buddhahood."

When we chant to the Gohonzon with the same single-minded determination and compassionately propagate the teachings, we can call forth the life state of Buddhahood inherent in the Gohonzon. In response, our own Buddha nature is awakened and manifested from within.

SGI President Ikeda says, "By tirelessly polishing our own lives in the midst of our daily affairs, confident that we have in ourselves the same wonderful state of life as the Gohonzon embodies, our lives come to shine with good fortune and benefit [28]." Ikeda Sensei describes this interaction between the external Gohonzon and the internal Buddha nature as a "responsive communion" between the Gohonzon and ourselves. This is the practice for attaining Buddhahood in one's present form. Sensei explains: "For this reason, when we chant *"Nam myoho renge kyo"* while practicing for ourselves and others, with the Gohonzon of *Nam myoho renge kyo* manifested by the Buddha as our Clear mirror, and with deep confidence in the Gohonzon existing in our own lives, *Myoho renge kyo* within us resonates with the *Myoho renge kyo* outside us, and the world of Buddhahood emerges within us [28]." In doing so, we reveal our true identity as that of a Buddha and begin to live based on a vow, enabling all people to awaken to this same inherent and irrefutable truth.

Platform sutra on Clear Mirror: The story about the Essence of Mind given in the Platform sutra is a wonderful melange of early Chan teachings, a virtual repository of the entire tradition up to the second half of the eighth century. At the heart of the sermon is the same understanding of the Buddha-nature.

This well-known story is in the contest for the succession of Ven. Hongren. The fifth Patriarch summoned all his followers and proposed a poem contest for his followers to demonstrate the stage of their understanding of the essence of mind. He decided to pass down his robe and teachings to the winner of the contest, who would become the sixth Patriarch. Shenxiu, the leading disciple of the fifth Patriarch, composed a stanza, but having no courage to present it to the master, one day at midnight about one o'clock in the morning, he wrote his stanza on the south corridor wall to remain anonymous. The other monks saw the stanza and commended it. Shenxiu's stanza is as follows:

Our body is a Bodhi tree.
And our mind a mirror bright.
Carefully we wipe them hour by hour
And let no dust alight.

The Patriarch was not satisfied with Shenxiu's verse, and pointed out that it did not show understanding of "fundamental nature and essence of mind." He gave Shenxiu a chance to submit another poem to demonstrate that he had entered the "gate of enlightenment," so that he could transmit his robe and the Dharma to Shenxiu, but the student's mind was agitated and could not write one more stanza.

Two days later, the illiterate Huineng, heard Shenxiu's stanza being chanted by a young attendant at the monastery and inquired about the context of the poem. The attendant explained to him the poem contest and the transmission of the robe and Dharma. Huineng asked to be led to the corridor, where he could also pay homage to the stanza. He asked a low-ranking official named Zhang Riyong from Jiangzhou to read the verse to him, and then immediately asked him to write down a stanza that he composed.

There is no Bodhi tree.
Nor stand of mirror bright.
Since all is void,
Where can the dust alight?

Next day the Patriarch came secretly to Huineng room, where the rice was pounded and said 'A seeker of a path risks his life for the Dharma. Is the rice ready?' "Ready long ago, only waiting for the sieve,' was a reply from Huineng. He knocked the mortar thrice with his stick and left. Knowing the meaning of the Patriarch's message, in the third watch of the night, Huineng went to his room. The Patriarch expounded the Diamond sutra to Huineng. When he reached to a sentence, 'One should use one's mind in such a way that it will be free from any attachment,' Huineng instantly became thoroughly enlightened, and realized that all things in the universe are the essence of mind itself [29].

With this basic background about Nichiren Buddhism and Ichinen sanzen, we shall try to explore the relativity of the 3,000 Realms with the 84,000 Dhammakkhanda in applied Buddhism for the cultivation of the wisdom and attainment of the enlightenment.

The objective of the 3,000 realms is to perceive the real nature of the phenomena. Let us analyze all the factors in terms of their requirement and role in achieving the objective of clear perception of reality i.e. the perception of the Noble eightfold path. It is also necessary to understand the limitation of the human mind to perceive the objectives, practical obstacles and challenges faced by the meditator on his progressive path of liberation.

The philosophical system of the three thousand realms in a single moment of life provides a basis for hope, for it posits that our reality at each moment is a function of our life state, that when our life state changes, the world itself appears in a new light. It tries to bring out the boundless possibilities of each person. It is a philosophy that promotes engagement with others and with the challenges of society and empowers one to squarely face and surmount obstacles [30].

2.9　Dhamma-Realization of the Truth

In the discourses the Buddha says that just as the great ocean there is but one taste, the test of salt, so in his doctrine and discipline there is but one taste, the taste of freedom, deliverance, emancipation (Vimutii-rasa). The taste of freedom and emancipation that flavours the Buddha's doctrine and discipline is the taste of spiritual freedom which means the freedom from suffering. Thus, the Buddha could say throughout his ministry, that "Previously monks, as also now I make known only suffering and the cessation of suffering.". This focal concern with the issue of suffering is evident form the formula of the four Noble truths which deals entirely with the problem of suffering.

Buddha's teachings on the conditioned worldly reality, the four Noble truths, dependent origination, and complete freedom from suffering are central to his philosophy and are intricately connected. According to the Buddha, the conditioned worldly reality is characterized by suffering. All things in the world are impermanent, and our attachment to these impermanent things causes us to suffer. This suffering is not limited to physical pain, but also includes mental anguish and dissatisfaction with life.

To penetrate the nature of this suffering, the Buddha taught the four Noble truths, the Noble truth of suffering (dukkha), the Noble truth of the cause of suffering (samudaya), the Noble truth of the cessation of suffering (nirodha) and the Noble truth of the path leading to the cessation of suffering (magga).

The first truth, the truth of suffering, acknowledges that all beings experience pain, frustration, and dissatisfaction. The second truth, the truth of the cause of suffering, identifies the root cause of this suffering as craving and attachment. The third truth, the truth of the cessation of suffering, asserts that it is possible to be free from suffering. And the fourth truth, the truth of the path leading to the cessation of suffering, outlines the Eightfold path which is a set of practices and principles that lead to the eradication of craving and attachment, and thus to the cessation of suffering.

The concept of Dependent origination is central to the Buddha's teachings. It explains the interdependent nature of all things and how suffering arises from this interconnectedness. According to dependent origination, all things arise in dependence upon other things. Our thoughts, feelings, and actions are shaped by our environment and the people around us. Our environment and the people around us, in turn, are shaped by our thoughts, feelings, and actions. This cycle of cause and effect leads to the arising of suffering.

Enlightenment, or complete freedom from suffering, can be attained by understanding the four Noble truths and practicing the Eightfold path. This involves recognizing the impermanence and interdependent nature of all things and letting go of our attachment and craving. By doing so, we can break the cycle of suffering and attain complete liberation from the conditioned worldly reality.

If the cultivation of insight, wisdom and liberation from suffering demands understanding of the four Noble truths and practicing the Eightfold path, a plausible question may be raised as to how it is possible to attain cultivation of wisdom and enlightenment via bypassing four noble truths.

In traditional Buddhist teachings, the four Noble truths and dependent origination are considered fundamental concepts that form the basis of the Buddhist path to liberation from suffering. They are taught as a means to understand the nature of suffering and its causes, and to guide practitioners towards the path of liberation. In contrast, the practice of chanting a mantra, such as *Nam myoho renge kyo* in Nichiren Buddhism, is considered a form of meditation and a means to focus the mind. The repetition of the mantra is said to help practitioners enter a meditative state, which can lead to inner transformation and spiritual awakening. Ichinen sanzen teaches that all things are interrelated and interconnected. It asserts that the ultimate reality can be experienced through the mind, and that this reality is inextricably linked to our everyday experiences. The goal of Ichinen sanzen is to awaken to this ultimate reality, or the Buddhahood, in order to attain complete liberation from suffering [20].

Nichiren Buddhists believe that the ultimate goal of the practice is to awaken to the ultimate reality, rather than simply understand the nature of suffering and its causes. They believe that the practice of chanting *Nam myoho renge kyo*, which is the primary practice that can lead to this awakening. The practice of chanting *Nam myoho renge kyo* is believed to cultivate wisdom, compassion, and inner transformation. By chanting, practitioners can connect with their innate Buddha nature, which is the ultimate reality within themselves. This connection leads to the realization that all things are interrelated and interconnected, and that we are all part of a greater whole. Nichiren Buddhists believe that this realization can lead to complete liberation from suffering by chanting *Nam myoho renge kyo*, that can overcome their negative karma and transform their lives. This transformation is not simply a change in behaviour or attitude, but a fundamental shift in consciousness that leads to complete liberation from suffering. While chanting a mantra can be a powerful tool for inner transformation and spiritual growth, it is important to note that it is not a substitute for understanding the four Noble truths and Dependent origination. These concepts are considered essential for cultivation of insight and for liberation from suffering.

However, it is also important to note that different Buddhist traditions may have different perspectives on the role of chanting in the path to liberation. In Nichiren Buddhism, for example, the practice of chanting *Nam myoho renge kyo* is considered a direct path to enlightenment, and is said to contain the essence of the Buddhist teachings.

Ultimately, whether it is possible to bypass the four Noble truths and Dependent origination through chanting a mantra is a matter of interpretation and individual belief. Some may argue that chanting can be a powerful tool for spiritual growth and liberation, while others may view it as a supplementary practice that is best approached in conjunction with a deeper understanding of Buddhist teachings.

The doctrine of the "Three thousand realms in a single thought" associated with the Lotus sutra relates its 100 worlds with the truth of impermanence, 1,000 factors with the truth of unsubstantiality, and the 3,000 realms with the truth of the Middle way. It's important to note that this concept is not found in all forms of Buddhism and is specific to certain schools and traditions. Although this concept illustrates the interconnectedness and interdependence of all phenomena, it seems to be deviated from the basic principles of the teachings, practice and comprehension of Buddhist meditative practices.

Chapter 3

3000 Realms

Analysis with the Buddha's Charter of Enquiry

"To remain indifferent to the challenges we face is indefensible. If the goal is noble, whether or not it is realized within our lifetime is largely irrelevant. What we must do therefore is to strive and persevere and never give up."

– Dalai Lama

The renowned Buddhist scholar Ven. T'ien-t'ai developed a meditative practice to enable people to perceive the boundless extent of their lives at each moment. He developed a theoretical system to describe this reality. He called this "Ichinen sanzen" which means "The three thousand realms in a single moment of life". A single moment of life or one mind or one thought" (ichinen) and three thousand (sanzen) was established by Ven. T'ien-t'ai in his "Great Concentration and Insight" on the basis of the phrase "the true aspect of all phenomena."

The Buddhist principle of "Ichinen sanzen" later transformed as a philosophical framework for Nichiren Buddhism, expressing why and how it is possible for ordinary human beings to attain Buddhahood amid the realities of daily life. Ven. Nichiren Daishonin illustrated "the Doctrine of three thousand realms in a single moment of life" in 1258, which was described by him as the heart and core of the Buddha's teachings and established a practice to enable all people to experience the state of Buddhahood in their daily lives. As per the practice of this belief, the practice of chanting "Nam myoho renge kyo" with faith in our inherent Buddha nature actualizes the principle of three thousand realms in a single moment of life, in the life of the practitioner. Ven. Nichiren believed the Lotus sutra as an important scripture in Mahayana Buddhism, and one of the Buddha's vital teachings, holding the key to happiness. The Lotus sutra clarifies that the world of Buddhahood, as with the other nine worlds, is equally inherent in the lives of all people and thus is a potential open to all within this lifetime [16,20].

3.1   3,000 Realm: Why Free enquiry?

Ichinen sanzen "Three thousand realms in a single moment of life", is a practice of mindfulness meditation where one has to develop complete awareness of one's own internal and external phenomena. For this purpose, variety of factors have been taken into consideration to construct the frame work of 3,000 realms that can be perceived by the meditator with his six sense bases. Let us now take all the factors of 3,000 realms for our phenomenal scrutiny and analysis. The Buddha was adamant that the information not to be accepted without question. He pushed for open minded verification based on logic and first-hand experience, accepting only that which demonstrated to be true. As per the 'Skill in Questions-How the Buddha Taught,' Ven. Bhikku Thanissaro (Geoffrey DeGraff) described the four-fold classification approach of the Buddha to answer the questions [31]. A discourse from Anguttara Nikaya *4:42*, in which the Buddha classified questions into four types of approaches depending on the response-strategy they deserved: "There are these four ways of answering questions. Which four? There are questions that should be answered categorically. There are questions that should be answered analytically. There are questions that should be answered with cross-questioning. There are questions that should be put aside. These are the four ways of answering questions.[1]"

Although the Buddha was a responsible, compassionate and skilled rhetorician, in teaching a path of practice, he meant for his words to be put into practice. To meet this end, he professed his discourses in the local dialect to the common people with clear meaning of his words with its precise interrelationship. As a matter of fact, Dhamma and khandha do not have its independent existence in the world unless and until experienced within the frame of body and mind. If it would be taken in this way, the prerequisite for the Dhammakkhandha or Dhamma aggregate is to have its practical aspect to be proven on the body and mind.

The Buddha's discourses and lessons on Dhamma are full of the right approaches befitting the particular situation as encountered by him during his preaching of Dhamma. When we read the account of the Buddha's last night, from Digha Nikaya-16 (DN-16), it's easy to sense the importance of his final teaching before entering total Nibbāna. "... Then the Buddha addressed the monks and said: This I tell you Bhikkus. "Vaya dhamma saṅkhārā, appamāden sampādetha- Decay is inherent in all conditioned things, work out your own liberation with diligence" [32]. These words call attention to themselves because they were the last, he ever said."

Then the Blessed One addressed the monks, "If even a single monk has any doubt or indecision concerning the Buddha, Dhamma, or Sangha, the path or the practice, ask. Don't later regret that 'The teacher was face-to-face with us, but we didn't bring ourselves to cross-question him in his presence."

When this was said, the monks were silent. A second time... A third time, the Blessed One said, third time, the monks were silent. Then the Blessed One addressed the monks, "Now, if it's out of respect for the Teacher that you don't ask, let a friend inform a friend." When this was said, the monks were silent. Then Ven. Ananda said to the Blessed One, "It's amazing, Lord. It's astounding. I'm confident that in this community of monks there isn't even a single monk who has any doubt or indecision concerning the Buddha, Dhamma, or Sangha, the path or the practice." "You, Ananda, speak out of confidence, while there is knowledge in the Tathagata that in this community of monks there isn't even a single monk who has any doubt or indecision concerning the Buddha, Dhamma, or Sangha, the path or the practice. Of these 500 monks, the most backward is a stream- winner, not destined for the planes of deprivation, headed to self- awakening for sure."

This passage shows how the Buddha, instead of enforcing an unquestioning acceptance of his teachings, had resolved his students' doubts by being open to their questions. The fact that this incident is placed right before the last teaching is a measure of how central this method was to his teaching, and how important it was to his followers who assembled the Canon.

It is necessary to see the relativity of the 3,000 realms with the viewpoint of the Buddha's tool-kit of investigation. The Kalama sutta is considered to be an important text in the Buddhist tradition because it deals with the subject of how to determine what is true and what is false. The Kalama sutta is a teaching given by the Buddha to the people of the Kalama town in ancient India. The sutta addresses the issue of skepticism and encourages the Kalamas to use their own experience and judgment, rather than blindly following tradition or authority, in determining what is true and beneficial.

One of the main themes of the sutta is the importance of personal experience in the pursuit of truth. The Buddha advises the Kalamas to "know for themselves" and to "investigate" rather than accepting things on faith or authority. This emphasis on experiential knowledge is consistent with the Buddha's emphasis on the importance of personal practice and the cultivation of inner wisdom [1].

Now, let us elaborate on all these variety of factors of 3,000 realms one by one in the context of the development of mindfulness for clear perception of the phenomena in terms of the soundness and credibility of the concept of the factors enumerated in the 3,000 realms.

3.2 Ten Worlds

The first component of the three thousand realms is the principle of the Ten Worlds, which describes the state or condition of our lives. They are, in ascending order of the degree of free will, compassion and happiness one feels: the worlds of (1) Hell, (2) Hunger (Hungry spirits), (3) Animality (animals), (4) Anger (asuras), (5) Tranquility (human beings), (6) Rupture (heavenly beings), (7) Learning (voice-hearers), (8) Realization (cause-awakened ones), (9) Bodhisattvas, and (10) Buddhahood.

World of Hell

The world of hell is a life state in which one is imprisoned by suffering and completely lacking in freedom. Living is itself painful, and everything we see is coloured by our unhappiness and misery.

Soundness and credibility of concept: The concept of "hell" is generally associated with religious or spiritual beliefs, and the idea of a literal, physical underworld where souls are punished after death is not supported by scientific evidence. Therefore, the existence of such a place cannot be validated through empirical observations or logical reasoning. Moreover, different religious traditions have different beliefs about the nature and characteristics of hell, and there is no consensus or objective evidence to support any of these beliefs. In many cases, the concept of hell is based on faith or revealed scripture, which is not subject to empirical testing or validation. From a psychological perspective, the concept of hell may be seen as a way to provide a moral framework or to create a sense of justice or accountability for one's actions.

However, the idea of eternal punishment in a place of suffering and torment is often considered inconsistent with concepts of forgiveness, compassion, and redemption, which are also central to many religious traditions. Therefore, while the idea of hell may have cultural, psychological, or spiritual significance for some individuals or communities, it cannot be practically validated or disproven by the human mind in a scientific sense.

World of Hunger (Hungry spirits)

The world of hungry spirits, or the life state of hunger, is a state where one is spiritually and physically tormented by insatiable craving.

Soundness and credibility of concept: The world of hungry spirits is a concept from Buddhism and refers to a realm in the cycle of rebirths where beings are consumed by insatiable cravings and desires. This realm is characterized by extreme suffering and a constant feeling of emptiness, as the beings are unable to satisfy their desires no matter how much they try. The concept of the world of hungry spirits cannot be practically validated by the human mind because it is not an empirical phenomenon that can be directly observed or measured. Rather, it is a metaphysical concept that is based on Buddhist teachings about the nature of existence and the cycle of rebirths.

The human mind is limited in its ability to comprehend certain concepts, especially those that are beyond the realm of direct experience. The world of hungry spirits, being a realm that is beyond the physical world and the realm of human experience, falls outside the scope of the human mind's ability to grasp.

The concept of the world of hungry spirits is not a part of mainstream scientific understanding or investigation. Science is based on empirical observation and experimentation, and the existence of the world of hungry spirits cannot be directly observed or tested using scientific methods.

Thus, the world of hungry spirits is a metaphysical concept that falls outside the scope of direct human experience and scientific investigation, and therefore cannot be practically validated by the human mind.

World of Animality (Animals)

The world of animals, or the life state of animality (reflecting the ancient Indian conception of the nature of animals) is characterized by foolishness in the sense of being moved by impulse and concerned only with immediate benefit and gratification. In this condition, the ability to make moral and ethical judgments is lacking. Because the worlds of hell, hungry spirits and animals all represent conditions of suffering, they are collectively known as the Three Evil Paths.

Soundness and credibility of concept: The world of animals, just like the world of humans, is a complex and diverse system with its own unique set of behaviours, instincts, and ways of communicating. However, while humans are capable of observing and studying the behaviour of animals, it is important to recognize that our understanding of the animal world is limited by our own perspective and cognitive abilities.

Firstly, animals have different sensory perceptions than humans. They have a wider range of hearing, sight, and smell, and may use these senses to communicate and interact with their environment in ways that we cannot fully comprehend. For example, some animals are able to detect changes in the earth's magnetic field, while others can see in the ultraviolet or infrared spectrum, which humans cannot perceive.

Animals have their own unique instincts and behavioural patterns that are shaped by their evolutionary history and environmental factors. While humans may be able to observe and understand some of these behaviours, we may not always be able to fully comprehend the reasons behind them or the complex interplay between different behaviours.

Since, animals have their own subjective experiences and emotions, which may be difficult or impossible for humans to fully understand or validate. For example, while we may observe that an animal is exhibiting signs of distress, we cannot truly know what that animal is feeling or experiencing on an emotional level.

Although humans may be able to observe and study the behavior of animals, our understanding of the animal world is limited by our own cognitive abilities and perspectives. It is important to recognize the limitations of our own understanding and to approach the study of animals with humility and respect for their unique perspectives and experiences.

World of Anger (Asuras)

In ancient Indian mythology Asura*s* were contentious demons. A characteristic of the world of Asuras, or the life state of anger, is an obsession with personal superiority or self-importance, a tendency to always compare oneself to others and want to be better than them. Another characteristic of this life state is the "perversity" of concealing one's true feelings in order to ingratiate oneself with others.

Soundness and credibility of concept: The world of demons, as described in various religious and cultural traditions, is often believed to be a realm that exists beyond the physical world that we can perceive with our senses. This world is thought to be populated by supernatural beings that possess powers and abilities that are beyond human understanding. There are several reasons why the world of demons cannot be experienced and validated by human beings:

Limited human perception: Human beings are limited in their ability to perceive the world around them. We can only perceive the physical world through our five senses, and anything that exists beyond that is beyond our comprehension.

Cultural and religious differences: The concept of demons and the supernatural varies widely across cultures and religions. What is considered a demon in one culture may be viewed as a different type of entity in another, and there is no consensus on the nature of these beings.

Lack of empirical evidence: While there are many anecdotal accounts of encounters with demons, there is no empirical evidence to support their existence. This makes it difficult to validate their existence and the experiences of those who claim to have encountered them.

Psychological explanations: Many experiences that are attributed to encounters with demons can be explained by psychological phenomena such as sleep paralysis, hallucinations, and delusions. These experiences can be very real to those who experience them, but they do not necessarily indicate the existence of demons.

Overall, the world of demons remains a subject of belief and faith for many people, but it cannot be experienced or validated through empirical means.

World of Tranquility (Human beings)

The world of human beings, or the life state of humanity, is a tranquil, calm, composed humane state. People in this condition understand the principle of cause and effect and are rational enough to know the difference between good and evil. This state of life is, however, susceptible to negative external conditions and cannot be sustained without a constant effort toward self-improvement and personal development.

Soundness and credibility of concept: The validation of the world of human beings can be achieved through various means, including scientific inquiry, critical thinking, and empirical evidence. Humans have developed various methodologies and approaches to better understand and validate their world, such as the scientific method, logical reasoning, and philosophical inquiry.

To validate the world of human beings, individuals must rely on verifiable evidence and sound reasoning. This can be achieved through systematic observation, experimentation, and analysis of data. For instance, scientists use various scientific methods, such as hypothesis testing, controlled experiments, and statistical analysis, to gather and validate knowledge about the natural world.

In addition to scientific inquiry, critical thinking is also essential to validate the world of human beings. Critical thinking involves analyzing and evaluating information to determine its accuracy, relevance, and reliability. By critically assessing information, individuals can separate facts from opinions, biases, and misconceptions, and make informed decisions based on evidence.

Moreover, philosophy provides a valuable framework for validating the world of human beings by analyzing fundamental concepts and principles. Philosophers use reasoning and logical arguments to explore concepts such as truth, ethics, and knowledge, and determine their validity.

Overall, to validate the world of human beings, individuals must use a combination of scientific inquiry, critical thinking, and philosophical inquiry to gather and analyze evidence, assess its validity, and make informed decisions based on the evidence.

World of Rupture (Heavenly beings)

In ancient India, it was believed that those who performed good acts in their present life would be reborn as deities in the heavenly realm. In Buddhism, the world of heavenly beings, or the life state of heaven, is regarded as a condition of joy or rapture experienced when our desires are fulfilled. However, such joy is not lasting. It fades and disappears with the passage of time and as situations change.

The worlds from hell to heavenly beings-the "six paths"-are easily influenced by external circumstances, so these life states are not truly free or autonomous. Buddhism encourages people to transcend the six paths and develop a self-determined state of happiness through Buddhist practice.

Soundness and credibility of concept: The nature and world of the heavenly beings, such as angels or gods, cannot be validated by human beings for several reasons.

Human beings have limited sensory abilities and cognitive capacity. Our understanding of the world is constrained by our five senses, which can only perceive a tiny fraction of the electromagnetic spectrum. Additionally, our cognitive abilities are limited, and we can only comprehend a small portion of the vastness of the universe. Therefore, we may not be able to perceive or understand the existence of other beings that exist outside of our sensory and cognitive capabilities.

The concept of heavenly beings varies greatly across cultures and religions. What one culture or religion may view as a heavenly being, another culture or religion may view as a myth or folklore. Therefore, it is difficult to validate the existence of heavenly beings since different cultures and religions have different beliefs and interpretations.

Empirical evidence is based on observations and experiments that can be repeated and verified by others. However, there is currently no empirical evidence that proves the existence of heavenly beings. Therefore, it is difficult to validate the existence of something that cannot be observed or tested through empirical means.

The belief in heavenly beings is often based on faith rather than empirical evidence or rational inquiry. While belief and faith can provide a sense of comfort and purpose for individuals, they cannot be used to validate the existence of heavenly beings in a scientific or objective manner.

In summary, the nature and world of the heavenly beings cannot be validated by human beings due to our limited perception, cultural and religious differences, lack of empirical evidence, and the role of belief and faith in the concept of heavenly beings.

World of Learning (Voice-hearers)

The world of voice-hearers is the life state attained by those who gain a partial awakening through hearing the Buddha's teachings. These groups of beings have Sotāpaññā.

Soundness and credibility of concept: The experiences of voice hearers, also known as auditory hallucinations, can be difficult for others to validate because they are subjective experiences that are unique to the individual experiencing them.

Normal human beings may have difficulty understanding the world of voice hearers because they have not personally experienced auditory hallucinations themselves. As a result, they may struggle to relate to or fully comprehend the lived experiences of those who do.

Furthermore, voice hearers may experience a wide range of different auditory hallucinations, which can vary in terms of the content, tone, and intensity of the voices they hear. This can make it challenging for others to fully grasp the nature of these experiences, as they are highly individualized and can be difficult to describe.

Ultimately, the world of voice hearers can only be validated by those who have experienced auditory hallucinations themselves, as they are the only ones who can truly understand the unique nature of these experiences. However, it is still important for others to show empathy and support for voice hearers, and to work to create a more inclusive and understanding society where these experiences are not stigmatized or dismissed.

World of Realization (Cause-awakened ones)

The world of cause-awakened ones refers to the life state attained by those who gain a partial awakening and realization through their own observations and effort. These two life states are characterized by an awareness of the principle of cause and effect and the truth that nothing in life is permanent. This is the basis of the realization that attachment to various things is a source of suffering and that to do away with attachment leads to liberation.

The limitation of these life states is a tendency toward self- centeredness and self-absorption. In the Mahayana Buddhist scriptures, such disciples were criticized by the Buddha for a kind of self-satisfaction that made them unwilling to extend themselves past the limits of their partial awakening to strive for the full enlightenment of the Buddha. The group of beings of this world may be compared with the Ariya-puggala Sotāpaññā, Sakkitagami, Anagāmi and Arahat.

Soundness and credibility of concept: The "world of cause" refers to a spiritual or mystical realm that is said to be accessible only to those who have achieved a certain level of awakening or enlightenment. This concept is often associated with various spiritual traditions, such as Buddhism, Hinduism, and Taoism.

The reason why the world of Cause cannot be validated by normal human beings is because it is said to be beyond the realm of ordinary perception and cognition. According to these traditions, the human mind is limited by its attachment to material things, sensory experiences, and conceptual thinking. The world of Cause, on the other hand, is said to be a realm of pure consciousness, where the limitations of the human mind do not apply.

Therefore, in order to access the world of Cause, one must undergo a transformation of consciousness that transcends the limitations of the ordinary human mind. This transformation is said to involve the cultivation of spiritual practices, such as meditation, prayer, and self-inquiry, which allow the individual to gradually detach from the material world and awaken to their true nature as pure consciousness.

Normal human beings, who are still bound by the limitations of their minds, cannot directly perceive or validate the existence of the world of Cause. However, they may be able to indirectly perceive its effects through the actions and teachings of awakened beings, who are said to be in touch with this higher realm of consciousness. Therefore, the world of Cause may be validated through its impact on human behavior, ethics, and values, rather than through direct perception or scientific investigation.

World of Bodhisattvas

People in the world of Bodhisattvas strive to attain the enlightenment of the Buddha. What distinguishes them is their aspiration for the enlightened life state manifested by their mentor, the Buddha, who works tirelessly to free people from suffering. Bodhisattvas are characterized by compassion and altruism-an empathy for the pain and sorrow of others and a desire to help relieve them of that suffering and find joy.

Soundness and credibility of concept: The nature and world of the Bodhisattvas cannot be validated by human beings because they exist beyond the realm of ordinary human experience and understanding. Bodhisattvas are beings who have attained a high level of spiritual development and have dedicated themselves to the welfare of all sentient beings, seeking to attain enlightenment for the benefit of all.

In Buddhist philosophy, the nature of reality is seen as being dependent on the individual's perception and is therefore subjective. Bodhisattvas are said to exist in a state of awareness beyond the ordinary human mind, and their actions are guided by a profound understanding of the nature of reality that is beyond the grasp of human intellect.

The teachings of the Buddha suggest that the ultimate nature of reality is non-dual and beyond all concepts and categories, including those of existence and non-existence, self and other. This means that the Bodhisattva's nature and world cannot be grasped by the ordinary dualistic mind, which operates within the realm of concepts and categories.

In summary, the nature and world of the Bodhisattvas are beyond the ordinary human experience and understanding and cannot be validated by human beings. They exist beyond the dualistic mind and the realm of concepts and categories, and their actions are guided by a profound understanding of the nature of reality that is beyond the grasp of human intellect.

World of Buddhahood

Lastly, the world of Buddhahood, describes the most supremely noble state of life that a living being can manifest. It is not, however, a superhuman or supernatural state of being. The term "Buddha" means "awakened one." What a Buddha is awakened to is the underlying principle of the "Mystic Law"-that all life possesses intrinsic, irreplaceable value, that all living beings are capable of harnessing unique strengths and creating good within themselves and the environment. In other words, each living being is itself a manifestation of the Mystic law. Those who awaken to this and take action based upon it are Buddhas.

Although the life state of Buddhahood is originally inherent in each of us, it is difficult to manifest in our daily lives. The Buddhist practice established by Ven. Nichiren (that of chanting Nam-myoho- renge-kyo, or devotion to the Mystic Law) is revolutionary in that it provides a means for all people to bring forth the world of Buddhahood at any time, regardless of their circumstances.

This life state of Buddhahood can be described in contemporary terms as a state of absolute and indestructible happiness unaffected by circumstantial changes or difficulties. Although this does not imply freedom from sufferings and problems, it does indicate possession of a vibrant, sturdy life force and abundant wisdom to challenge and overcome all the sufferings and difficulties we may encounter. Most importantly, however, in the words of Daisaku Ikeda, attaining Buddhahood means "to solidify in our lives a spirit of yearning for the happiness of oneself and others, and to continuously take constructive action with that spirit." It is a life state of ultimate hope and fulfilment.

Soundness and credibility of concept: In Buddhism, the nature and world of the Buddhas refer to the ultimate reality or truth that lies beyond the ordinary world of human experience. It is said to be a state of perfect peace, wisdom, and compassion that can be achieved through spiritual practice.

According to Buddhist teachings, the normal human mind is limited by its conditioning and attachment to subjective experiences and perceptions. It is subject to delusions and false perceptions, which lead to suffering and dissatisfaction. Therefore, the nature and world of the Buddhas cannot be fully grasped or understood by the normal human mind.

Buddhism teaches that spiritual practice, such as meditation, mindfulness, and ethical living, can help to gradually transform the human mind and enable it to experience glimpses of the ultimate reality. However, even with such practice, the ultimate truth can never be fully comprehended by the human mind because it is beyond the scope of our ordinary understanding and language.

In other words, the nature and world of the Buddhas are beyond the reach of normal human cognition because they lie outside the realm of our conditioned perceptions and concepts. They are not something that can be validated or grasped by the normal human mind alone, but rather require a profound transformation of consciousness through spiritual practice [21].

3.3   Extended Ten Worlds

The Lotus Sutra is distinct from other teachings also because it expounds the mutual possession of the Ten Worlds, clarifying that each of the Ten

Worlds encompasses all of the other worlds. This indicates that life is not fixed in one of the Ten Worlds but at any moment can manifest any one of them. Because of this principle, it is possible for us to change our state of life, for although we may "inhabit" a particular world, the other nine are present, though dormant, in our lives.

Which of the Ten Worlds will manifest at any given moment depends on our response to the influences in our environment. One's life state may fluctuate from one moment to the next, but from a broader perspective, there is always one state or several states around which our activities revolve and to which we are most likely to revert.

The mutual possession of the Ten Worlds implies that all individuals have the potential to manifest Buddhahood at any given moment. Through continuing effort in Buddhist practice-practicing for the happiness of oneself, dismantling one's prejudices and mistaken beliefs, polishing the inherent qualities of wisdom and compassion- we can solidify the world of Buddhahood inherent within our life. Buddhahood is not an abstract idea; it reveals itself tangibly in our daily behavior in the form of compassion, wisdom and our efforts to establish happiness for ourselves and others.

Attaining Buddhahood does not mean eradicating the lower nine worlds. Instead, under the influence of our inherent Buddhahood, the positive aspects of these worlds become manifest, contributing to the construction of happiness for ourselves and others [33].

3.4   Ten Factors of Life

Together with the ten worlds and their mutual possession, the next component of the three thousand realms is the principle of "the ten factors of life." While the ten worlds describe life's differing expressions, the ten factors describe elements common to all things. It explains how the law of cause and effect activates any of the ten worlds.

All life equally possesses the same ten factors, regardless of which of the ten worlds it manifests. The ten factors are (1) appearance, (2) nature, (3) entity, (4) power, (5) influence, (6) inherent causes, (7) external causes, (8) latent effects, (9) manifest effect, and (10) consistency from beginning to end.

The first three factors (appearance, nature and entity) describe the life entity, which manifests the ten worlds. The next six (power, influence, internal cause, relation, latent effect and manifest effect) describe the law of cause and effect-the way in which the ten worlds become manifest in the entity. Thus, a life "entity" has attributes that can be perceived by the senses (appearance) and attributes that cannot (nature).

The tenth factor, consistency from beginning to end, means that the ten factors are consistent for each of the ten worlds. Most saliently, this means that Buddhahood, a life state of unwavering happiness, is inherently present in our lives as an internal cause, and when we come in contact with a "relation" that opens that internal cause, we fully flower and harness the workings of the world of Buddhahood in our lives.

Appearance: Briefly, this is the way you look. This is not fixed as you can smile and appear one way or scowl and appear another. You can wear certain clothes and look different from when you wear other types of clothing. There are some aspects of appearance which are not changeable such as eye color, or skin color (well not so much generally), height once fully grown, hair color (well not permanently for the most part), hair or no hair. I would add gender except in certain circumstances.

Soundness and credibility of concept: Enlightenment refers to a state of spiritual awakening or realization, where an individual transcends their ego and gains a deep understanding of the nature of reality. Personal appearance, which includes physical characteristics such as height, weight, skin color, facial features, and clothing style, is not a relevant factor for achieving enlightenment.

Enlightenment is an internal transformation that occurs within an individual's consciousness. It has nothing to do with external factors such as appearance or material possessions. The path to enlightenment is about cultivating inner qualities such as compassion, wisdom, and mindfulness through practices of meditation, self-reflection, and service to others.

It is also worth noting that enlightenment is not reserved for a specific group of people or certain physical appearances. Anyone can achieve enlightenment, regardless of their appearance or background. In fact, many enlightened beings throughout history have come from diverse backgrounds and have looked very different from one another.

In short, personal appearance is not a relevant factor for enlightenment. Enlightenment is an internal transformation that can be achieved by anyone, regardless of their physical appearance. It is about cultivating inner qualities and developing a deeper understanding of the nature of reality.

Nature: Nature refers to the inherent qualities and characteristics of a phenomenon. It is the fundamental essence that gives rise to the appearance. Discerning the true nature of things often requires deep insight and contemplation.

This is how you are, not who you are. This includes such things as pessimistic, optimistic, daring, bold, shy, extrovert, introvert, gregarious, quick learner, visual learner, literal learner, learner by doing rather than instruction, adventurous, laid back, easy going, excitable. These are not always fixed, though for some people they may seem to be such. And further they are not always the same in any of us, we can be one way at one time and another in other instances. We can be both shy and gregarious, introverted and extroverted.

Soundness and credibility of concept: Enlightenment is a state of profound understanding or realization that transcends ordinary consciousness and leads to a greater sense of clarity, peace, and wisdom. Whether personal nature is a relevant or irrelevant factor for enlightenment depends on how one defines personal nature and how it influences one's spiritual journey.

Personal nature refers to the unique combination of personality traits, life experiences, and cultural background that shape an individual's perspective, values, and behaviour. From this perspective, personal nature could be seen as a relevant factor for enlightenment because it affects how one perceives and responds to spiritual teachings, practices, and experiences.

For example, someone who has a strong analytical mind may find it easier to understand and integrate complex philosophical concepts, while someone who is more emotionally sensitive may be more attuned to the subtle nuances of spiritual experiences. Similarly, someone who has had traumatic life experiences may need to work through deep emotional wounds in order to fully embrace spiritual growth, while someone who has had a relatively stable life may have fewer barriers to overcome.

However, personal nature can also be an irrelevant factor for enlightenment if one recognizes that the true nature of consciousness is beyond the limitations of the individual self. From this perspective, enlightenment is not something that can be attained through personal effort or mastery of certain techniques, but rather it is a realization of the innate nature of awareness that is already present in every moment.

In this sense, personal nature can be seen as a temporary construct that obscures the deeper reality of who we are. By letting go of attachment to our personal nature and opening up to the infinite potential of consciousness, we can experience a profound shift in perspective that leads to enlightenment.

Ultimately, whether personal nature is relevant or irrelevant for enlightenment depends on how one approaches the spiritual path. For some, personal nature may be an important aspect of self-discovery and growth, while for others it may be a temporary obstacle to be transcended.

Entity: The entity represents the substantive aspect or underlying reality of a phenomenon. It is the "thing-in-itself" that exists independently of our perceptions. Grasping the entity can be challenging as it goes beyond mere appearances and delves into the essence of existence. This is our total complete self, it can include genetics, disposition to certain diseases, blood type, physical strength, emotional strength, internal organs, demeanor as a total.

Soundness and credibility of concept: The cultivation of wisdom and enlightenment is not dependent on our physical or genetic makeup, but rather on our inner state of awareness, consciousness, and perception. While our genetics and physical attributes may influence our experience in the world, they do not determine our capacity for spiritual growth or understanding.

Enlightenment and wisdom are about transcending our limited sense of self and connecting with a deeper, more universal truth that transcends our physical existence. This means that our genetics, disposition to certain diseases, blood type, physical strength, emotional strength, internal organs, and demeanor are all ultimately irrelevant to the pursuit of wisdom and enlightenment.

While these physical factors may influence our experiences in the world and shape our individual perspective, they are not the essence of who we are. True wisdom and enlightenment come from recognizing the fundamental nature of consciousness, which is present in all beings regardless of physical form.

In fact, some spiritual traditions teach that our physical and genetic makeup can be a distraction from the path of enlightenment, as we may become attached to our identity and cling to certain beliefs or characteristics as defining aspects of ourselves. By letting go of these attachments and opening up to the infinite potential of consciousness, we can experience a profound shift in perspective that leads to greater wisdom and understanding.

Therefore, while our physical and genetic makeup may shape our experience in the world, they are ultimately irrelevant to the pursuit of enlightenment and the cultivation of wisdom. These qualities may influence how we approach the spiritual path, but they do not determine our capacity for spiritual growth or realization of our true nature.

Power: Power refers to the inherent potential or capacity of a phenomenon to act and influence its surroundings. Understanding the power of a phenomenon involves recognizing the dynamic and transformative aspects that shape its interactions with other phenomena.

Power is not always only about physical or mental strength. It includes our ability to persevere, to challenge ourselves, to introspect, to reflect, (our nature may affect our willingness or tendency to do so even if we may have great power as an ability). Our ability to lead others, for good or ill, our skill with other people can be a power again for good or ill. Our ability to see our strengths and use them skillfully or not is a power even when the actual power may be limited. A person may not have the power to do something yet may be able to accomplish the goal through the power of working with others again for good or for ill.

Soundness and credibility of concept: Our power, ability to persevere, to challenge ourselves, to introspect, to reflect, and to lead others can all be relevant factors in the cultivation of wisdom and enlightenment, depending on how we use them.

On one hand, these qualities can be valuable tools for self-discovery and growth. For example, the ability to persevere through challenging situations can help us develop resilience and deepen our understanding of our own strengths and limitations. The ability to introspect and reflect can help us identify patterns in our thoughts and behaviour, and gain greater insight into our motivations and desires. And the ability to lead others can help us develop compassion, empathy, and a sense of responsibility towards others.

However, these qualities can also be obstacles to spiritual growth if we become attached to them as defining aspects of our identity. For example, if we become overly identified with our power or ability to lead, we may lose sight of the deeper, more universal truths that transcend our individual accomplishments. Similarly, if we become too focused on challenging ourselves and pushing our limits, we may lose sight of the importance of stillness, surrender, and letting go.

Ultimately, the relevance of these qualities for the cultivation of wisdom and enlightenment depends on how we approach them. If we use them as tools for self-discovery and growth, while also recognizing their limitations and the need for humility and surrender, they can be valuable assets in our spiritual journey. However, if we become attached to them as defining aspects of our identity or use them as a means to bolster our ego, they can become obstacles to our spiritual growth and realization.

Influence: Influence pertains to the effects or impact a phenomenon has on its environment or other phenomena. Determining and comprehending the extent and nature of influence can be complex, as it involves considering various interdependencies and causal relationships. What are we doing, what are we accomplishing or trying to accomplish, is the activity physical, mental, emotional, spiritual, is the activity for self or for others are some ways to consider activity.

Soundness and credibility of concept: The soundness of the concept of "influence" as a factor of life in Ichinen sanzen. Within these realms, influence is seen as a pervasive and dynamic force that affects a person's life in various ways. Here's a brief overview of how influence is understood in this context:

Influence of One's Environment: According to Nichiren Buddhism, the environment we are in, including the people and circumstances surrounding us, exerts a significant influence on our lives. This influence can be positive or negative, depending on the nature of the environment.

Influence form One's Karma: Karma, is the accumulation of causes and effects from one's past thoughts, words, and actions. This karma influences the present and future circumstances of an individual's life. Positive karma can lead to good fortune, while negative karma can lead to suffering.

Influence from One's mind: The nature of one's thoughts and intentions in this moment can also have a profound influence on the course of one's life. Positive, compassionate thoughts are believed to attract positive outcomes, while negative, destructive thoughts may lead to adversity.

The concept of influence is considered sound and credible, as it is deeply rooted in the teachings of Ven. Nichiren Daishonin and has been practiced by millions of people for centuries. However, it's essential to recognize that belief in this concept is a matter of faith and personal conviction.

Belief in the power of influence is subjective and can vary widely among different individuals and belief systems. Ultimately, the soundness and credibility of the concept of influence in Ichinen sanzen depend on one's faith in Nichiren Buddhism and their personal experiences and interpretations of how this concept operates in their life.

Inherent causes: This factor relates to the internal factors or conditions that contribute to the existence and functioning of a phenomenon. Identifying and understanding the internal causes requires a deep understanding of the underlying mechanisms and processes at play.

There is a cause which precedes every cause to some extent. There is a primary cause in all things, what is that in each of the situations we engage in and how does that impact all the other ten factors. One primary cause is the difference between self and others, between self and environment, between self as a physical entity and self as a spiritual entity and self as a complete undifferentiated complete entity. Where is the primary cause directed inward versus outward, towards oneself or towards others, includes or excludes others, benefits others or only self all are primary causes beneath initial traditional activities. Also, a primary cause is human, non-human animal, plant, or even alien.

Soundness and credibility of concept: In the Ichinen sanzen philosophy, "Inherent cause," refers to the fundamental karmic forces that shape our destiny and influence our experiences.

The relevance of the primary cause for the cultivation of wisdom and enlightenment depends on how we understand its role in our lives. From a Buddhist perspective, karma is understood as the result of our past actions and intentions, which have created an ongoing chain of cause and effect that shapes our current experiences.

In this context, the primary cause can be seen as a fundamental force that shapes our destiny and influences our experiences in the world. However, from the perspective of wisdom and enlightenment, the goal is to transcend the limitations of our past karma and cultivate a deeper understanding of the nature of reality.

This means that while the primary cause may be relevant to our current experiences and circumstances, it is ultimately irrelevant to the pursuit of wisdom and enlightenment. Instead, the focus is on cultivating a deeper awareness of the present moment, recognizing the impermanent and interconnected nature of all phenomena, and developing a sense of universal compassion and wisdom that transcends the limitations of our past karma.

In this sense, while the primary cause may play a role in shaping our experiences and influencing our path in life, it is ultimately an irrelevant factor for the cultivation of wisdom and enlightenment. The focus is on cultivating a deeper understanding of the nature of reality and developing a sense of universal compassion and wisdom that transcends the limitations of our past actions and intentions.

External causes: There are factors which take place outside ourselves and often outside our control. Is it raining, if so, did you think to bring an umbrella? Failing to consider environmental causes can lead to death such as by heat exhaustion and stroke, or freezing to death, starvation, disease and illness. Sometimes the environment is beyond our control but what is within our control may be able to mitigate the effects of the environment. Sometimes it cannot, such as an earthquake, typhoon, airplane crash, fire, terrorist attack. In all cases we do ever act independent of our environment even if we may fail to consider it.

Soundness and credibility of concept: The external causes are mostly environment factor is both relevant and irrelevant in the cultivation of wisdom and enlightenment, depending on how it is understood and approached in spiritual practice.

On the one hand, the external factors are relevant because they shape our perceptions, attitudes, and behaviors. Our external environment can either support or hinder our spiritual growth and development. For example, being surrounded by positive influences such as wise teachers, supportive friends, and natural beauty can help us cultivate a calm and clear mind, deepen our understanding of the nature of reality, and foster compassion and wisdom. On the other hand, being surrounded by negative influences such as violence, materialism, and ignorance can hinder our spiritual progress and lead us astray from the path of wisdom and enlightenment.

Ichinen sanzen emphasizes the interconnectedness of all phenomena, including the external factors. According to this philosophy, everything that we experience in our environment is a manifestation of our own life and consciousness. Therefore, by changing our inner state of mind, we can transform our environment and create a more conducive atmosphere for spiritual growth and development.

The external causes can also be seen as irrelevant in the cultivation of wisdom and enlightenment. Ultimately, the attainment of wisdom and enlightenment is an internal process that depends on our own efforts and understanding, rather than external conditions. No matter what the environment is like, we have the potential to awaken our true nature and realize our full spiritual potential.

Therefore, while the external causes are important in the cultivation of wisdom and enlightenment, it is not the only factor or the determining factor. Our own efforts, intentions, and understanding also play a crucial role in this process.

Latent effect: Latent effects refer to the potential consequences or outcomes that are not immediately apparent but may manifest in the future. Recognizing and predicting latent effects requires a comprehensive understanding of the system and its dynamics.

There are factors which take place outside ourselves and often outside our control. Is it raining, if so, did you think to bring an umbrella? Failing to consider environmental causes can lead to death such as by heat exhaustion and stroke, or freezing to death, starvation, disease and illness. Sometimes the environment is beyond our control but what is within our control may be able to mitigate the effects of the environment. Sometimes it cannot, such as an earthquake, typhoon, airplane crash, fire, terrorist attack. In all cases we do ever act independent of our environment even if we may fail to consider it.

Soundness and credibility of concept: The concept and the idea of "Latent effects" suggests that every action, thought, or intention has consequences that may not immediately manifest but can influence one's future experiences. These latent effects are believed to be an integral part of the cycle of karma, and they contribute to the continuous cycle of birth and rebirth.

From the standpoint of Nichiren Buddhism and its practitioners, believe that understanding and addressing these latent effects through sincere practice, chanting, and seeking enlightenment can lead to positive transformations in one's life.

At its core, the concept suggests that our lives are a reflection of our inner state, and that our thoughts, feelings, and actions have a direct impact on the world around us. This means that everything that happens, whether it is immediately observable or not, is seen as a manifestation of our inner state.

On the other hand, the concept of "latent effects" can also be irrelevant because true wisdom and enlightenment are said to transcend the realm of cause and effect altogether. In this view, the ultimate goal of spiritual practice is to achieve a state of pure awareness that is free from the limitations of our conditioned thinking and habits. In this state, the distinction between cause and effect becomes irrelevant, as we become one with the interconnected web of all phenomena.

Overall, the concept of "latent effect" in Ichinen sanzen philosophy serves as a reminder of the interdependence of all things and the importance of cultivating awareness and wisdom in order to live a fulfilling life.

Manifest effects: Manifest effects are the observable consequences or outcomes of a phenomena. While these effects may be easier to recognize, tracing them back to their underlying causes and understanding the broader implications can still be a complex task.

It's what happens, seen, unseen, known, unknown, immediately observable or seemingly manifest later (all effects manifest instantly only some may not be observed instantly).

Soundness and credibility of concept: The concept of "manifest effect" plays a significant role in the cultivation of wisdom and enlightenment. At its core, the idea of Ichinen sanzen suggests that our lives are a reflection of our inner state, and that our thoughts, feelings, and actions have a direct impact on the world around us. This means that everything that happens, whether it is immediately observable or not, is seen as a manifestation of our inner state.

In this context, the concept of "manifest effect" can be both relevant and irrelevant to the cultivation of wisdom and enlightenment. It could be relevant because our experiences and the consequences of our actions can serve as powerful teachers, helping us to develop insight and wisdom about ourselves and the world around us. By observing the effects of our thoughts, feelings, and actions, we can learn to better understand our own nature and the nature of reality.

On the other hand, the concept of "manifest effect" can also be irrelevant because true wisdom and enlightenment are said to transcend the realm of cause and effect altogether. In this view, the ultimate goal of spiritual practice is to achieve a state of pure awareness that is free from the limitations of our conditioned thinking and habits. In this state, the distinction between cause and effect becomes irrelevant, as we become one with the interconnected web of all phenomena.

Overall, the concept of "manifest effect" in Ichinen sanzen philosophy serves as a reminder of the interdependence of all things and the importance of cultivating awareness and wisdom in order to live a fulfilling life.

Consistency from beginning to end: The concept of "Consistency from beginning to end" in Ichinen sanzen is a fundamental principle in the practice, particularly in the context of chanting the mantra Nam-myoho-renge-kyo. This principle emphasizes the importance of maintaining a consistent and sincere practice throughout one's life, from the beginning of their Buddhist practice to the very end. It is closely related to the broader concept of "faith, practice, and study" in Nichiren Buddhism.

Soundness and credibility of concept: This concept depend largely on one's personal belief system and their commitment to the teachings of Nichiren Buddhism. Here are some key points to consider:

Spiritual Practice: Consistency in spiritual practice is a common principle in many religious and philosophical traditions. The idea is that regular and sincere practice leads to spiritual growth and enlightenment.

In Nichiren Buddhism, consistency in chanting Nam- myoho-renge-kyo is believed to help individuals tap into their innate Buddha nature.

Personal Belief: The credibility of this concept largely depends on an individual's belief in Nichiren Buddhism and its teachings. Those who follow this faith often find value and meaning in maintaining consistent practice throughout their lives.

Experiential Evidence: Some practitioners may claim to have experienced positive changes in their lives as a result of consistent practice, which can strengthen their belief in the concept. However, personal experiences can vary widely, and what works for one person may not work for another.

Skepticism: From a more skeptical perspective, the concept of "Consistency from beginning to end" may be seen as a form of confirmation bias, where individuals attribute positive outcomes in their lives solely to their religious practice. Skeptics may question the causal relationship between consistent practice and life outcomes.

The Ichinen sanzen diagram shows how the ten worlds, the mutual possession of the ten worlds, the ten factors, and the three realms all combine to provide insight into the incredible beauty and complexity of life at any given moment (Fig. 2.1 and 2.2). The three realms, then, represent the actual world of the individual. They are not separate but, rather, are an integrated whole which simultaneously manifests any of the Ten worlds.

3.5 The Three Realms of Existence

The final component of the three thousand realms is the principle of the "three realms of existence." This concept views life from three different standpoints and explains the existence of individual lives in the real world.

The three realms are (1) the realm of the five aggregates (form, perception, conception, volition, and consciousness; form corresponds to the physical aspect of life, the other four components to the mental aspect), (2) the realm of living beings (the individual living being, formed of a temporary union of the five components, that manifests or experiences any of the Ten worlds), and (3) the realm of the environment (the individual environment that supports the existence of the living being). The third component views life and explains the existence of individual in the real world.

These three realms of existence can also be described as the desire realm, the form realm, and the formless realm. The desire realm is the realm in which humans, animals, and other sentient beings lives, while the form and formless realms are the realms inhabited by higher beings who have attained higher levels of existence through their practice. The three realms, represent the actual world of the individual. They are not separate but, rather, are an integrated whole which simultaneously manifests any of the Ten worlds.

The Realm of the Aggregates: Within the desire realm, the realm of the five components (also known as the five aggregates) is of particular importance to the cultivation of wisdom and enlightenment. The five components are:

1. Form (rūpa) - the physical body and its sense organs.
2. Perception (vedanā) - the experience of sensation and feeling.
3. Conception or labeling (saññā) - the recognition and identification of objects
4. Volition or mental formations (saṅkhārā) - the mental processes that create thoughts and actions.
5. Consciousness (viññanā) - the awareness of one's surroundings and experiences.

According to Buddhism, these five components are impermanent and constantly changing, and they are not a permanent self or soul. By understanding this impermanence and non-self-nature, one can cultivate wisdom and enlightenment.

For example, through the practice of mindfulness and meditation, one can observe the impermanent nature of the five components, and by doing so, gain insight into the nature of reality. This can lead to the realization that all phenomena are empty of inherent existence, and that attachment to these components is the cause of suffering.

In addition, by understanding the interdependence and interconnection of the five components, one can also develop compassion and empathy for others. This understanding can lead to the realization that all beings are interconnected and that the suffering of one being affects all beings.

Overall, the realm of the five components plays a critical role in the cultivation of wisdom and enlightenment in Buddhism, as it provides a framework for understanding the impermanence and non-self-nature of reality, and for developing compassion and empathy for all beings. The difficulty arises because these components are not separate entities but are interconnected and interdependent. They constantly influence and condition each other, making it challenging to discern their individual contributions to our experiences and existence. Moreover, the nature of consciousness itself is complex and elusive, making it difficult to fully comprehend its workings and its role in shaping our perception of reality. Abhidhamma intricately defines the realm of five aggregates (khandhā) and it require the six sensory bases of the body and mind to perceive its real nature of impermanence and unsubstantiality.

The Realm of Living beings: This realm refers to the diverse array of sentient beings that inhabit the world. Each living being has its own unique experiences, perspectives, and karmic tendencies. Understanding this realm involves recognizing the inherent interconnectedness and shared experiences of all living beings.

However, comprehending the realm of living beings can be challenging due to the sheer diversity and complexity of sentient existence. Each individual possesses a unique combination of factors such as karma, past experiences, and present circumstances that shape their current state. The multifaceted nature of living beings makes it difficult to categorize or generalize their experiences, and true understanding requires empathy, deep observation, and the ability to transcend one's own limited perspective.

The Realm of the Environment: This realm pertains to the external world and the conditions in which living beings exist. It includes the physical environment, social structures, cultural systems, and various external factors that shape our experiences and interactions. Understanding this realm involves recognizing the intricate web of cause and effect that operates on a collective level.

Comprehending the realm of the environment can be challenging because it encompasses a vast array of factors and influences. The environment is constantly changing and evolving, and its impact on living beings is complex and multifaceted. Additionally, the interdependence between the realm of living beings and the realm of the environment adds another layer of complexity, as they mutually shape and influence each other.

In this way, one's life condition at any given moment is determined by three elements: the mutual possession of the Ten Worlds (10 worlds × 10 worlds = 100 worlds), the ten factors of life and the three realms of existence. Therefore, the dimensions that exist in this world are the number that results from multiplying these elements, or 3,000. This also means that any single life has the potential to express 3,000 dimensions.

Ten suchnesses is the second volume of three volume set on Ichinen sanzen, "Three thousand states of mind in a moment of existence." During our everyday service people recite the ten suchnesses, or Junnyoze as part of Chapter II from the Lotus sutra. The author of the book, Ryusho Jeffus Shonin mentions in the blurb: "Because there is not much written about the ten aspects or the ten suchnesses, I thought it might be useful to explain them so people can have a better idea of the depth and the complexity of not just the ten suchnesses but also the concept of Ichinen sanzen, three thousand states of mind in a moments existence, a fundamental teaching of the Lotus Sutra as identified by Chih'I [33]." Here the author clears that there is not much information as a written document about the details of the factors that encompasses Ichinen sanzen. Such unavailability of the information many a time obstruct the meditator to perceive the worldly phenomena in its real nature of impermanence and unsubstantiality. In many a case it may lead to blind faith among the believers which takes them far away from the path of their insight and wisdom.

3.6   Objective of 3,000 Realms

The philosophy of Ichinen sanzen, also known as the "Three thousand realms in a single moment of life," is a concept that originated in the Lotus sutra, a key scripture in Mahayana Buddhism. The basic idea of Ichinen sanzen is that every single moment of our lives contains the potential for enlightenment, and that this potential is present in all beings and things in the universe.

The main objective of Ichinen sanzen philosophy is to help individuals understand and cultivate this potential for enlightenment within themselves. This is achieved through the practice of mindfulness and the cultivation of compassion and wisdom. By focusing on the present moment and cultivating a sense of compassion and understanding for all beings, one can begin to realize the interconnectedness of all things and the ultimate nature of reality.

Ichinen sanzen philosophy is the idea that all beings have the potential to become Buddhas, or fully enlightened beings. This belief emphasizes the idea that everyone has the capacity for enlightenment, regardless of their background or circumstances. It is believed that through the practice of mindfulness and the cultivation of compassion and wisdom, individuals can work towards realizing their full potential and becoming enlightened.

In addition to support individuals understand and cultivate their own potential for enlightenment, Ichinen sanzen philosophy also emphasizes the importance of sharing this understanding with others. By spreading the teachings of the Lotus sutra and the concept of Ichinen sanzen, practitioners can help others realize their own potential and work towards enlightenment as well. This sense of interdependence and shared responsibility is an important aspect of Ichinen sanzen philosophy.

Overall, the objectives of Ichinen sanzen philosophy can be summarized as helping individuals understand and cultivate their own potential for enlightenment, and sharing this understanding with others in order to help all beings realize their own potential and work towards enlightenment. This is achieved through the practice of mindfulness and the cultivation of compassion and wisdom, and is based on the belief that all beings have the capacity to become fully enlightened.

Buddhism's ultimate goal has always been to enable people to attain Buddhahood, or enlightenment. Early Buddhists believed, however, that achieving this highest state of life required carrying out incredible efforts over countless lifetimes.

3.7   Perception of 3,000 Realms

In Buddhism, the concept of the "3,000 realms in a single moment of life" refers to the idea that all possible experiences, thoughts, and states of being exist within us at every moment. This concept is related to the broader framework of the "ten worlds, ten life factors, and three realms."

The "ten worlds" refer to ten possible states of being that one can experience at any given moment. These include Hell, Hunger, Animality, Anger, Humanity, Heaven, Learning, Realization, Bodhisattva, and Buddhahood. Each of these states represents a different level of consciousness or awareness, and they are arranged hierarchically with Buddhahood being the highest state.

The "ten life factors" refer to the various components that make up our lives, including perception, cognition, volition, consciousness, and others. These factors are seen as interconnected and interdependent, and they shape our experiences of the ten worlds.

Finally, the "three realms" refer to the three categories of existence: the realm of desire, the realm of form, and the realm of formlessness. These realms are not physical places, but rather represent different levels of consciousness and awareness.

In this conceptual framework, the clear perception of the 3000 realms in reality is practically impossible because our experiences are shaped by our current state of consciousness and awareness. Our perception of reality is filtered through our current state, and we can only perceive those aspects of reality that are consistent with our current level of consciousness.

For example, someone in the state of Hell may perceive the world as a place of suffering and despair, while someone in the state of Buddhahood may perceive the world as a place of equanimity and enlightenment. These perceptions are shaped by the individual's current state of consciousness and awareness, and they cannot fully comprehend the experiences of other states.

The interconnectedness of the ten life factors means that our experiences are shaped not only by our current state of consciousness but also by our past experiences and actions. These factors create a complex web of causality that makes it impossible to fully comprehend all the possible experiences and states of being in the 3,000 realms.

Hence the conceptual framework of ten worlds, ten life factors, and three realms makes it practically impossible to have a clear perception of the 3,000 realms in reality because our experiences are shaped by our current state of consciousness and awareness, as well as by our past experiences and actions. This means that we can only perceive a limited subset of the possible experiences and states of being in the 3,000 realms.

3.8   Limitations of Human Mind

While the concept of Ichinen sanzen, "3,000 realms in a single moment," may be profound and intellectually stimulating, it is important to recognize the limitations of the human mind in fully grasping and comprehending this concept. The human mind is finite and limited in its capacity to process and understand complex ideas and concepts, and Ichinen sanzen may be beyond the scope of our ability to fully comprehend.

The human mind is conditioned by its own experiences and perceptions, which can influence and shape our understanding of reality. This means that our understanding of the 3,000 realms in a single moment may be limited by our own biases, perspectives, and limited experiences. Furthermore, the concept of Ichinen sanzen involves an understanding of the interconnectedness of all things, which is a complex and abstract idea that may be difficult for the human mind to fully grasp and comprehend.

Therefore, although the concept of Ichinen sanzen may be a profound and intellectually stimulating idea, it is important to recognize the limitations of the human mind in fully grasping and comprehending this concept.

3.9   Practical Obstacles in Perception of 3,000 Realms

It is thought to be a state of enlightenment in which an individual is able to perceive the interconnectedness and interdependence of all things in the universe simultaneously. There are many practical obstacles that can make it difficult for individuals to achieve this state.

Primary practical obstacle to achieving Ichinen sanzen is the time and effort required to cultivate the necessary skills and mindset. Achieving enlightenment and developing a deep understanding of the interconnectedness of all things requires dedicated practice and discipline, and this can be a difficult and time-consuming process.

Many individuals may not have the time or resources to commit to this level of practice, making it difficult for them to achieve Ichinen sanzen.

Another practical obstacle is the lack of guidance and support from experienced teachers and mentors. Achieving Ichinen sanzen is not a process that can be completed on one's own, and it requires the guidance and support of those who have already achieved this state. Without access to these resources, it can be difficult for individuals to develop the necessary skills and understanding to achieve Ichinen sanzen.

There may be societal or cultural barriers that make it difficult for individuals to pursue Ichinen sanzen. In some societies, there may be a lack of understanding or acceptance of the concept, or there may be social or economic pressures that prevent individuals from devoting the necessary time and energy to the pursuit of enlightenment.

As per the concept of Ichinen sanzen, it is thought that an individual can perceive the interconnectedness and interdependence of the ten worlds. There are specific limitations and challenges that make it difficult to fully perceive these ten worlds simultaneously. Individuals who wish to perceive the ten worlds may need to spend many years learning and practicing the principles of Buddhism. This necessitates a strong foundation in Buddhist teachings and practices. However, the Buddha denies mysticism and in Buddhism, the Buddha is often seen as a teacher who rejected mysticism and instead focused on practical, experiential methods for attaining enlightenment. One of the key ways in which the Buddha rejected mysticism was by emphasizing the importance of personal experience and direct perception in attaining enlightenment. Rather than relying on supernatural or mystical powers, the Buddha taught that enlightenment could be attained through the cultivation of mindfulness, concentration, and other mental qualities. He also rejected the idea of salvation through faith in a deity or other external power, and instead taught that each individual was responsible for their own enlightenment.

In this way, the Buddha promoted a practical, experiential approach to enlightenment that was grounded in the realities of the present moment. He encouraged his followers to investigate and observe their own minds and experiences, and to use the tools of mindfulness and insight to gain a deeper understanding of the nature of reality. Through this process, practitioners could discover for themselves the truth of the Buddha's teachings and attain enlightenment.

Overall, the Buddha's emphasis on the practical, experiential nature of enlightenment represents a significant departure from traditional mystical or supernatural approaches to spiritual growth. By rejecting these elements and focusing on the realities of the present moment, the Buddha provided a path for ordinary individuals to attain enlightenment and end suffering through their own efforts.

In fact, the concept of the ten worlds itself is difficult for a common analytical mind of human beings to perceive, comprehend and understand on the tract of the time. As the human mind is trained to comprehend and analyze all the physical and mental phenomena as it appears and pass away on the screen of his worlds of sensations, the ten worlds described in the concept of the Ichinen sanzen may be a mere imaginary world without any practical sensory experience.

Another specific challenge is the need for a clear and focused mind. In order to perceive the ten worlds simultaneously, an individual must be able to let go of distractions and ego-driven desires and focus solely on the present moment. This requires a high level of mental discipline and concentration, which can be difficult to achieve for many people.

Yet another challenge is the need for a strong connection to one's inner self. In order to fully grasp the interconnectedness of the ten worlds, an individual must be able to see beyond their own ego and connect with their true self. This requires a deep level of self-awareness and introspection, which can be challenging for some people to develop.

There are limitations and challenges specific to each of the ten worlds. For example, the concept of hell may be difficult for some people to understand or comprehend due to cultural or personal beliefs. Similarly, the concept of heavenly beings may be difficult for some people to accept due to their own beliefs about the nature of reality.

The concept of the "mystic law of the perception of ten worlds," is a central teaching in Nichiren Buddhism. It refers to the idea that all beings possess the potential to manifest any of the ten worlds within their own lives, depending on their state of mind at any given moment.

According to Nichiren Buddhism, the world of hell governs a state of extreme suffering and torment. The world of hungry spirits is a state of craving and desire. The world of animality is associated with ignorance and lack of consciousness. The world of anger synonymous to a state of hatred. The world of humanity runs through a state of ordinary, everyday consciousness. The world of heaven is full of a state of joy and bliss. The world of learning denotes a state of striving for enlightenment. The world of realization is experience of a state of enlightenment. The world of Bodhisattva is a state of compassion and altruism. Lastly the world of Buddhahood is the consummation state of complete and perfect enlightenment.

Nichiren Buddhism profess that all beings are capable of manifesting any of these ten worlds within their own lives, depending on the state of their minds at any given moment. Comprehending the ten worlds within Ichinen sanzen can be challenging due to several reasons:

Complexity: The ten worlds encompass a wide range of human experiences and states of mind, from the lowest world of Hell to the highest world of Buddhahood. Each world represents a different level of consciousness, and understanding the intricacies and nuances of each world requires deep contemplation and study.

Subjectivity: The ten worlds are not distinct, separate realms but rather interwoven and mutually inclusive aspects of our subjective experience.

Each individual can fluctuate between different worlds based on their thoughts, actions, and circumstances. This fluidity makes it difficult to clearly define and comprehend each world.

Fluctuation: Individuals can move through different worlds, depending on their thoughts, actions, and circumstances. This fluctuation can make it challenging to grasp the boundaries and distinctions between the worlds.

Dualities and Interconnectedness: The Ten worlds are not separate and independent from one another. They are interconnected, and one can contain elements of others. This interplay of dualities and the complex web of interconnectedness can make it difficult to grasp each world in isolation.

Personal Transformation: The concept of the Ten Worlds suggests that individuals have the potential to transcend lower worlds and attain higher states of consciousness. However, this transformation requires deep inner work, self-reflection, and spiritual practice, which can be challenging to undertake.

Cultural context: Nichiren Buddhism, from which the concept of Ichinen sanzen originates, has its own unique terminology, symbolism, and worldview. These cultural aspects may be unfamiliar to individuals not well-versed in Nichiren Buddhism, making it harder to grasp the full depth and meaning of the ten worlds.

Experiential nature: The ten worlds are not merely intellectual concepts but are meant to be experienced and realized through one's own practice and awakening. It is through personal introspection, meditation, and self-reflection that one can begin to directly perceive and understand the nature of these worlds.

In this way, the concept of the mystic law of the perception of ten worlds is central to the practice of Nichiren Buddhism, as it teaches that all beings have the potential to manifest any of the ten worlds within their own lives, and that through the practice of chanting and contemplation, they can ultimately attain the highest state of enlightenment. Within this belief, it is thought that an individual can perceive the interconnectedness and interdependence of all things.

The above philosophical framework within Nichiren Buddhism that aims to describe the complexity and interconnectedness of the universe. It encompasses ten factors that are believed to exist in all phenomena.

In conclusion, while the concept of Ichinen sanzen is a noble and potentially transformative goal, there are practical obstacles that can make it difficult to achieve. These obstacles include the need for a strong foundation in Buddhist teachings and practices, a clear and focused mind, and a strong connection to one's inner self. Despite these challenges, individuals who are committed to the path of Buddhism may be able to overcome these obstacles and achieve a deeper understanding of the interconnectedness of all things.

3.10 Mantra Recitation and Perception of Reality

In Buddhism, chanting of mantras are often used as a form of meditation practice to cultivate wisdom and enlightenment. Besides this Theravada chanting of the suttas, we should keep in mind about the Mahayana tradition which includes Vajrayana, Tantrayana, Sahajayana, Kalcakrayana and some other sects. This tradition holds a major part in Indian sub-continent as well as far east and south-east Asian countries. To understand the Buddhist chanting as a whole, one should study both the traditions.

However, it is important to understand that the recitation of a mantra alone cannot replace the perception of reality. On the other hand, the recitation of mantras is a form of meditation that can help to cultivate concentration, mindfulness, and insight. Mantras are a tool to focus the mind and develop awareness of the present moment. They are often used in combination with other meditation practices, such as visualization, to deepen one's understanding of the nature of reality.

While mantras can be a powerful tool for cultivating wisdom and enlightenment, they cannot replace the direct perception of reality. Mantras are a means to an end, rather than an end in themselves. They can help us to develop the concentration and insight necessary to perceive reality directly, but ultimately, it is the direct experience of reality that leads to true wisdom and enlightenment. The direct perception of reality requires a deep level of insight and wisdom that comes from the practice of ethical conduct, contemplation, and meditation.

3.11   "Nam Myoho Renge Kyo" and "Om Mani Padme Hum"

"*Nam Myoho Renge Kyo*" and "*Om Mani Padme Hum*" are both Buddhist chants related to Lotus sutra which is referred to as the Mystic law of the Lotus. "*Nam Myoho Renge Kyo*" is a root mantra of Nichiren Buddhism, chanted before the Gohonzon, a mandala. The meaning of the mantra of Nichiren Buddhism may be described as "Devotion to the wonderful Law of the Lotus". The Tibetan mantra "*Om Mani Padme Hum*" means "Praise to the Jewel in the Lotus". It is understood that both the mantras are derived from the title of the text of the Saddharma Pundarik sutra.

"*Om Mani Padme Hum*" is the Tibetan adaptation of the title of the Lotus sutra. It is the root mantra for Tibetan Buddhists associated with Ven. Avalokiteśvara, an entity of Bodhisatva. It is chanted in the Tibetan monasteries, inscribed on the flags and carved on stones of the walls. "Om is an Indian mystic incantation. "Padme" means Lotus flower. "Mani" means jewel. "Hum" means the spirit of enlightenment.

It seems that Tibetan Buddhism has a common link with Nichiren Buddhism through the Lotus sutra through its main mantra, implicitly referring to the "Law of the Lotus". The common thread in these two mantras is the word Lotus, not in terms of the flower, but in term of teachings offered in the Nichiren and Tibetan Buddhism by Ven. Nichiren and by Ven. Avalokitasvara.

However, Tibetan Buddhism does not correlate and associate the essence of the Lotus sutra with the observation of all the 3,000 phenomena in a single moment as established by Ichinen sanzen. There is also no frame of factorial design of the worldly phenomena in their meditative practices.

These chanting are purely sincere prayers, an exercise of gratitude and also inadvertently a breathing exercise which brings calmness, serenity and bliss to the mind of a meditator. The chanter of the mantra puts out his best thoughts while exercising the activity. Chanting either mantra almost surely help one connect to something bigger, and one feels the flow of happy chemicals whatever it is that these states bring out in us.

3.12   Ichinen Sanzen and Dhammakkhandha

In "Great Concentration and Insight," T'ien-t'ai states that life at each moment is endowed with the Ten Worlds. At the same time, each of the Ten Worlds are endowed with all Ten Worlds, so that an entity of life actually possesses one hundred worlds. Here we may associate the relativity of the principle of Ichinen sanzen with the philosophy of Dhammakkhandha. In the chapter of "Calculation of 84,000 Dhammakkhandha," we have arrived to 3,000 Dhammakkhandha by multiplication of the five elements of aggregates (Khandha) with 120 [60+60=120] elements of Sense spears (Āyatana) and five elements of hindrances to make total of 3000.

It seems that 10 worlds of the Ichinen sanzen means 10 'Loke' or 'Worlds of Sense spears. These 10 worlds of sense spears associate with the six internal and six external sense spears amounting to the total of 12 sense spears (Āyatana). These 12 worlds of sense spears and 10 worlds of sense spears (10 loke) becomes 120 worlds. The entity of life actually interplays in these 120 worlds of the sense spears. These when correspond with the five aggregates (Khanda) and five hindrances (Nīvaraṇa) comes to the total sum of 3000 realms. It is a fact that these three thousand realms of existence are all possessed by life in a single moment. If there is no life, that is the end of the matter but, if there is the slightest bit of life, it contains all the three thousand realms.

There have been records that Ven. T'ien-t'ai during his "Great Concentration and Insight," practiced Buddhist meditation and through this meditation the principle of the 3000 realms would have been absorbed as Ichinen-sanzen.

The Buddha states that Satipaṭṭhānā, four foundations of establishing mindfulness is the only teaching (Ekāyano maggo). This teaching gives us a comprehensive view of how life operates as the oneness of body and mind, the oneness of life and its internal and external environment. For the attainment of enlightenment, the 3000 realms of the world further associate with seven factors of enlightenment (Bojjhaṅga) and four Noble truths of suffering (Sacca) to further correspond them to 84,000 Dhammakkhanda explained by the Buddha in Mahāsatipatthānā sutta. Therefore, the principle of three thousand realms in a single moment of life, which forms the basis for Nichiren Buddhism may be reassessed and reconstituted in the light of the 84,000 Dhammakkhandha of Buddhism.

Although Ichinen sanzen speaks about 3,000 realms of the world, the Zen meditation accepts the principle of 84,000 Dhamma hooks for the progressive meditation. All people possess within their lives these 84,000 Dhamma aggregates and that all people, without exception, possess the world of Buddhahood, or the potential of enlightenment for liberation from suffering.

The author firmly believes that the calculation of the "three thousand realms" to see the entire phenomenal world in a single moment of life shall be better suited to the triad of Khandhā [5] x Āyatana [60+60=120] x Nīvaraṇa [5] = 3,000 Dhammakkhandha. For a Satipatthānā meditator it is not uncommon to see the entire phenomenal world in a single moment of life. In the entire external and internal phenomenal world, all the dhamma and khandhā does not have its true relevance unless and until it is practically experienced within the framework of the body and mind. If this is possible, then only the framework of the four noble truths and the relativity and interconnectivity of the dependent origination can be perceived. On the ground of these realities, there is no space for any imaginary mystic phenomenal world in this domain as it cannot be perceived and experienced on the body and mind of an individual on the path of the cultivation of wisdom and enlightenment.

3.13   Fundamental teachings of the Buddha: Noble Truths and Dependent Origination

The four Noble truths and Dependent origination are fundamental teachings in Buddhism, and they are considered essential for understanding the nature of reality and achieving enlightenment. The four Noble truths state that suffering exists, the cause of suffering is attachment and craving, suffering can be overcome, and the path to the cessation of suffering is the Eightfold path. Dependent origination explains the interdependent nature of all phenomena, and how our actions and intentions shape our experiences.

It is not possible to bypass these teachings and still achieve a clear perception of reality or cultivate wisdom and enlightenment in the Buddhist tradition. The four Noble truths and Dependent origination are foundational teachings that form the basis of Buddhist practice and philosophy. They provide a framework for understanding the nature of suffering and the path to liberation from it. Without an understanding of these teachings, it is difficult to cultivate the necessary insight and wisdom to develop a clear perception of reality.

Perception of reality is the direct experience of the present moment, which is free from the influence of concepts, thoughts, and emotions. It is the direct realization of the true nature of reality, which is beyond words and concepts. This realization requires a deep level of insight and wisdom that comes from the practice of meditation, contemplation, and ethical conduct.

3.14   Living in Present Moment

To live in the present moment is to live in reality. Moments that have passed are no longer real, only memory. Similarly, moments yet to come are unreal; you can only have expectations, fears and hopes of the future.

Living in the present moment means to be fully aware of whatever you experience at this very moment, here and now - by objectively observing the reality within and without your own body and mind. Pleasant, unpleasant memories of the past and hopes, insecurity, fears of the future fill one's mind with attractions or aversions and takes you away from reality of the present moment. A life not lived in reality of the present, is a life of delusion. Delusions defile the mind, and the deluded, impure mind leads to misery and unhappiness.

As the mind has a habit to roll in thoughts of the past or future, strong determination and steadfast efforts are needed to change this habit pattern of the mind. One has to stop the mind constantly wandering into the past or future and train to remain in reality of the present.

The wonderful practice of Buddhist meditations like Vipassana and Zen, enables the mind to live in the present moment. The Buddha therefore proclaims- "*Attā hi attano nātho, attā hi attano gati*" You are your own master; you make your own future.

Every thought arises with a sensation in the body, a pleasant or unpleasant biochemical reaction. The deepest part of the mind-where conditioning takes root-is constantly reacting to these sensations, and has nothing to do with objects in contact with sense organs.

3.15   Vipassana-Unique, Infinitely Beneficial for Mindfulness

Blindly reacting to bodily sensations is a real cause of our suffering, not external objects, persons, or happenings. The real cause of happiness or misery is within an individual, not outside. Therefore, the objective of the Buddhist practice is awareness of constantly changing bodily sensations, from moment to moment, experiencing this inner reality of sensations arising, passing away, with equanimity of the true, impermanent nature of things, every moment. Present moment is nothing but an offspring of the past moments. Likewise, the future is an offspring of the present moment. When the present moment is full of wisdom, the future will be full of happiness.

Chapter 4
Satipaṭṭhānā

Foundation for 3,000 Realms

There is no need to run, strive, search or struggle. Just be. Just being in the moment in this place is the deepest practice of meditation. Most people cannot believe that just walking as if you have nowhere to go is enough."

– Thich Nhat Hanh

The Mahāsatipaṭṭhānā sutta is a Buddhist text that is widely regarded as one of the most important teachings on mindfulness within the Sutta Pitaka, a collection of scriptures within the Pali Canon. This sutta, which is also known as the "foundational sutta" for the practice of mindfulness meditation, outlines four foundations of mindfulness, which are referred to as the "four satipaṭṭhānās." These four major divisions are categorized as mindfulness of the body (Kāyānupassanā), mindfulness of feelings (Vedanānupassanā), mindfulness of the mind (Cittānupassanā), and mindfulness of mental contents (Dhammānupassanā) [34]. The Mahāsatipaṭṭhānā sutta has been discussed in details in the authors book, "Encounter with Satipaṭṭhāna: 84,000 Dhammakkhandha of Buddhism." The reference of this book has been quoted quite often throughout this book [35]. The brief overview of the Mahāsatipaṭṭhānā sutta has been given as follows:

Evaṃ me sutaṃ Ekaṃ samayaṃ bhagavā kurūsu viharati kammāsadhammaṃ nāma kurūnaṃ nigamo. Tatra kho bhagavā bhikkhū āmantesi, 'Bhikkhavo' ti. 'Bhaddante' ti te bhikkhū bhagavato paccassosuṃ. Bhagavā etadavoca.

Katame cattāro? Idha, bhikkhave, bhikkhu kāye kāyānupassī viharati ātāpī sampajāno satimā, vineyya loke abhijjhādomanassaṃ. Vedanāsu vedanānupassī viharati ātāpī sampajāno satimā, vineyya loke abhijjhādomanassaṃ. Citte cittānupassī viharati ātāpī sampajāno satimā, vineyya loke abhijjhādomanassaṃ. Dhammesu dhammānupassī viharati ātāpī sampajāno satimā, vineyyaloke abhijjhādomanassaṃ.

... ...

... ... 'Ekāyano ayaṃ, bhikkhave, maggo sattānaṃ visuddhiyā, sokaparidevānaṃ samatikkamāya, dukkhadomanassānaṃ atthaṅgamāya, ñāyassa adhigamāya, nibbānassa sacchikiriyāyayadidaṃ cattāro satip atthānā' ti. Iti yaṃ tamvuttaṃ, idametaṃ paṭicca vuttaṃ ti. Idamavoca bhagavā. Attamanā te bhikkhū bhagavato bhāsitaṃ abhinanduṃ ti.

"I have heard thus, at one time the Sublime One was dwelling among the Kurus at Kammāsadhamma, a market town of the Kuru people. There the Sublime One addressed the monks thus: "Monks," and they replied, "Yes Venerable Sir!" Then the Sublime One spoke as follows.

Which are these four? Here, monks, a monk dwells with diligence, clear understanding and mindfulness of impermanence, perceiving body as just the body (not I, not mine, not self but just as phenomena), keeping away from craving and aversion towards the world [of mind and matter]; he dwells with diligence, clear understanding and mindfulness of impermanence, perceiving feelings as just the feelings (not I, not mine, not self but just as phenomena), keeping away from craving and aversion towards the world [of mind and matter]; he dwells with diligence, clear understanding and mindfulness of impermanence, perceiving mind as just the mind (not I, not mine, not self but just as phenomena), keeping away from craving and aversion towards the world [of mind and matter]; he dwells with diligence, clear understanding and mindfulness of impermanence, perceiving mental contents as just the mind contents (not I, not mine, not self but just as phenomena), keeping away from craving and aversion towards the world [of mind and matter]. ……It is for this reason that it was said: "Monks, this is the one and the only way, for the purification of beings, for the overcoming of sorrow and lamentation, for the cessation of physical sufferings and mental grief, for walking on the noble path of truth, for the realization of enlightenment: that is to say, the four progressions of mindfulness. Thus, the Sublime One spoke. With rejoiced, the monks welcomed the words of the Sublime One.

Summary of the Mahasatipaṭṭhānā sutta: The sutta is delivered by the Blessed One at Kuru's Kammāsadhamma, a market town of the Kuru people. He teaches the bhikkhus about the four progressions of mindfulness which the Blessed One proclaimed as, the one and the only way, for the purification of beings, for the overcoming of sorrow and lamentation, for the cessation of physical sufferings and mental grief, for walking on the noble path of truth, for the realization of enlightenment.

The Blessed One explains, progression of mindfulness on contemplation of the body (Kāyānupassanā) on six aspects of the body namely, on in and out breathing (Ānāpāna); on means of deportment (Iriyāpatha); on establishing clear understanding (Sampajāna); on reflection on bodily impurities (Patikūlamanasikāra); on reflection on bodily elements (Dhātumanasikāra); and on the nine charnel-ground contemplations (Navasivathika).

The Blessed One explains, progression of mindfulness on contemplation of three different sensation of feelings (Vedanānupassana), experiencing a pleasant (sukhaṃ) sensation of feeling, an unpleasant (dukkhaṃ) sensation of feeling, and a neither- unpleasant-nor-pleasant (adukkhamasukhaṃ) sensation of feeling. The Blessed One explains, progression of mindfulness on contemplation of eight different types of the mind state (Cittānupassanā)- a monk knows clearly mind state with craving as mind state with craving (sarāgaṃ), mind state free from craving (vītarāgaṃ); mind state with aversion (sadosaṃ), mind state free from aversion (vītadosaṃ); mind state with delusion (samohaṃ), mind state free from delusion (vītamohaṃ); contracted mind state (saṅkhittaṃ), distracted mind set (vikkhittaṃ); mind state as expanded one (mahaggataṃ), unexpanded mind state (amahaggataṃ); surpassable (sa-uttaraṃ) mind state; unsurpassable (anuttaraṃ) mind; concentrated mind state (samāhitaṃ), unconcentrated mind state (asamāhitaṃ); mind state temporarily free from defilement (vimuttaṃ), a mind state not free from defilement (avimuttaṃ).

The Blessed One explains, progression of mindfulness on contemplation of the mental contents (dhammānupassanā) on five different aspects of the mind contents (dhamma), namely on five hindrances (nīvaraṇa), five aggregates (khandhā), six sense spheres bases (āyatana), seven factors of enlightenment (bojjhaṅga), and on four Noble truths (Ariyasacca).

At the end of the sutta the Buddha assures about the results of the establishing of awareness that whosoever practices the fourfold foundations of mindfulness, in this manner, that person shall expect one of the two results. In this very life that noble one should attain the highest wisdom (Arahatship) or, if any trace of aggregates remains, the state of non-returner (Anagāmi). The time period for these attainments has been mentioned from the seven years to the lowest as less as seven days.

4.1 Comprehensive Structure of Mahāsatipaṭṭhānā Sutta

The Mahāsatipaṭṭhānā sutta begins by explaining that the practice of mindfulness is essential for achieving spiritual development and liberation. It states that through the cultivation of mindfulness, one can gain insight into the true nature of the self and the world, and eventually achieve liberation from suffering. The sutta then goes on to provide detailed instructions for the cultivation of mindfulness with respect to each of the four mindfulness of the body (kāyā), feelings (vedanā), mind (cittā) and mind contents (dhammā) as illustrated in Fig. 4.1.

In terms of mindfulness of the body, the sutta teaches that one should focus one's attention on the breath, as well as on various bodily sensations such as posture, movement, and physical sensations. With regard to mindfulness of feelings, the sutta advises practitioners to pay attention to their feelings of pleasure, pain, and neutrality, and to understand that these feelings are impermanent and not a true reflection of the self. In terms of mindfulness of the mind, the sutta teaches that one should observe the various states of the mind, including thoughts, emotions, and mental states, and to understand that these are also impermanent and not a true reflection of the self. Finally, with regard to mindfulness of mental objects, the sutta advises practitioners to focus on the various objects of their thoughts and attention, such as sights, sounds, smells, tastes, and physical sensations, and to understand that these too are impermanent and not a true reflection of the self. The sutta also emphasizes the importance of ethical conduct as a support for mindfulness practice. It states that one should strive to cultivate virtues such as non-harming, non-stealing, and non-lying, and to avoid actions that cause harm or suffering to oneself or others.

Overall, the Satipaṭṭhānā sutta is a powerful and timeless teaching that continues to be a central part of the Buddhist tradition. It provides a clear and practical guide for cultivating mindfulness and gaining insight into the true nature of reality, and offers a path to spiritual development and liberation from suffering.

Now let us perform the critical analysis (Dhammāvichaya) as to how the various divisions and subdivisions of the four foundations of mindfulness can put to the test of the Aggregates (Khandha) of Mind content (Dhammā).

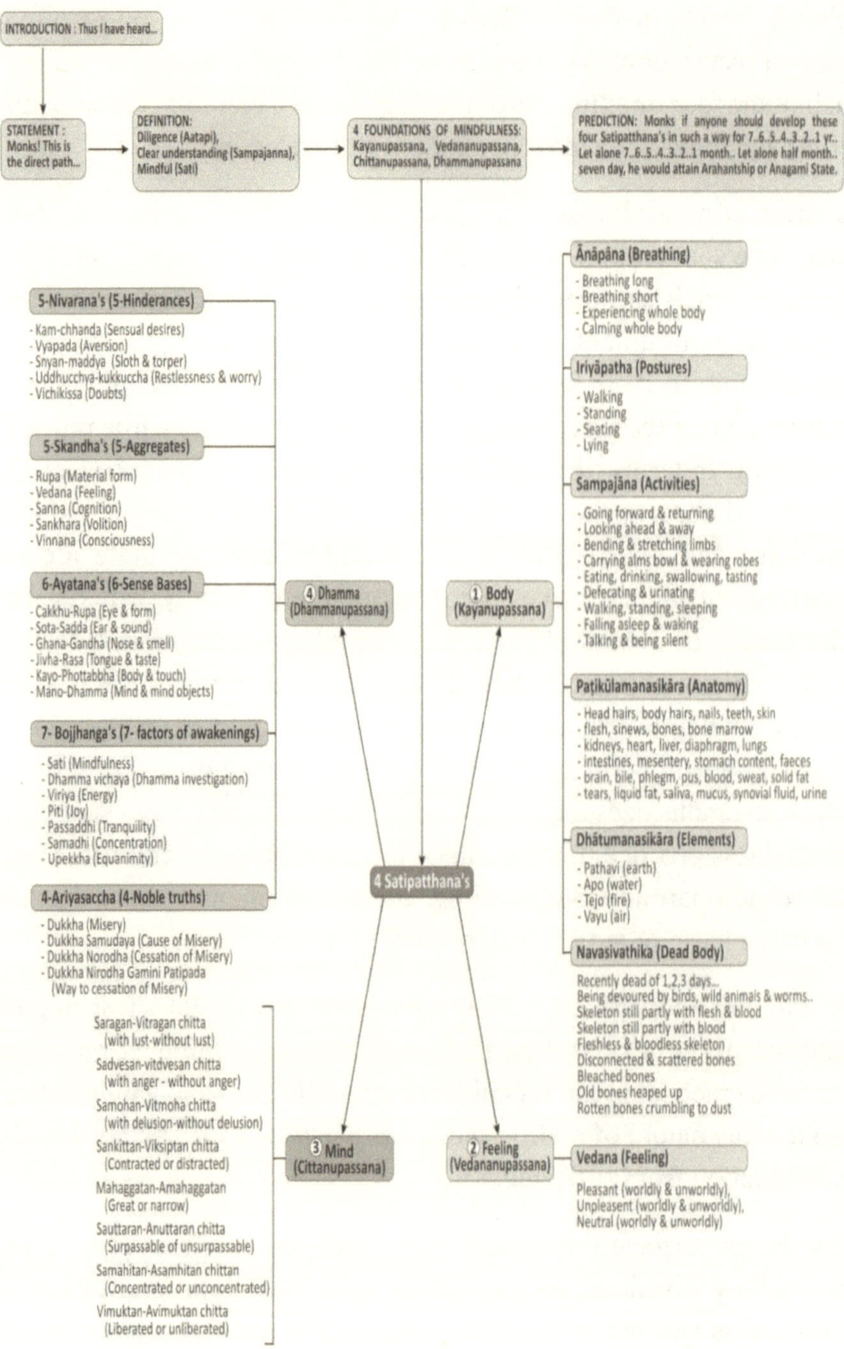

Fig. 4.1: The comprehensive structure of the Mahāsatipaṭṭhānā sutta

4.2 Progression of Mindfulness on Contemplation of the Body: Kāyānupassanā

Kāyānupassanā-satipaṭṭhāna means mindfulness is firmly established on the six bodily physical phenomena which are associated with all routine activities of the human body, such as in and out breathing (ānāpāna), means of deportment (iriyāpatha), establishing clear understanding (sampajāna), reflection on bodily impurities (patikūlamanasikāra), reflection on body elements (dhātumanasikāra) and reflection on the fates of the dead body in its natural disposition (navasivathika). This relativity is indicated in Fig. 4.2.

These above six subdivisions of Kāyānupassanā are known as six sections (Pabba) namely Ānāpāna pabba, Iriyāpatha pabba, Sampajāna pabba, Patikūlamanasikāra pabba, Dhātumanasikāra pabba and Navasivthika pabba. The six subdivisions of Kāyānupassanā cannot be regarded as khandha or dhammā because they reflect the ongoing life processes of the body rather than the deeper insights into the nature of existence. They serve as essential practices for developing mindfulness and insight, ultimately leading to a greater understanding of the khandha and dhammā that constitute the path to liberation. It can also be said that these activities do or don't require the base of mindfulness and the meditator, who first use the Ānāpāna as the first pabba for the awareness and for development of mindfulness leaves it for penetrating the higher realms of the Sātipaṭṭhāna meditation VIZ. for the mindfulness of bodily postures), bodily activities, bodily impurities, bodily elements) and variety of states through which the dead body eventually passes during its natural disposition.

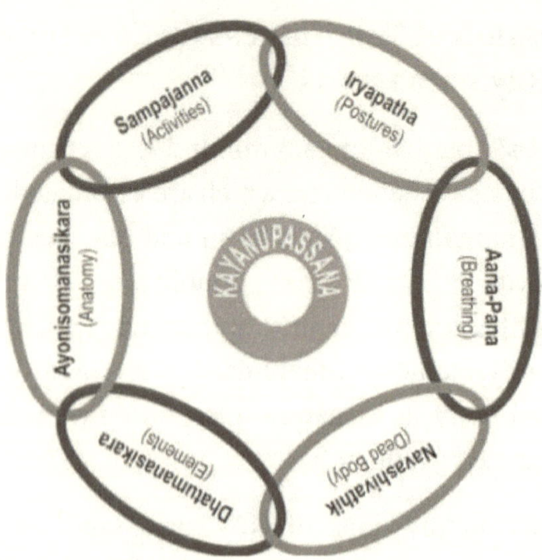

Fig. 4.2: Connectivity of six Kāyānupassanā division of Mahāsātipaṭṭhāna

During all these stages of the contemplations, a monk reflects regarding his own body, "Indeed, this body is of the same nature, it will become like that and cannot be escaped from these stages.

4.3 Progression of Mindfulness on Contemplation of the Feelings: Vedanānupassanā

Vedanānupassanā is of three types and the feelings (bodily or mental) that one experiences can be unpleasant, pleasant or neither unpleasant nor pleasant in its characteristics. Each of these three feelings can be further seen as either sensual-of the householder life or non- sensual of renunciate life. None of the above three Vedanānupassanā (sensation of feeling) as illustrated in Fig. 4.3, can be referred to as khandha or dhammā as they are the expressions of mind-body duo that can be perceived by the seeker even in the absence of mindfulness. The various sections of the Vedanānupassanā had been explained very well in the Mahāsātipaṭṭhāna sutta.

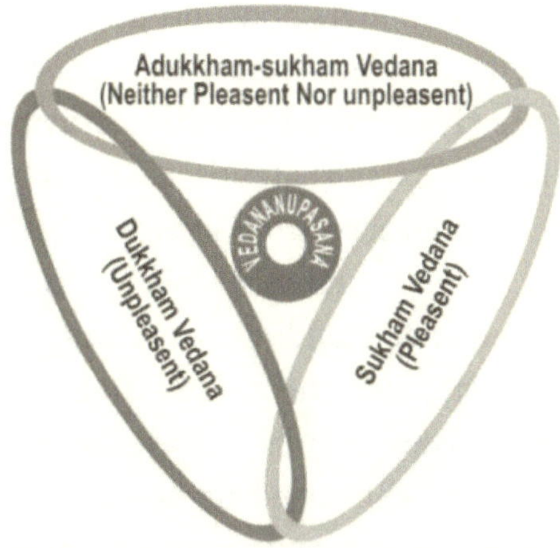

Fig. 4.3: Connectivity of three Vedanānupassanā of Mahāsātipaṭṭhāna

4.4 Progression of Mindfulness on Contemplation of the Mind: Cittānupassanā

Cittānupassanā consists of the eight types of consciousness in the mind (chittā) which have been illustrated for its connectivity in Fig. 4.4. In Mahasatipaṭṭhana sutta the Buddha expounded mindfulness of the mind as follows:

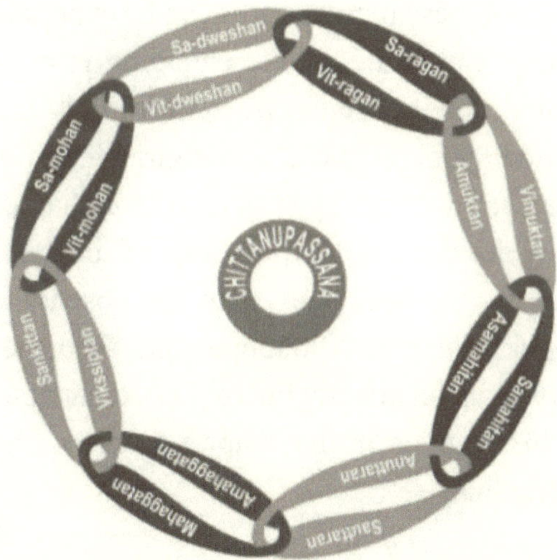

Fig. 4.4: Connectivity of eight types of Cittānupassanā of Mahāsātipaṭṭhāna

"Here, monks, a monk understands properly mind with craving (greedy) as mind with craving, he understands properly mind free from craving (not greedy) as mind free from craving; he understands properly mind with aversion (hateful) as mind with aversion, he understands properly mind free from aversion (not hateful) as mind free from aversion; he understands properly mind with delusion as mind with delusion, he understands properly mind free from delusion as mind free from delusion; he understands properly shortened or upset (contracted/distracted) as shortened or upset mind, he understands properly not shortened or upset mind (not contracted/distracted) mind as not shortened or upset mind; he understands properly expanded mind as expanded mind, he understands properly unexpanded mind as unexpanded mind; he understands properly surpassable (not supreme) mind as surpassable mind, he understands properly unsurpassable (supreme) mind as unsurpassable mind; he understands properly concentrated mind as concentrated mind, he understands properly unconcentrated mind as unconcentrated mind; he understands properly liberated mind as liberated mind, he understands properly not liberated mind as not liberated mind."

The first four pairs of these mental states can be experienced both during meditation sessions and while we are engaging in everyday activities. The last four pairs focus on states we achieve only through dedicated meditation practice. None of the above eight Chittānupassanā (mental states) can be referred to as aggregates (khandha) or mind content (dhammā) as they are the usual expressions of the mind-body duo that can be perceived by the seeker even in the absence of mindfulness. If one becomes skillful with Cittānupassanā then the mind is ready for the contemplation on the realm of Dhammānupassanā. (detailed explanation of this is given in the chapter-5 on the khandha, dhammā and dhammakkhandha).

4.5 Progression of mindfulness on contemplation of the Mental contents: Dhammānupassanā

The fourth foundation of Mindfulness is Dhammānupassanā Sātipaṭṭhāna which means mindfulness which is firmly established on mental phenomena or mind content (dhammā). It is categorized in five sections as five hindrances (nīvaraṇa), five aggregates (khandha), six sense bases (āyatana), seven factors of enlightenment (bojjhaṅga) and four Noble truths' (ariyasacca) of Dhammā. In this Dhammānupassanā, the Buddha categorically explained all the possible Dhammā that can be perceived by the human mind that makes the base of mind contents. Let us discuss all these Dhammā to understand the exact base of these mind contents. These various sections of the Dhammānupassanā can be elaborated in details to understand its cause and effect on the worlds of the sense bases as follows:

4.5.1 The Five Hindrances (Nīvaraṇa Dhammā)

The five obstacles in particular which block the road to spiritual progress, are reffered to as the hindrances (nīvaraṇa), are often mentioned as follows:

1. Sensual desire (kāmacchanda),
2. Ill-will (vyāpāda),
3. Sloth and torpor (thinamiddha),
4. Restlessness and remorse (uddhaccakukkuccassa),
5. Skeptical doubt (vicikicchā).

They are called "hindrances" because they hinder and envelop the mind in many ways, obstructing its development of tranquility and insight. According to the Buddhist teachings, spiritual development is twofold: through tranquility and through insight. Tranquility is gained by complete concentration of the mind during the meditative absorptions. For achieving these absorptions, the overcoming of the five hindrances, at least temporarily, is a preliminary condition. It is especially in the context of achieving the absorptions, the Buddha often instruct about five hindrances to his monks.

"Here, monks, a monk, whenever sense desire is present in him, he understands properly that, "Sense desire (aversion/sloth and torpor/ agitation and remorse/doubt) is present in me." Whenever sense desire (aversion/sloth and torpor/agitation and remorse) is absent from him, he understands properly that, "Sense desire (aversion/ sloth and torpor/agitation and remorse/ doubt) is absent from me." He understands properly, how sense desire (aversion/sloth and torpor/ agitation and remorse/ doubt) that has not yet arisen in him, comes to arise. He understands properly, how sense desire (aversion/sloth and torpor/agitation and remorse) that has now arisen in him, gets eradicated. He understands properly, how sense desire (aversion/ sloth and torpor/agitation and remorse/ doubt) that has now been eradicated, will in future no longer arise in him." Information about the five hindrances have been taken here directly with the courtesy of Ven. Ajahn Brahmavamso from the Buddhist Society of Western Australia, Newsletter, April-1999 [36].

The major obstacles to successful mindfulness meditation and liberating insight take the form of one or more of the five hindrances. The whole practice leading to enlightenment can be well expressed as the effort to overcome the five hindrances, at first suppressing them temporarily in order to experience the progress of jhana and insight, and then overcoming them permanently through the full development of the Noble eightfold path.

Sensory Desire (Kāmacchanda)

Sensory desire refers to that particular type of wanting that seeks for happiness through the five senses of sight, sound, smell, taste and physical feeling. It specifically excludes any aspiration for happiness through the sixth sense of mind alone.

In its extreme form, sensory desire is an obsession to find pleasure in such things as sexual intimacy, good food or fine music. But it also includes the desire to replace irritating or even painful five-sense experiences with pleasant ones, i.e. the desire for sensory comfort.

The comprehension of sensory desires has been described in details by the Buddha in Mahā-dukkhakkhandha sutta (Majjhim Nikaya-14) [37]. Once the wanderers of other persuasions questioned the monks that they too, describe the comprehension of sensuality, forms and feelings. What is the difference, the distinction, the distinguishing factor between the Buddha's comprehension and others, in terms of his teaching and others, Buddha's message and others? Unable to answer it, the monks came to the Buddha and wanted to learn the meaning of these words from him. The Buddha said, "Monks, when the wanderers of other persuasions say this, they are to be told, with regard to sensuality, forms and feelings, what is the allure, the drawback and the escape? They will not be able to answer because it lies outside their range.

What is the allure of sensuality? The five strings of sensuality, forms/sounds/smell/taste/tactile sensations - cognizable via the eye/ear/nose/tongue/body- agreeable, pleasing, charming, endearing, fostering desire and enticing. Whatever pleasure or joy arises in dependence on these five strands of sensuality, that is the allure of sensuality.

In the Mahadukkhakkhandha sutta, the Buddha explains- "And what is the drawback of sensuality? Withstanding all hardships for earning livelihood, grieving if one gains no wealth while thus working, even if one gains wealth while thus working, experience of pain & distress in protecting the wealth - This drawback too in the case of sensuality, this mass of hardship visible here & now, has sensuality for its reason, sensuality for its source, sensuality for its cause, the reason being simply sensory desires [37].

The Buddha compared sensory desire to taking out a loan. Any pleasure one experiences through these five senses must be repaid through the unpleasantness of separation, loss or hungry emptiness which follow relentlessly when the pleasure is used up. As with any loan, there is also the matter of interest and thus, as the Lord Buddha said, the pleasure is small compared to the suffering repaid.

In meditation, one transcends sensory desire for the period by letting go of concern for this body and its five-sense activity. Some imagine that the five senses are there to serve and protect the body, but the truth is that the body is there to serve the five senses as they play in the world ever seeking delight. Indeed, the Lord Buddha once said, "The five senses are the world" and to leave the world, to enjoy the other worldly bliss of absorption (jhana), one must give up for a time all concern for the body and its five senses.

When sensory desire is transcended, the mind of the meditator has no interest in the promise of pleasure or even comfort with this body. The body disappears and all the five senses get switched off. The mind becomes calm and free to look within. The difference between the five-sense activity and its transcendence is like the difference between looking out of a window and looking in a mirror. The mind that is free from five sense activity can truly look within and see its real nature. Only from that can wisdom arise as to what we are, from where and why?

Ill Will (Vyāpāda)

Ill will refers to the desire to punish, hurt or destroy. It includes sheer hatred of a person, or even a situation, and it can generate so much energy that it is both seductive and addictive. At the time, it always appears justified for such is its power that it easily corrupts our ability to judge fairly. It also includes ill will towards oneself, otherwise known as guilt, which denies oneself any possibility of happiness. In meditation, ill will can appear as dislike towards the meditation object itself, rejecting it so that one's attention is forced to wander elsewhere.

The Lord Buddha likened ill will to being sick. Just as sickness denies one the freedom and happiness of health, so ill will denies one the freedom and happiness of peace.

Ill will is overcome by applying Mettā, loving kindness. When it is ill will towards a person, Mettā teaches one to see more in that person than all that which hurts you, to understand why that person hurt you (often because they were hurting intensely themselves), and encourages one to put aside one's own pain to look with compassion towards the other. But if this is more than one can do, Mettā to oneself leads one to refuse to dwell in ill will to that person, so as to stop them from hurting you further with the memory of those deeds.

Similarly, if it is ill will towards oneself, Mettā sees more than one's own faults, can understand one's own faults, and finds the courage to forgive them, learn from their lesson and let them go. Then, if it is ill will towards the mediation object (often the reason why a meditator cannot find peace) Mettā embraces the meditation object with care and delight. For example, just as a mother has a natural Mettā towards her child, so a meditator can observe their breath, say, with the very same quality of awareness. Then it will be just as unlikely to lose the breath through forgetfulness as it is unlikely for a mother to forget her baby in the shopping mall, and it would be just as improbable to drop the breath for some distracting thought as it is for a distracted mother to drop her baby! When ill will is overcome, it allows lasting relationships with other people, with oneself and, in meditation, a lasting, enjoyable relationship with the meditation object, one that can mature into the full embrace of absorption.

Sloth and Torpor (Thinamiddha)

Sloth and torpor refer to that heaviness of body and dullness of mind which drag one down into disabling inertia and thick depression. The Lord Buddha compared it to being imprisoned in a cramped, dark cell, unable to move freely in the bright sunshine outside. In meditation, it causes weak and intermittent mindfulness which can even lead to falling asleep in meditation without even realizing it!

Sloth and torpor are overcome by rousing energy. Energy is always available but few know how to turn on the switch, as it were. Setting a goal, a reasonable goal, is a wise and effective way to generate energy, as is deliberately developing interest in the task at hand. A young child has a natural interest, and consequent energy, because its world is so new. Thus, if one can learn to look at one's life, or one's meditation, with a 'beginner's mind' one can see ever new angles and fresh possibilities which keep one distant from sloth and torpor, alive and energetic. Similarly, one can develop delight in whatever one is doing by training one's perception to see the beautiful in the ordinary, thereby generating the interest which avoids the half-death that is sloth and torpor.

The mind has two main functions, 'doing' and 'knowing'. The way of meditation is to calm the 'doing' to complete tranquility while maintaining the 'knowing'. Sloth and torpor occur when one carelessly calms both the 'doing' and the 'knowing', unable to distinguish between them.

Sloth and torpor are a common problem which can creep up and smother one slowly. A skillful meditator keeps a sharp look-out for the first signs of sloth and torpor and is thus able to spot its approach and take evasive action before it's too late. Like coming to a fork in a road, one can take that mental path leading away from sloth and torpor. Sloth and torpor are unpleasant states of body and mind, too stiff to leap into the bliss of Jhana and too blinded to spot any insights. In short, it is a complete waste of precious time.

Restlessness and Remorse (Uddhaccakukkuccassa)

Restlessness refers to a mind which is like a monkey, always swinging on to the next branch, never able to stay long with anything. It is caused by the fault-finding state of mind which cannot be satisfied with things as they are, and so has to move on to the promise of something better, forever just beyond. The Lord Buddha compared restlessness to being a slave, continually having to jump to the orders of a tyrannical boss who always demands perfection and so never lets one stop.

Restlessness is overcome by developing contentment, which is the opposite of fault-finding. One learns the simple joy of being satisfied with little, rather than always wanting more. One is grateful for this moment, rather than picking out its deficiencies. For instance, in meditation restlessness is often the impatience to move quickly on to the next stage. The fastest progress, though is achieved by those who are content with the stage they are on now. It is the deepening of that contentment that ripens into the next stage. So be careful of 'wanting to get on with it' and instead learn how to rest in appreciative contentment. That way, the 'doing' disappears and the meditation blossoms.

Remorse refers to a specific type of restlessness which is the kammic effect of one's misdeeds. The only way to overcome remorse, the restlessness of a bad conscience, is to purify one's virtue and become kind, wise and gentle. It is virtually impossible for the immoral or the self-indulgent to make deep progress in meditation.

Skeptical Doubt (Vicikicchā)

Doubt refers to the disturbing inner questions at a time when one should be silently moving deeper. Doubt can question one's own ability "Can I do this?", or question the method "Is this the right way?", or even question the meaning "What is this?" It should be remembered that such questions are obstacles to meditation because they are asked at the wrong time and thus become an intrusion, obscuring one's clarity.

The Lord Buddha likened doubt to being lost in a desert, not recognizing any landmarks. Such doubt is overcome by gathering clear instructions, having a good map, so that one can recognize the subtle landmarks in the unfamiliar territory of deep meditation and know which way to go. Doubt in one's ability is overcome by nurturing self-confidence with a good teacher. A meditation teacher is like a coach who convinces the sports team that they can succeed. The Lord Buddha stated that one can, one will, reach jhana and enlightenment if one carefully and patiently follows the instructions. The only uncertainty is 'when'! Experience also overcomes doubt about one's ability and also doubt whether this is the right path. As one realized for oneself the beautiful stages of the path, one discovers that one is indeed capable of the very highest, and that this is the path that leads one there.

The doubt that takes the form of constant assessing "Is this jhana?" "How am I going?", is overcome by realizing that such questions are best left to the end, to the final couple of minutes of the meditation. A jury only makes its judgement at the end of the trial, when all the evidence has been presented. Similarly, a skillful meditator pursues a silent gathering of evidence, reviewing it only at the end to uncover its meaning.

The end of doubt, in meditation, is described by a mind which has full trust in the silence, and so doesn't interfere with any inner speech. Like having a good chauffeur, one sits silently during the journey out of trust in the driver.

Any problem which arises in meditation will be one of these five hindrances, or a combination. So, if one experiences any difficulty, use the scheme of the five hindrances as a 'check list' to identify the main problem. Then you will know the appropriate remedy, apply it carefully, and go beyond the obstacle into deeper meditation.

When the five hindrances are fully overcome, there is no barrier between the meditator and the bliss of jhāna. Therefore, the certain test that these five hindrances are really overcome is the ability to access Jhāna.

4.5.2 The Five Aggregates (Khandha)

The five Aggregates (khandhā) [34, 35] includes the Form (rūpa), Feeling (vedanā), Perception (saññā), Mental formation (saṅkhārā) and Consciousness (viññāṇa). These five aggregates have been summarized in Fig. 4.5.

The Buddha explains the five aggregates (khandha) and the practice of the observation of the five aggregates as follows:

Kathaṃ ca pana, bhikkhave, bhikkhu dhammesu dhammānupassī viharati pañcasu upādānakkhandhesu?

How, monks, does a monk dwell, observing form, sensation, perception, mental formation and consciousness as regards the five aggregates of clinging?

Idha, bhikkhave, bhikkhu,

'...iti rūpam, iti rūpassa samudayo, iti rūpassa atthangamo; iti vedanā, iti vedanāya samudayo, iti vedanāya atthangamo; iti saññā, iti saññāya samudayo, iti saññāya atthangamo; iti sankhārā, iti sankhārānam samudayo, iti sankhārānam atthangamo; iti viññānam, iti viññānassa samudayo, iti viññānassa atthangamo ti.'

Here, monks, a monk understands properly: "Such is form (matter) such is the arising of matter, such is the passing away of matter; such are sensations, such is the arising of sensations, such is the passing away of sensations; such is perception, such is the arising of perception, such is the passing away of perception; such are reactions (mental formations), such is the arising of reactions, such is the passing away of reactions; such is consciousness, such is the arising of consciousness, such is the passing away of consciousness."

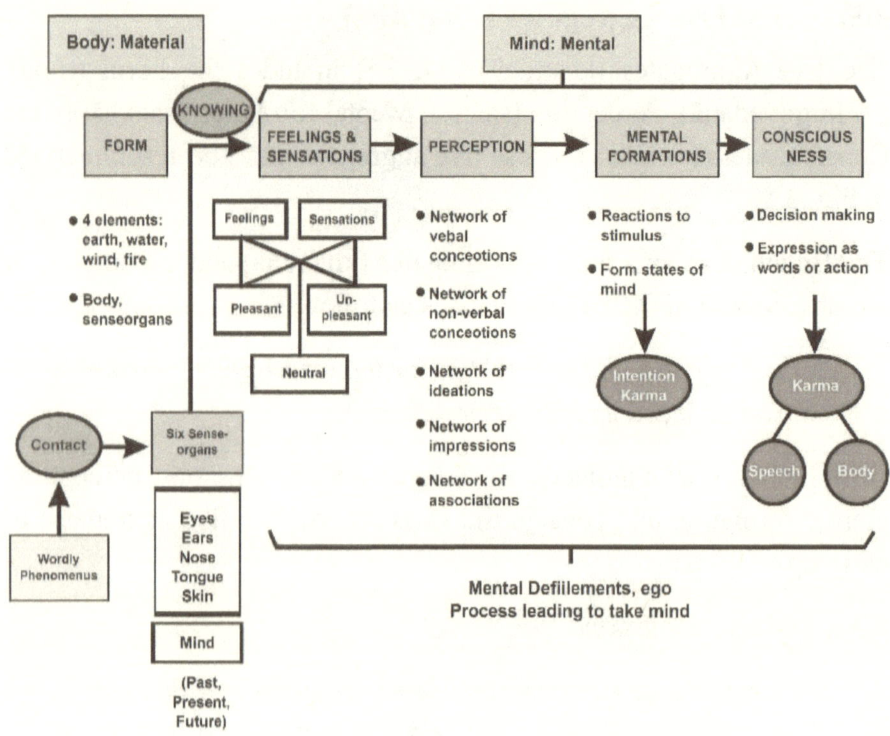

Fig. 4.5: Summary of the five Aggregates (khandha)

Form or Matter (Rūpa)

The aggregate of the form of matter is called Rūpa. It covers everything that appears in the material world of visual form, sound, smell, taste and texture. The material form that is responsible for developing the particular sensation constitute the rūpa khandha. However, when on notes the activity of 'going', 'standing', 'sitting', 'rising', 'falling', one would realize that these actions are matter or rūpa. Changes in the matter cannot be cognized easily being the constancy of the shapes and forms but in fact it also remains in the constant flux of rising and passing away.

Visual form, the first of the sense objects means the various colours and shapes that appear before our eyes. Broadly speaking, colours may be divided into primary colours - which according to the Abhidhamma are white, red, yellow and blue - and secondary colours, they may be pleasant, unpleasant or neutral.

Sounds, the objects of the ears, may occur naturally or be man-made, or they may be a combination of the two, such as when a person beats a drum. A lot of sounds are just meaningless noise, but some impart meaning. In the case of the latter, they might be a vehicle for ordinary notions, or else the sublime, liberating message of the Dhamma. As with sights, sounds can be pleasant, unpleasant or neutral.

Smells or odours can be natural or artificial, and once again, pleasant, unpleasant or neutral.

Tastes are said to be of six kinds, roughly translated as sweet, sour, bitter, hot, astringent and pungent.

Textures, or tactile sensations, may be felt on the body's surface or in its interior. Interior 'textures' include hunger and thirst, and the feelings that come with being ill or deeply relaxed. In this investigation, form means our physical bodies. More generally, it is all that we can see, hear, smell, taste and touch, and also the subtle faculties that do the seeing, hearing, smelling, tasting and touching.

Feeling/Sensation (Vedanā)

The aggregate of feelings is called vedanā khandha but it does not mean emotional feelings, but something more like sensations. These are said to be the painful, pleasant and neutral sensations in the body and the pleasant or unpleasant sensations in the mind. (It is said that neutral sensations of the mind are not counted separately, because they are indistinguishable from the neutral sensations of the body.) We are always experiencing sensations, mostly neutral ones, but also painful and pleasant. They can also be thought of as the sensations that occur based on sense impressions. A sense object such as incense would belong under the khandha of form, but the sensation created when we smell it belongs in this category. In this case, it would most likely be a pleasant sensation.

According to the teachings, feelings are important because they are the basis for attachment and aversion, which lie at the heart of many of the conflicts between lay people, who have not renounced mundane concerns.

Neuroscience of desire has scientifically proved that dopamine, a signaling agent in brain which is crucial to memory formation, helps the individual to remember experiences both positive and negative i.e. pleasant and painful. This stamped-in memory gives the person the motivation to repeat pleasurable experiences.

Perception (Saññā)

The aggregate of perception is called Saññā khandhā. Perception means the apprehension of a specific object, as circumscribed and distinct from something else. On the conceptual level, this means the recognition of identities or names, and on the sensory level it means the sixfold discernment of the five physical sense objects and of the mental objects. It is the awareness of the object's distinctive mark. In case of repeated perception of an object these marks are recognized and the saññā functions as memory.

Technically, perception is defined as 'that which grasps or identifies characteristics. Perception could be non-conceptual, in the case of the five physical senses, or conceptual, as in the perception of thoughts and ideas.

In all these cases, perception can either be 'discerning' or 'non-discerning'. The five non-conceptual sense perceptions are regarded as discerning when they are operating normally and perceiving their proper objects: colours/shapes, sounds, smells, tastes and textures. Mental perception is said to be discerning when it distinguishes identities or names. This happens when (a) mind recognizes an object and associates it with its name, and (b) the mind knows what is referred to when a name is given.

Perception is non-discerning when the sense organ in question is fully functional but there is no object. This occurs in states of deep meditative absorption, and also when the mind is unable to identify and name objects, as, for example, when you encounter something for the first time and therefore do not recognize it. This is the common experience of children.

Mental perception is also non-discerning when it does not know what is referred to when names are given as, for example, when an unknown language is heard. There are as many types of perception as there are phenomena. Perceptions are subjective experiences, and are said to be important because they are the basis for disagreement and controversy, leading to conflict amongst the perceivers.

Mental Formation or Reaction (Sankhārā)

The mental formation aggregate is called sankhārā khandhā. Sankhārā refers to "conditioned things" or "dispositions, mental imprint". The khandha of mental formations is a little complicated concept but if we just limit ourselves to mental formations, then it basically refers to thoughts and emotions, or what are technically referred to as the 'mental states. Buddhist concept of khandha says that all aggregates in the world-physical or mental, and all phenomena, are conditioned things. Since conditioned things and dispositions are perceptions and do not have real essence, they are impermanent and cannot be the reliable sources of pleasure. Understanding the significance of this reality is wisdom.

In the other sense, sankhārā khandha refers to the form-creating faculty of mind. It is part of the doctrine of Dependent origination (Paticcasamutpada). In this sense, the term sankhārā is karmically active volition or intention, which generates rebirth and influences the realm of rebirth. Sankhārā herein is synonymous with karma, and includes actions of the body, speech and mind.

Consciousness (Viññāna)

The consciousness aggregate is called viññāna khandha. Consciousness here refers to the consciousness of impressions from the five senses, and also consciousness of mental objects, like thoughts, ideas and emotions. The consciousness of the five senses (seeing, hearing, smelling, tasting, and touching) are non-conceptual. Then the information is fed to the mental consciousness, where concepts can enter in. Visual consciousness registers only colours and shapes. It does not recognize particular colours, which is the function of the khandha of perception. Nor does it identify certain colours as pleasant, which is done by the feeling khandha.

The followers of the "Mind Only" school identified eight types of consciousness. In addition to the consciousness of the five senses and the mind, they spoke of a 'defiled mental consciousness and the famous 'all-ground consciousness', or "alaya viññāna".

The defiled mental consciousness is closely connected with the ego, and is where the notion of 'I' and 'mine' enters into experience. It is absent in the meditation of noble beings, but never ceases in the mind stream of an ordinary being. This seventh consciousness relates very closely to our 'self-image'. After we receive data from the senses, and process them with the sixth consciousness, the defiled mental consciousness asks whether or not this experience fits with how we have come to think of ourselves-our 'image', in other words. This means there is a lot of judgment here, paving the way for attachment and aversion.

The "Storehouse consciousness" (alaya viññanā) is described as 'mere knowing, an unspecified apprehension, the object of which is general and uncircumscribed'. It is often likened to a storehouse, in which we keep all our habits and instincts, the imprints or 'seeds' of our actions which will ripen into future experiences. "*Aññā tra paccayā natthi viññānassa sambhava*". Herein viññāna includes rūpā, vedanā, saññā, sankhāra and viññāna, which transform into new nama-rūpā from existence to existence.

In its broadest sense, form is spoken of in terms of causal and resultant forms. Causal forms are the elements of earth, water, fire and wind, and then the resultant forms - which are made from these elements - are said to include the five sense faculties and their objects, as well as a slightly more problematic category called 'imperceptible forms', which we do not need to go into here. While noting 'thinking', 'knowing' or 'realizing', one may also come to know that this is consciousness. It is also impermanent since it arises and passes away incessantly.

Five khandhas are the five psycho-physical aggregates, which according to Buddhist philosophy are the basis for self-grasping. In its broadest sense, form (rūpa) is spoken of in terms of causal and resultant forms. Causal forms are the elements of earth, water, fire and wind, and then the resultant forms – which are made from these elements – are said to include the five sense faculties and their objects.

4.5.3   Six Sense Bases (Āyatana Dhammā)

Saḷāyatana means the six sense bases, that is, the sense organs and their objects. These six sense bases are external as well as internal to form total 12 sense bases of perception and 120 worlds of the six sense bases. The concept of the 120 worlds is very important to understand the entirety of the dhammakkhandha concept. The concept of the 120 worlds of the six sense bases although seriously understood and contemplated in the vipassana meditation, its mathematical correlativity with the other components of the dhammanupassana was not seriously understood. This seems to be a main reason for missing the concept of the 84,000 dhammakkhandha in the 2,550 years of Buddhism.

The Worlds (Loke) of Sense Bases

It is important to understand the exact meaning of the word 'Loke' which is synonymous to the English word 'World'. The Buddha has categorically avoided anything imaginary and illusive as a base of consciousness and considered all the experiences associated with the body and mind. These six-sense organ based sensory and perceptive phenomena are transitory in its nature. Therefore, all the sensory and perceptive phenomena which have the universal nature of impermanence (anicca), suffering (dukkha), and unsubstantiality (anatta) is the domain of the world (loke). Within the circumference of these sense organs the human consciousness exercises its experiences and not beyond it.

Modern science has always been exploratory towards the materialistic scales of the suffering while dealing with the health conditions of the body and mind, its diseases that creates unhappiness and its treatment that brings back the individual to normalcy. The mental agonies and distresses which are the major cause of the misery and grief are also measured with materialistic scales. So, the overall measure of the suffering is mechanized without any human element of happiness and peace.

The Buddha looks towards this universal truth of suffering (dukkha) with the human element and tries to resolve this universal issue for resetting an individual in happiness and peace. Here lies the whole difference. The Buddha use the measure of impermanence (anicca), suffering (dukkha), and unsubstantiality (anatta) to enroute an individual through the reality of the consciousness. For this purpose, he further takes the help of the faculty of the ardence (ātāpī), comprehenesion (sampajañña), and mindfulness (sati), to delve in the depth of the impermanence, suffering, and unsubstantiality to annihilate suffering from the root causes. The root causes of attractions (kāmacchanda), aversions (vyāpādo) towards the ongoing phenomena which springs up and resides with the ignorance (avijjā). Thus, the Buddha takes an individual beyond the hindrances of the attractions and aversions to merge the consciousness with the unbound external dhand internal universe where there is the end of suffering.

So, the worlds that the Buddha emphasizes are the worlds of eyes, ears, nose, tongue, skin and mind. The Buddha has used the supermicroscopic mind to evaluate the phenomena of the consciousness. He has used the piercing mind as a tool to break down the feeble consciousness in its components of five aggregates i.e. mind (nama) and matter (rūpa) where nama has been further fragmented in sensation (vedana), perception (saññā), mental formation (saṅkhārā) and consciousness (viññāṇa). It is a greatest discovery of the Buddha to expand and breakup the transitory, momentary phenomenon of the consciousness which has been completely overlooked by the modern psychiatry. The Buddha did not stop at this point but he further enquired to explore the real nature and phenomena of consciousness of the six internal and six external sensory organs and their interconnectivity to keep the perception of the flow of craving intact throughout the life of an individual.

4.6　How the Buddha breaks the consciousness in fragments?

It is very important and inspiring to see, how the Buddha made the divisions in the most transitory phenomenon of the consciousness? By breaking the consciousness in ten sequential occurrences that goes on at the time of the consciousness building. These ten sequential chains of the phenomenon that occurs in dependence upon each other merge in a flash of a moment with each other to make an illusion that it is just one consciousness but in fact it is the chain of the occurrences. These ten divisions of each existing phenomenon of consciousness have been called by the Buddha as the worlds of the internal and external sensory organs (āyatana loke). These worlds of the sense organs have been illustrated in Fig. 4.6.

These six internal and six external worlds of sensory phenomenon have been extrapolated in hundred and twenty worlds of the consciousness. These chains of the occurrences of the individual phenomenon have a vast domain in this material existence (samsāra). This vast domain of the sequential phenomena has been referred to as these worlds (loke) by the Buddha, where there is no chance for any imagination to creating phenomena that pulls on the threads of consciousness.

Sensory Reception

Human sensory reception is a media by which humans react to changes in the external and internal environments. Ancient philosophers called the human senses "the windows of the soul," and Aristotle described five senses-sight, hearing, smell, taste and touch. The sensory imputes coming into a physical body through the five sense bases go to specific brain regions. This has been well- researched by scientists over the past hundred years. The following fig. 4.6, shows the specific areas of the brain that analyze the data from the five senses. These five senses are also present in the animals in more or less evolved conditions and that is enough for the normal, natural living on earth.

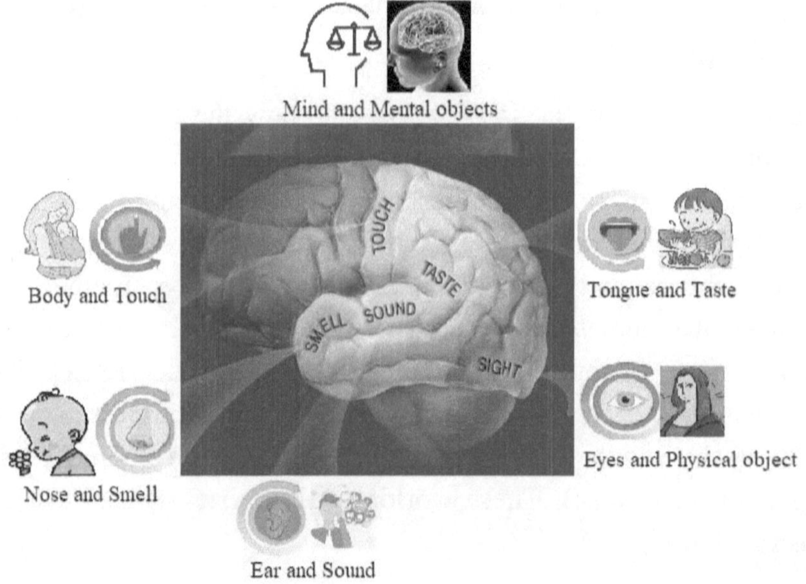

Fig. 4.6: Human Brain and its six sensory bases

Buddhism considers brain as an interface between mind and body. The Buddha accommodated 'mind' as a sixth sensory organ which works both as an independent sensory base for the Dhamma and also as the coordinator for all the other five sensory streams. The exploration of the mind as a base for all the sensory streams including the Dhamma opens the world of spirituality for the human being. That is the difference between the other animals and human beings. This unique quality of human mind equips him with the ways and means to clearly understand the interplay of the mind and matter, to probe into the impermanent and unsubstantial nature of existence. It helps him to see beyond the realms of the worldly phenomena to attain the supreme wisdom and enlightenment.

4.7   120 Worlds of Six Sense Bases

Six internal and six external worlds of sensory phenomena have been illustrated in Table-4.1, by breaking it in its ten sequential and integral part without which the perception phenomena of the specific consciousness cannot be continued. Clear understanding and mindfulness of this interlinking phenomena is very essential to understand the nature of reality of the material and mental world.

We would like to follow Ikeda's constructive and value-creating approach by presenting in this book our attempt to build a bridge between the wisdom of Nichiren Buddhism and the knowledge of modern science.

Sense organs: Sense organs are referred to as specialized organs capable of helping us perceive this world. Sense organs act as an integral part of our lives, and it is one of the only ways that could enable us to perceive our environment. These organs provide us with the required information to interpret through a network of nerves and various other organs in response to multiple physical phenomena.

Much of this information comes through the sensory organs namely the eyes, ears, nose, tongue, and skin. The nervous system receives and process information about the world outside in order to react, communicate, and keep the body healthy and safe. Specialized cells and tissues within these organs receive raw stimuli and translate them into signals the nervous system can use. Nerves relay the signals to the brain, which interprets them as sight (vision), sound (hearing), smell (olfaction), taste (gustation), and touch (tactile perception).

Table 4.1: Summary of six sensory bases and their phenomena

Eye World (Chakkhu Loke)	Ear World (Sotaṃ Loke)	Nose World (Ghānaṃ Loke)	Tongue World (Jivhā Loke)	Body World (Kayā Loke)	Mind World (Mano Loke)
Eye (Chakkhu)	Ear (Sotaṃ)	Nose (Ghānaṃ)	Tongue (Jivhā)	Body (Kayaṃ)	Mind (Manaṃ)
Visual objects (Rūpa)	Sound (Sadda)	Smell (Gandha)	Taste (Rasa)	Touch (Photthabha)	Mind content (Dhamma)
Eye consciousness (Chakkhu viññanā)	Ear consciousness (Sota viññanā)	Nose consciousness (Ghān viññanā)	Tongue consciousness (Jivha viññanā)	Body consciousness (Kaya viññanāa)	Mind consciousness (Mano viññanā)
Eye Contact (Chakkhu Sampassa)	Ear Contact (Sota Sampassa)	Nose Contact (Ghān Sampassa)	Tongue Contact (Jivha Sampassa)	Body Contact (Kaya Sampassa)	Mind Contact (Mano Sampassa)

Continued...

Feeling of Eye (Chhakkhusampass aja vedanā)	Feeling of Ear (Sotasampassa ja vedanā)	Feeling of Nose (Ghānasampass aja vedanā)	Feeling of Tongue (Jivhasampassa ja vedanā)	Feeling of Body (Kayasampas s-aja vedanā)	Feeling of Mind (Manosampas s-aja vedanā)
Perception of Visual objects (Rūpa Saññā)	Perception of Sound (Sadda Saññā)	Perception of Smell (Gandha Saññā)	Perception of Taste (Rasa Saññā)	Perception of Touch (Photthabha Saññā)	Perception of Mind contents (Dhamma Saññā)
Mental reaction of visual object (Rūpa Sanchetana)	Mental reaction of Sound (Sadda Sanchetana)	Mental reaction of Smell (Gandha Sanchetana)	Mental reaction of Taste (Rasa Sanchetana)	Mental reaction of Touch (Phottabbha Sanchetana)	Mental reaction of Mind content (Mano Sanchet-ana)
Craving of visual objects (Rūpa Taṇhā)	Craving of Sound (Sadda Taṇhā)	Craving of Smell (Gandha Taṇhā)	Craving of Taste (Rasa Taṇhā)	Craving of Body (Phottabbha Taṇhā)	Craving of Mind content (Dhamma Taṇhā)
Thought conception of visual object (Rūpa Vitakka)	Thought conception of Sound (Sadda Vitakka)	Thought conception of Smell (Gandha Vitakka)	Thought conception of Taste (Rasa Vitakka)	Thought conception of Touch (phottabbha Vitakka)	Thought conception of Mind Content (Dhamma Vitakka)
Rolling in thoughts of visual objects (Rūpa Vichara)	Rolling in thoughts of Sound (Sadda Vichara)	Rolling in thoughts of Smell (Gandha Vichara)	Rolling in thoughts of Taste (Rasa Vichara)	Rolling in thoughts of Touch (Phottabbha Vichara)	Rolling in thoughts of Mind contents (Dhamma Vichara)

4.7.1　20 Worlds of Eye (Cakkhu Loke)

Eye and Sense of visual forms: The eyes are positioned in the orbits of the skull, protected by bone and fat. The white part of the eye is the sclera which protects interior structures and surrounds a circular portal formed by the cornea, iris, and pupil. The transparent cornea allow light to enter the eye, and curved to direct it through the pupil behind it. The pupil is actually an opening in the coloured disk of the iris. The iris dilates or constricts, adjusting how much light passes through the pupil and onto the lens. The curved lens then focuses the image onto the retina, the eye's interior layer. The retina is a delicate membrane of nerves containing photoreceptor cells of rods and cones. These cells translate light into nervous signals. The optic nerve carries the signals from the eye to the brain, which interprets them to form visual images.

Eye has been placed by the Buddha as the first sensory organ which by its contact with its external visual object generate the visual sensation referred to as the feeling of the eye (cakkhusamphassajā vedanā) which further continue to link next linking of the mind to complete the deca-world process of perception of the external world. This eye works with the same efficiency for the world within, therefore, it opens up the other deca-world of the internal eye. These 20 worlds of the eye are sequentially arranged here one after another as per their appearance in the process of the deca-world of eye consciousness as given in Table-4.2. This world of 'cakkhu loka' (the realm of the eye or sensory perception) culminates in the development of dibba-cakkhu (divine eye or clairvoyance) through the purification and transcendence of ordinary sensory experience. By mastering deep meditative states and cultivating insight, a meditator transcends the limitations of physical sight, gaining the ability to perceive subtle and distant phenomena beyond ordinary vision. This abhiññā (higher knowledge) reflects the expansion of consciousness into supramundane realms, transcending the limitations of sensory experience.

Table 4.2: 20 Worlds of the eye

Sr. No.	10 Worlds of internal eye (10 Ajjhattika chakkhu loke)	10 Worlds of external eye (10 Bahiresu chakkhu loke)
1.	World of internal eye (Ajjhattika cakkhu loke)	World of external eye (Bahiresu cakkhu loke)
2.	World of internal visual objects (Ajjhattika rūpa loke)	World of external visual objects (Bahiresu rūpa loke)
3.	World of internal eye consciousness (Ajjhattika cakkhuviññāṇaṃ loke)	World of external eye consciousness (Bahiresu cakkhuviññāṇaṃ loke)
4.	World of internal eye contact of visual objects (Ajjhattika cakkhusamphasso loke)	World of external eye contact of visual objects (Bahiresu cakkhusamphasso loke)
5.	World of internal feeling of visual objects (Ajjhattika cakkhusamphassajā vedanā loke	World of external feeling of visual objects (Bahiresu cakkhusamphassajā vedanā loke)
6.	World of internal perception of visual objects (Ajjhattika rūpasaññā loke	World of external perception of visual objects (Bahiresu rūpasaññā loke)
7.	World of internal mental reaction (Ajjhattika Rupasañcetanā loke	World of external mental reaction (Bahiresu Rupasañcetanā loke)
8.	World of internal craving after mental objects (Ajjhattika rupataṇhā loke)	World of external craving after mental objects (Bahiresu rupataṇhā loke)
9.	World of internal thought conception of visual objects (Ajjhattika rupavitakko loke)	World of external thought conception of visual objects (Bahiresu rupavitakko loke)
10.	World of internal rolling in thoughts of visual objects (Ajjhattika rūpavicāro loke)	World of external rolling in thoughts of visual objects (Bahiresu rūpavicāro loke)

Ophthalmology and vision science excels in the study of physical eye, vision and treatment of eye disorders. The human vision system takes information from the external world in the form of light that strikes the eye's retina after reflecting off of the visual objects. Somehow the system takes the two-dimensional information from the retina and recreates a three-dimensional world of rupā in experience.

However, science of ophthalmology is unaware of the complete world of the internal and external eye, eye consciousness and how the world of the eye and visual objects works out the whole world of craving associated with the visual objects.

4.7.2   20 Worlds of Ear (Sotam Loke)

Ear and sense of sound: Spoken words, music, laughter, car honks-all reach the ears as sound waves in the air. The outer ear funnels the waves down the ear canal to the tympanic membrane also known as the "ear drum". The sound waves beat against the tympanic membrane, creating mechanical vibrations in the membrane. The tympanic membrane transfers these vibrations to three small bones, known as auditory ossicles, found in the air-filled cavity of the middle ear. These bones-the malleus, incus, and stapes carry the vibrations and knock against the opening to the inner ear. The inner ear consists of fluid-filled canals, including the spiral-shaped cochlea. As the ossicles pound away, specialized hair cells in the cochlea detect pressure waves in the fluid. They activate nervous receptors, sending signals through the cochlear nerve toward the brain, which interprets the signals as a specific sound.

The Buddha places ear as the second sensory organ of the six sense bases which by its contact with its external auditory objects generate the perception of sound referred to as the world of the feeling of the ear (Sotasamphassajā vedanā loke)) which further continue to link next linking of the mind to complete the deca-world process of perception of the external world. This ear works with the same efficiency for the world within, therefore, it opens up the other deca- world of the internal ear. These 20 worlds of the ear are sequentially arranged here one after

Table 4.3: 20 worlds of the Ear

Sr. No.	10 worlds of internal ear (10 Ajjhattika sotam loke)	10 worlds of external ear (10 Bahiresu sotam loke)
1.	World of internal ear (Ajjhattika sotam loke)	World of external ear (Bahiresu sotam loke)
2.	World of internal sound (Ajjhattika sadda loke)	World of external sound (Bahiresu sadda loke)
3.	World of internal auditory consciousness (Ajjhattika sotaviññāṇaṃ loke)	World of external auditory consciousness (Bahiresu sotaviññāṇaṃ loke)
4.	World of internal ear contact of auditory objects (Ajjhattika sotasamphasso loke)	World of external ear contact of auditory objects (Bahiresu sotasusamphasso loke)
5.	World of internal feeling of auditory object (Ajjhattika sotasamphassajā vedanā loke)	World of external feeling of auditory objects (Bahiresu sotasamphassajā vedanā loke)
6.	World of internal perception of sound (Ajjhattika saddasaññā loke)	World of external perception of sound (Bahiresu saddasaññā loke)
7.	World of internal mental reaction of sound (Ajjhattika saddasañcetanā loke	World of external mental reaction of sound (Bahiresu saddasañcetanā loke)
8.	World of internal craving after sound (Ajjhattika saddataṇhā loke)	World of external craving after sound (Bahiresu saddataṇhā loke)
9.	World of internal thought conception of sound (Ajjhattika Saddavitakko loke)	World of external thought conception of Sound (Bahiresu Saddavitakko loke)
10.	World of internal rolling in thoughts of Sound (Ajjhattika saddavicāro loke)	World of external rolling in thoughts of Sound (Bahiresu saddavicāro loke)

another as per its appearance in the process of the deca-world of ear consciousness as given in Table 4.3.

This world of 'sotam loka' (the realm of the ear or auditory perception) culminates in the development of 'dibba-sota' (divine ear or clairaudience) through the refinement and transcendence of ordinary hearing. By attaining deep meditative states and purifying the mind, a meditator gains the ability to perceive subtle and distant sounds beyond the range of physical hearing. This abhiññā (higher knowledge) reflects the expansion of consciousness into supramundane realms, transcending the limitations of sensory experience.

However auditory science is unaware of the complete world of the internal and external ear, auditory consciousness and how the world of the ear and sound works out the whole world of craving associated with the sound.

4.7.3   20 Worlds of Nose (Ghanam Loke)

Nose and Sense of smells: The sense of smell initiates with specialized nerve receptors located on hairlike cilia in the epithelium at the top of the nasal cavity. When we sniff or inhale through the nose, some chemicals in the air bind to these receptors. That triggers a signal that travels up a nerve fibre, through the epithelium and the skull bone above, to the olfactory bulbs. The olfactory bulbs contain neuron cell bodies that transmit information along the cranial nerves, which are extensions of the olfactory bulbs. They send the signal down the olfactory nerves, toward the olfactory area of the cerebral cortex.

Nose is the third sensory organ of the six sense bases which by its contact with its external olfactory objects generate the perception of smell referred to as the world of the feeling of the nose (ghanasamphassajā vedanā loke)) which further continue to link and pass on the information to the next olfactory connection of the mind to complete the deca-world process of perception of the external world of nose.

This nose works with the same efficiency for the world within, therefore, it opens up the other deca-world of the internal nose. These 20 worlds of the nose are sequentially arranged here one after another as per its appearance in the process of the deca-world of nose consciousness as given in Table 4.4.

Olfaction, or the sense of smell, is the process of creating the perception of smell. The study of the physiology and other aspects of olfaction is known as osphresiology. Chemical molecules emanating from the source are carried away by air current. These molecules come in contact with the specialized anatomical structure, where an interaction occurs and the signals of the particular odour are conveyed to the brain. These characters of the odour are stored in the memory.

Basic science of olfaction which deals with the perception of smell. However, it is unaware of the complete world of the internal and external nose, olfactory consciousness and how the world of the nose and smell works out the whole world of craving associated with the smell.

4.7.4 20 Worlds of Tongue (Jivhā Loke)

Tongue and sense of taste: The top of the tongue contains small bumps known as papillae. Many of them, including circumvallate papillae and fungiform papillae, contain taste buds. When we eat, chemicals from food enter the papillae and reach the taste buds. These tastants stimulate specialized gustatory cells inside the taste buds, activating nerve receptors. The receptors send signals to fibres of the facial, glossopharyngeal, and vagus nerves. Those nerves carry the signals to the medulla oblongata, which relays them to the thalamus and cerebral cortex of the brain.

Tongue is the fourth sensory organ of the six sense bases which by its contact with its external objects of taste generate the perception of taste referred to as the world of the feeling of the tongue (jivhā- samphassajā vedanā loke) which further continue to link and pass on the information

Table 4.4: 20 Worlds of the nose

Sr. No.	10 Worlds of internal nose (10 Ajjhattika ghanam loke)	10 Worlds of external nose (10 Bahiresu ghanam loke)
1.	World of internal nose (Ajjhattika ghanam loke)	World of external nose (Bahiresu ghanam loke)
2.	World of internal olfactory objects (Ajjhattika gandha loke)	World of external olfactory objects (Bahiresu gandha loke)
3.	World of internal nose consciousness (Ajjhattika ghanaviññāṇaṃ loke)	World of external nose consciousness (Bahiresu ghanaviññāṇaṃ loke)
4.	World of internal nose contact of olfactory objects (Ajjhattika ghanasamphasso loke)	World of external nose contact of olfactory objects (Bahiresu ghanasamphasso loke)
5.	World of internal nose feeling of olfactory objects (Ajjhattika ghanasamphassajā vedanā loke	World of external nose feeling of olfactory objects (Bahiresu ghanasamphassajā vedanā loke)
6.	World of internal perception of olfactory objects (Ajjhattika gandhasaññā loke)	World of external perception of olfactory objects (Bahiresu gandhasaññā loke)
7.	World of internal mental reaction to olfactory objects (Ajjhattika gandhasañcetanā loke)	World of external mental reaction to olfactory objects (Bahiresu gandhasañcetanā loke)
8.	World of internal craving after olfactory objects (Ajjhattika gadhataṇhā loke)	World of external craving after olfactory objects (Bahiresu gandhataṇhā loke)
9.	World of internal thought conception of olfactory objects (Ajjhattika gandhavitakko loke)	World of external thought conception of olfactory objects (Bahiresu gandhavitakko loke)
10.	World of internal rolling in thoughts of olfactory objects (Ajjhattika gandhavicāro loke)	World of external rolling in thoughts of olfactory objects (Bahiresu gandhavicāro loke)

to the next connection of the mind to complete the deca-world process of perception of the external world of tongue.

This tongue works with the same efficiency for the world within, therefore, it opens up the other deca-world of the internal tongue. These 20 worlds of the tongue are sequentially arranged here one after another as per its appearance in the process of the deca-world of tongue consciousness as given in Table 4.5.

The mechanism of taste is very complicated which starts on the tongue, where thousands of taste buds come in contact with the gustatory objects. Taste is just one component of our perception of flavour. Flavour, originally thought to depend on the combined sensation of both the taste and smell of a food, in two ways: directly through the nose, which is orthonasally, or retronasally, which is "when we chew the food, vaporizing chemicals in the food stimulate the odour-sensing cells of nose from the back through olfaction." In addition, the colour, taste, texture to touch, and crunching sound as one chew are all integrated in the brain to give us the delicious flavour of a food. The combined mechanism of the stimulation of the food through all five of our senses as illustrated in Fig. 4.6.

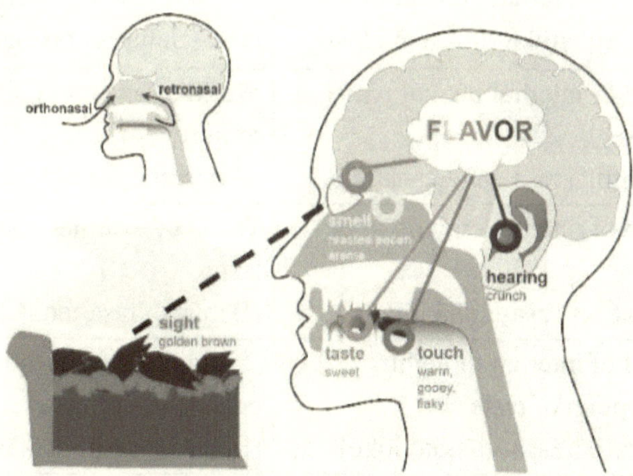

Fig. 4.7: Human perception of flavor: Combined sensual information from all six of our sense organs.

In the Padhāna Sutta the Buddha describes the world of the tongue (jivha loke) and taste (rasa loke) and craving for various tastes and food (rasa tanha loke) as the fourth of the ten soldiers of Māra which

Table 4.5: 20 Worlds of the tongue

Sr. No.	10 Worlds of internal tongue (10 Ajjhattika jivhā loke)	10 Worlds of external tongue (10 Bahiresu jivhā loke)
1.	World of internal tongue (Ajjhattika jivhā loke)	World of external tongue (Bahresu jivhā loke)
2.	World of internal taste (Ajjhattika rasa loke)	World of external taste (Bahiresu rasa loke)
3.	World of internal tongue consciousness (Ajjhattika jivhā-viññāṇaṃ loke)	World of external tongue consciousness (Bahiresu jivhā-viññāṇaṃ loke)
4.	World of internal tongue contact of taste (Ajjhattika jivhā-samphasso loke)	World of external tongue contact of taste (Bahiresu jivhā-samphasso loke)
5.	World of internal feeling of taste (Ajjhattika jivhā-samphassajā vedanā loke	World of external feeling of taste (Bahiresu jivhā-samphassajā vedanā loke)
6.	World of internal perception of taste (Ajjhattika rasasaññā loke	World of external perception of taste (Bahiresu rasasaññā loke)
7.	World of internal mental reaction of tatse (Ajjhattika rasa-sañcetanā loke	World of external mental reaction of tatse (Bahiresu rasa-sañcetanā loke)
8.	World of internal craving after taste (Ajjhattika rasa-taṇhā loke)	World of external craving after taste (Bahiresu rasa-taṇhā loke)
9.	World of internal thought conception of taste (Ajjhattika rasa-vitakko loke)	World of external thought conception of taste (Bahiresu rasa-vitakko loke)
10.	World of internal rolling in thoughts of taste (Ajjhattika rasa-vicāro loke)	World of external rolling in thoughts of taste (Bahiresu rasa-vicāro loke)

works as the destroyer of meditation. When very tasty, delicious food is eaten it stimulate more craving for food? For a common person it is not possible to eat without any appreciation of the taste of the food. Only the arahant (fully liberated person) can do this [38, 39].

4.7.5   20 Worlds of Body (Kayo Loke)

Body and sense of touch: Skin is considered as the biggest sensory organ of the body. It consists of three major tissue layers namely, the outer epidermis, middle dermis, and inner hypodermis. Specialized receptor cells within these layers detect tactile sensations and relay signals through peripheral nerves toward the brain. The presence and location of the different types of receptors make certain body parts more sensitive. These receptors detect touch, pressure, and vibration and the free endings of specialized nerves that feel pain, itch, and tickle.

Body is the fifth and largest sensory skin cover including all the organs of the body involved as a sensory organ of the six sense bases which by its contact with its external objects, generate the perception of sensation referred to as the world of the feeling of the body (kayo- samphassajā vedanā loke) which further continue to link and pass on the information to the next connection of the mind to complete the deca-world process of perception of the external world of body. This body works with the same efficiency for the world within, therefore, it opens up the other deca-world of the internal body. These 20 worlds of the body are sequentially arranged here one after another as per its appearance in the process of the deca-world of body consciousness as given in Table 4.6.

Our skin acts as the protective barrier between our internal body systems and the outside world. Skin is the body's largest sensory organ that works by "sense of touch." Our world and sense of touch (Photthabha loke) is controlled by a huge network of nerve endings and touch receptors in the skin known as the somatosensory system. It provides a wealth of information about the external environment to the brain. Most importantly, this sense of touch lets us feel physical

Table 4.6: 20 Worlds of the body

Sr. No.	10 Worlds of internal body (10 Ajjhattika kayo loke)	10 Worlds of external body (10 Bahiresu kayo loke)
1.	World of internal body (Ajjhattika kayo loke)	World of external body (Bahiresu kayo loke)
2.	World of internal touch (Ajjhattika phoṭṭhabbā loke)	World of external touch (Bahiresu phoṭṭhabbā loke)
3.	World of internal body consciousness (Ajjhattika kayo-viññāṇaṃ loke)	World of external body consciousness (Bahiresu kayo-viññāṇaṃ loke)
4.	World of internal body contact (Ajjhattika kayo-samphasso loke)	World of external body contact (Bahiresu kayo-samphasso loke)
5.	World of internal feeling of body (Ajjhattika kayo-samphassajā vedanā loke)	World of external feeling of body (Bahiresu kayo-samphassajā vedanā loke)
6.	World of internal perception of touch (Ajjhattika phoṭṭhabbā-saññā loke)	World of external perception of touch (Bahiresu phoṭṭhabbā-saññā loke)
7.	World of internal mental reaction of touch (Ajjhattika phoṭṭhabbā-sañcetanā loke)	World of external mental reaction of touch (Bahiresu phoṭṭhabbā-sañcetanā loke)
8.	World of internal craving after touch (Ajjhattika phoṭṭhabbā-taṇhā loke)	World of external craving after touch (Bahiresu phoṭṭhabbā-taṇhā loke)
9.	World of internal thought conception of touch (Ajjhattika phoṭṭhabbā-vitakko loke)	World of external thought conception of touch (Bahiresu phoṭṭhabbā-vitakko loke)
10.	World of internal rolling in thoughts of touch (Ajjhattika phoṭṭhabbā-vicāro loke)	World of external rolling in thoughts of touch (Bahiresu phoṭṭhabbā-vicāro loke)

pain-a necessity for avoiding injury, disease and danger. This system is responsible for all the sensations we feel cold, hot, smooth, rough, pressure, tickle, itch, pain, vibrations and many more.

However, science of somatosensory system is unaware of the complete world of the internal and external body, body consciousness and how the world of the body (kayo loke) and tactile objects (photthabha loke) and works out the whole world of craving associated with the tactile objects (photthabha tanhā loke).

4.7.6 20 Worlds of Mind (Mano Loke)

Mind and sense of Dhamma: Mind in itself works as one of the sensory organs that perceive the Dhamma. The creation and function of the mind are the complex and not completely understood by the modern science. It is widely accepted that the mind arises from the activity of the brain which is responsible for processing, generating thoughts, emotions and consciousness.

In Buddhism, the concept of "mind" is often referred to as "mana" or "citta." The understanding of the mind in Buddhism is quite nuanced and differs from Western philosophical and psychological perspectives. Here are some key aspects of the mind (mana) in Buddhism:

1. The stream of consciousness: In Buddhism, the mind is seen as a constantly changing and flowing stream of mental states, thoughts, feelings, and perceptions. It is not considered a fixed or permanent entity but rather a dynamic process.

2. The threefold nature of mind: According to Buddhist teachings, the mind has a threefold nature:

   - Cosciousness (viññana) This aspect of the mind is responsible for the awareness of objects and experiences. It arises in response to sensory inputs and mental processes.

   - Mental factors (cetasika): These are various mental states or factors that accompany consciousness, including emotions, intentions, and volitions. There are numerous mental factors, and they interact to shape our thoughts and actions.

- Primary consciousness (viññanā) This is the foundational awareness that underlies the other mental states and provides the basic awareness of an object.

3. Impermanence: One of the core teachings of Buddhism is the impermanent nature of all things, including the mind. The mind is seen as constantly changing, with thoughts and mental states arising and passing away. This impermanence is essential to the Buddhist understanding of suffering and the path to liberation.

4. No-self (anattā): Buddhism teaches the concept of "anattā" or "anatman," which means there is no permanent, unchanging self or soul. The mind is not considered a self or a fixed identity but rather a process of ever-changing mental states.

5. Mindfulness and meditation: Buddhism places great emphasis on the practice of mindfulness and meditation as a means to understand and transform the mind. Through meditation, individuals can gain insight into the nature of the mind, its patterns, and the causes of suffering. This insight is crucial on the path to enlightenment.

6. Karma: The mind is seen as a crucial factor in the creation of karma, which is the law of moral cause and effect. The intentions and actions generated by the mind have consequences, influencing one's future experiences.

In Buddhism, the ultimate goal is to gain insight into the true nature of the mind and matter, i.e. the nama and rupā, through that insight and to achieve liberation from suffering. The understanding of the mind in Buddhism is a central aspect of its teachings and practices. Mind is the last but all-pervasive sensory base which rules over the other previously discussed five sense bases. Buddha explain the

Table 4.7: 20 Worlds of the mind

Sr. No.	10 Worlds of internal mind (10 Ajjhattika mano loke)	10 worlds of external mind (10 Bahiresu mano loke)
1.	World of internal mind (Ajjhattika mano loke)	World of external mind (Bahiresu mano loke)
2.	World of internal mental contents (Ajjhattika dhamma loke)	World of external mental contents (Bahiresu dhamma loke)
3.	World of internal mind (Ajjhattika manoviññāṇaṃ loke)	World of external mind (Bahiresu Manoviññāṇaṃ loke)
4.	World of internal mind contact of mental contents (Ajjhattika manosamphasso loke)	World of external mind contact of mental contents (Bahiresu manosamphasso loke)
5.	World of internal feeling of mind (Ajjhattika manosamphassajā vedanā loke)	World of external feeling of mind (Bahiresu manosamphassajā vedanā loke)
6.	World of internal perception of mental contents (Ajjhattika dhammasaññā loke	World of external perception of mental contents (Bahiresu dhammasaññā loke)
7.	World of internal mental reaction (Ajjhattika dhammasañcetanā loke	World of external mental reaction (Bahiresu dhammasañcetanā loke)
8.	World of internal craving after mental contents (Ajjhattika dhammataṇhā loke)	World of external craving after mental contents (Bahiresu dahmmataṇhā loke)
9.	World of internal thought conception of mental contents (Ajjhattika dahmmavitakko loke)	World of external thought conception of mental contents (Bahiresu dhammavitakko loke)
10.	World of internal rolling in thoughts of mental contents (Ajjhattika dhammavicāro loke)	World of external rolling in thoughts of mental contents (Bahiresu dhammavicāro loke)

sovereignty of the mind referring it as the supreme, as all the sensory worlds of the other sense organs as well as its own are culminated in the mind and executed by the mind. Buddha says, "All that we are is the result of our thought: it is founded on our thoughts and made up of our thoughts."

The contact of mind with its external objects generates the perception of the mental content referred to as the world of the feeling of the body (Mano-samphassajā vedanā loke) which further continue to link and pass on the information to the next connection of the mind to complete the deca-world process of perception of the external world of mind. The mind works with the same efficiency for the world within, therefore, it opens up the other deca-world of the internal mind. These 20 worlds of the mind are sequentially arranged here one after another as per its appearance in the process of the deca- world of tongue consciousness as given in Table 4.6.

The mind (mana) is the set of faculties including cognitive aspects such as consciousness, imagination, perception, thinking, intelligence, judgement, language and memory. It is also a repository non-cognitive aspect of the subconscious mind, emotion and instinct. As per the scientific interpretation on the basis of the physicality of an individual person, the mind is produced at least in part by the brain. All the objects sensed by the mind are the mental contents. Therefore, all the mental contents that makes the feeble, average, stronger or everlasting impressions on the mind can be termed as the dhamma.

However, science of mind is unaware of the complete world of the internal and external mind (mano loke), mind consciousness (mano viññaṇā loke) and how the world of the mental objects (dhammā loke) and their feeling (manosamphassajā vedanā loke) works out the whole world of craving of the mental objects (dhammā tanhā loke) associated with the mental objects.

The Buddha explains the working of the six external and six internal sense bases [34, 35] as follows:

"Kathaṃ ca pana, bhikkhave, bhikkhu dhammesu dhammānupassī viharati chasu ajjhattikabāhiresu āyatanesu"?

"How, monks, does a monk dwell, observing mental contents in mental contents, as regards the six internal and external sense spheres"?

Idha, bhikkhave, bhikkhu cakkhum (sotam/ghānam/ jivham/ kāyam/manam) ca pajānāti, rūpe (sadde/ gandhe/ rase/ phoṭṭhabbe/dhamme) ca pajānāti, yam ca tadubhayam paticca uppajjati samyojanam tam ca pajānāti, yathā ca anuppannassa samyojanassa uppādo hoti tam ca pajānāti, yathā ca uppannassa samyojanassa pahānam hoti tam ca pajānāti, yathā ca pahīnassa samyojanassa āyatim anuppādo hoti tam ca pajānāti".

"Here, monks, a monk understands properly the eye (ear/nose/tongue/ body/mind), he understands properly the visible object (sound/ smell/taste/touch/contents of the mind) and he understands properly the bondage that arises dependent on these two. He understands properly how the bondage that has not yet arisen, comes to arise. He understands properly how the bondage that has now arisen, gets eradicated. He understands properly how that bondage that has now been eradicated, will in future no longer arise". These six internal and six external sense bases, their objects and functions are illustrated in Table 4.8.

The six sense bases constitute 18 dhatu - the six sense bases, their six sense objects, and the six sense consciousnesses. They all function through the five aggregates. The eighteen dhātus can be arranged into six triads, where each triad is composed of a sense object, a sense organ, and sense consciousness.

The first five sense organs (eye, ear, nose, tongue, body) are derivates of form. The sixth sense organ (mind) is part of consciousness. The first five sense objects (visible forms, sound, smell, taste, touch) are also derivatives of form. The sixth sense object (mental object) includes

Table 4.8: Six internal and six external Sense bases, their objects and functions

Sr. No.	Internal sense bases *(Ajjhattika Ayatanesu)*	External sense bases *(Bāhiresu Ayatanesu)*	Objects	Function
1.	Internal Eye (*Cakkhum*)	External Eye	Visible object (Rūpa)	Vision
2.	Internal Ear (*Sotam*)	External Ear	Sound (Sadda)	Hearing
3.	Internal Nose (*Ghānam*)	External Nose	Smell (*Gandha*)	Olfaction
4.	Internal Tongue (*Jivham*)	External Tongue	Taste (*Rasa*)	Taste
5.	Internal Body (*Kaya*)	External Body	Touch (*Photthabba*)	Touch
6.	Internal Mind (*Mana*)	External Mind	Mental content (*Dhamma*)	Thought

form, feeling, perception and mental formations. The six sense bases make the total 18 dhatus with their specific consciousness (viññāṇa) and subjects (sense objects).

4.8 120 Worlds of Six Sense Bases (Loke)

While explaining the meaning of "loko" the Buddha said, '*Tam yeva cittam, pañca pi upādānakkhandhā loko ayam vuccati loko*' meaning 'For sure it is the world of one's mind, also the world of the five constituents (of mind and body) that provide fuel for attachment, this is said to be 'world' [22].

The world of one's mind and the world of the five constituents (of mind and body) is represented by the six external sense spears and the six internal sense spears, constitutes 60 external loke + 60 internal loke to the total of 120 loke as given in Table 8.4. All the senses had to pass through this sensory process of 10 levels of sense bases i.e. sense organ (ayatana), its sense object, its consciousness (viññāṇā), its contact (samphasso), its feeling (samphassajāvedanā), its perception (saññā), its cognition (sañcetanā), its craving (taṇhā), its thought conception (vitakko), and its rolling in thoughts (vicāro) so as to generate the strong saṅkhārā in the mind. In a process of perception this whole reaction may take place in a flash of second, but the process works with such quick intricacy internally that one could not take the cognizance of the in between intermediates in between the sense organ (āyatana) and the thought (vichara) that comes through perception. During the first perception, this process of cognition and volition may cease to occur if any one of the intermediate of the above deca-world would not work or be absent. However, after the process of saṅkhārā formation is over, one may skip the intermediate of vitakko as the process of recognition is over in the first perception.

Two thousand and six hundred years ago, without the aid of any external aid other than the worldly experiences, solely by means of his mental power, the Buddha realized the truth that there is no solidity in our apparently gross body and in the entire material world. This solidity is only the apparent truth, the manifest truth. It appears to be so. The ultimate truth is that everything in the material world is made up of innumerable tiny little sub-atomic particles, which are so minute that they cannot be seen with the naked eye. Buddha termed them as kalāpa [36]. Even this kalāpa is not permanent, not solid.

Observing the combustion-oscillation of these kalapa at every moment he discovered that, at the actual level, there is no solidity in the entire universe, that all material phenomena are made up of tiny *kalāpas* (sub-atomic particles) that arise and pass away with such great rapidity that they give the appearance of solidity. These *kalāpas*, the basic building blocks of the material universe are nothing but mere vibrations. The Buddha sees the entire universe in the flux of impermanence as indicated in Upacālā sutta:

Sabbo ādīpito loko, sabbo loko padhūpito; sabbo pajjalito loko, sabbo loko pakampito.

"The entire world is in flames, the entire world is going up in smoke; The entire world is burning, the entire world is vibrating" [40].

'Sabbo pajjalito loko, sabbo loko pakampito'. - 'The entire universe is nothing but combustion and vibration'. Here the Buddha use the term 'loko' for the whole world of perception that includes all the worldly phenomena the of the five great aggregates (khandha) with the six internal and six external sense bases (āyatana).

In the yet another discourse popularly known as the Fire sermon [41], in Adittapariyaya Sutta (Samyutta Nikaya: 35.28), the Buddha explains, what is on fire?

'All things, O Bhikkhus, are on fire. And what, O Bhikkhus, are all these things which are on fire?'

'The eye, O Bhikkhus, is on fire; forms are on fire; eye-consciousness is on fire; impressions received by the eye are on fire; and whatever sensation, pleasant, unpleasant, or indifferent, originates in dependence on impressions received by the eye, that also is on fire.'

'And with what are these on fire?'

'With the fire of passion, say I, with the fire of hatred, with the fire of infatuation; with birth, old age, death, sorrow, lamentation, misery, grief, and despair are they on fire.'

'The ear is on fire; sounds are on fire...the nose is on fire; odours are on fire...the tongue is on fire; tastes are on fire...the body is on fire; things tangible are on fire...the mind is on fire; mind contents are on fire...mind-consciousness is on fire; impressions received by the mind are on fire; and whatever sensation, pleasant, unpleasant, or indifferent, originates in dependence on impressions received by the mind, that also is on fire.'

Table 4.9: 120 Worlds of six internal and six external sense bases.

Iyatana	Constitution of 60 External loke + 60 Internal loke to the total of 120 loke					
	Chakkhu	Sotam	Ghanam	Jivha	Kayo	Mano
Viññāṇā	Chakkhu- viññāṇā	Sota- viññāṇā	Ghana- viññāṇā	Jivha- viññāṇā	Kaya- viññāṇā	Mano- viññāṇā
Sense object	Rupa	Sadda	Gandha	Rasa	Phoṭṭhabbā	Dhamma
Samphasso	Chakkhu- samphasso	Sota- samphasso	Ghana- samphasso	Jivha- samphasso	Kaya- samphasso	Mano- Samphasso
Samphassa jā vedanā	Rupa- samphassa jā vedanā	Sota- samphassa jā vedanā	Ghana- samphassa jā vedanā	Jivha - samphassa jā vedanā	Kaya- samphassa jā vedanā	Mano- samphassa jā vedanā
Saññā	Rupa- saññā	Sadda – saññā	Gandha- saññā	Rasa- saññā	Phoṭṭhabbā – saññā	Dhamma- saññā
Sañcetanā	Rupa sañcetanā	Sadda Sañcetanā	Gandha- sañcetanā	Rasa- sañcetanā	Phoṭṭhabbā – sañcetanā	Dhamma- Sañcetanā
Taṇhā	Rupa- taṇhā	Sadda - taṇhā	Gandha- taṇhā	Rasa- taṇhā	Phoṭṭhabbā - taṇhā	Dhamma- taṇhā
Vitakko	Rupa- Vitakko	Sadda – vitakko	Gandha- vitakko	Rasa- vitakko	Phoṭṭhabbā – vitakko	Dhamma- Vitakko
Vicāro	Rupa- vicāro	Sadda – vicāro	Gandha- vicāro	Rasa- vicāro	Phoṭṭhabbā – vicāro	Dhamma- vicāro

'Perceiving this, O Bhikkhus, the learned and noble disciple conceives an aversion for the eye, conceives an aversion for forms, conceives an aversion for eye- consciousness, conceives an aversion for the impressions received by the eye; and whatever sensation, pleasant, unpleasant, or indifferent, originates in dependence on impressions received by the eye, for that also he conceives an aversion. Conceives an aversion for the ear, conceives an aversion for sounds...conceives an aversion for the nose, conceives an aversion for odours...conceives an aversion for the tongue, conceives an aversion for tastes...conceives an aversion for the body, conceives an aversion for things tangible... conceives an aversion for the mind, conceives an aversion for ideas, conceives an aversion for mind- consciousness, conceives an aversion for the impressions received by the mind; and whatever sensation, pleasant, unpleasant, or indifferent, originates in dependence on impressions received by the mind, for this also he conceives an aversion. And in conceiving this aversion, he becomes divested of passion, and by the absence of passion he becomes free, and when he is free, he becomes aware that he is free; and he knows that rebirth is exhausted, that he has lived the holy life, that he has done what it behooved him to do, and that he is no more for this world.'

If asked at what point the Tathagata has cut off the chain of birth and death? It is at the point of sañña. It is sañña that transform into pañña and provides an individual, the ability to recognize each and every sensual perception with the understanding of aniccha, dukkha, anatta, uppado-vyayo dhamma. Hence from here onward it does not allow the mind to develop due attachment or aversion against the perception and the ongoing process of the formation of saṅkhārā and the kamma stops. As the habit of mind changes to see the things in its real nature thus brings the process of saṅkhārā formation to standstill and kamma changes into ineffective kamma (ahosi kamma).

4.9 Calculation of 3,000 Dhammakkhandha

The author of this book has extensively explored the concept of the dhammakkhandha in his book on 84,000 Dhammakkhandha of Buddhism [35]". This concept of the 3,000 Dhammakkhandha is a part of the same concept.

Various factors of the Dhammanupassana used for the calculation of 84,000 dhammakkhandha are Nīvaraṇa-Khandha- Āyatana - Bojjhaṅga-Saccha. These factors have been summarized as follows:

I. Nīvaraṇa Pabba [5]: Kāmacchando, Vyāpādo, Thinmiddha, Uddhaccakukkucca, Vicikicchā Cluster of Dukkha Triplet: Nīvaraṇa Pabba [5] × Khanda Pabba [5] × Āyatana Pabba [60+60=120] makes the total sum of the 3,000 Dhammakkhandha as illustrated in Fig. 4.8.

II. Khanda Pabba [5]: Rūpa, Vedanā, Saññā, Saṅkhārā, Viññāṇa

III. Āyatana Pabba: External and Internal Āyatana Loke (12×10=120): Cakku, Sotam, Ghanam, Jivha, Kayo, Mano

   1. Cakkhu Āyatana (20): Cakkhu, Cakkhu viññāṇaṃ, Rūpa, Cakkhusamphasso, Cakkhusamphassajā vedanā, Rūpa saññā, Rūpa sañcetanā, Rūpa taṇhā, Rupavitakko and Rūpa vicāro.

   2. Sotam Āyatana (20): Sotam, Sota viññāṇaṃ, Sadda, Sota-Sadda samphasso, Sotasamphassajā vedanā, Sadda saññā, Sadda- sañcetanā, Sadda taṇhā, Sadda vitakko and Sadda vicāro.

   3. Ghanam Āyatana (20): Ghanam, Ghana viññāṇaṃ, Gandha, Ghana samphasso, Ghanasamphassajā vedanā, Gandha saññā, Gandha sañcetanā, Gandha taṇhā, Gandha vitakko and Gandha vicāro.

   4. Jivham Āyatana (20): Jivham, Jivha viññāṇaṃ, Rasa, Jivha samphasso, Jivhasamphassajā vedanā, Rasa saññā, Rasa sañcetanā, Rasa-Tanha, Rasa-Vitakko and Rasa vicāro.

5. Kayo Āyatana (20): Kayo, Kaya- viññāṇaṃ, Photthabba, Kaya samphasso, Kayasamphassajā vedanā, Photthabba saññā, Photthabba sañcetanā, Photthabba taṇhā, Photthabba vitakko and Photthabba vicāro.

6. Mano Āyatana (20): Mano, Mano viññāṇaṃ, Dhamma, Mano samphasso, Manosamphassajā vedanā, Dhamma saññā, Dhamma sañcetanā, Dhamma taṇhā, Dhamma vitakko and Dhamma vicāro.

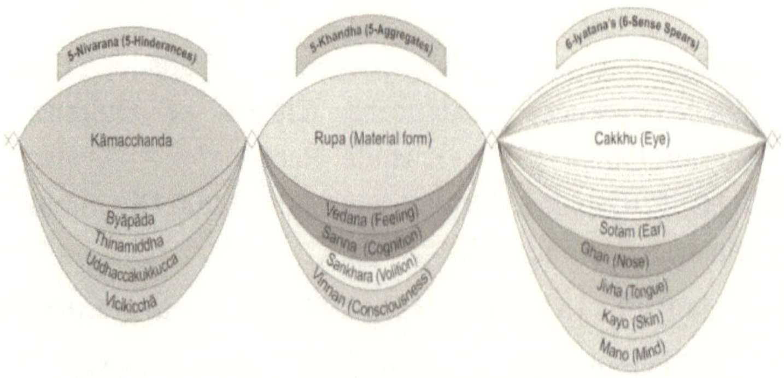

Fig. 4.8: Presentation of Inter-connectivity of Nīvaraṇa -Khandha-Āyatana.

Nīvaraṇa [5] × Khanda [5] × Āyatana [60+60=120] = [5] × [5] × [120] = 3,000 Dhammakkhandha.

4.10   Worldly phenomena and 3,000 Dhammakkhandha

It is very important to understand, as to why the Buddha emphasizes on the perception of the five hindrances, five aggregates and the worlds of the six sense spears? What would happen if the person doesn't pay heed to these six-sense based day to day experiences? As a matter of fact, human mind cannot avoid all the six-sense based day to day experiences. It is a natural process of human sensory organs and its master mind which generate the myriads of the pleasant, unpleasant or indifferent experiences that develops the minds attitude of affection towards the pleasant sensations and aversion towards the unpleasant sensations. At all the levels of critical observation of the experiences of deca-world sequence of consciousness with mindfulness is the tool to pierce into the real nature of the physical and mental world. It breaks down the web of ignorance and wrong views about the real nature of things which are generally taken as permanent and substantial. This way of observing the deca-world sequence of consciousness with diligence, comprehension and mindfulness gives a strong blow to the blind faith and opens up a mind to the practical understanding of the nature of the worlds as impermanent and unsubstantial.

These 3,000 aggregates of the sensory and mental contents are the practical exercises in the laboratory of the body and mind. It has the very important objectives of cultivation of the wisdom on the path of enlightenment.

4.11 Objective of 3,000 Dhammakkhandha

The principal objective of perception of 3,000 Dhammakkhandha is the same as that of the Ichinen sanzen to observe the "Three Thousand Realms in a Single Moment of Life." This is also based on the idea that every single moment of our lives contains the potential for enlightenment, and that this potential is present in all beings and things in the universe.

However, cultivation of mindfulness is a crucial factor in progressing on the path towards rūpa jhana, arūpa jhana, and ultimately, liberation form suffering. Here are the steps involved:

1. Establishing mindfulness: The first step is to establish mindfulness by bringing one's attention to the present moment and observing one's thoughts, feelings, and bodily sensations without judgment.

2. Concentration: Once mindfulness is established, the meditator needs to develop concentration by focusing on a single object, such as the breath. This helps to still the mind and reduce distractions.

3. First jhana: With continued practice, the meditator may enter the first jhana, characterized by intense joy and happiness, and a one-pointed concentration on the chosen object of meditation.

4. Second jhana: The meditator then progresses to the second jhana, characterized by a deep sense of tranquility and equanimity, as well as a heightened concentration.

5. Third and fourth jhanas: The meditator then progresses to the third and fourth jhanas, characterized by even deeper states of equanimity and concentration.

6. Arūpa jhanas: After achieving the fourth jhana, the meditator can progress to the arupa jhanas, which are states of meditation focused on formless objects such as infinite space, infinite consciousness, nothingness, and neither perception nor non- perception.

7. Liberation from suffering: Through continued practice and cultivation of mindfulness, the meditator can ultimately achieve liberation from suffering, which is characterized by a deep understanding of the nature of reality and the cessation of suffering.

Although Ichinen sanzen philosophy is to help individuals understand and cultivate this potential for enlightenment within themselves and also believe that it is achieved through the practice of mindfulness and the cultivation of compassion and wisdom. By focusing on the present moment and cultivating a sense of compassion and understanding for all beings, one can begin to realize the interconnectedness of all things and the ultimate nature of reality but the progressive path of the enlightenment is not planned.

Buddhism's ultimate goal has always been to enable people to attain Buddhahood, or enlightenment. Early Buddhists believed, however, that achieving this highest state of life required carrying out incredible efforts over countless lifetimes.

4.12 Reconstruction of the 3,000 Realms with Dhammakkhandha

Human mind perceives the phenomena of the internal and external world with the aid of the six sense bases. The perception process of these sensory organs i.e. eye, ear, nose, tongue, skin and mind with their subjects is a very intricate coordination explored by the Buddha to see the reality of the phenomena. This intricate interplay of the sense organ with the aggregates was used by the Buddha as a tool to see the reality of all the phenomena as impermanent, suffering and unsubstantial. First of all, it is necessary for an enquiring mind to be open to see a real nature of the phenomena happening inside and outside world without impartial and pure mind. The Buddha has dissected the process of sensory phenomena into a rapid sequence of ten distinct events. It is very important to understand this chain of sequential relay that has the ability to open up the real nature of all the phenomena. Real nature of the phenomena is often obscured for the mind suffused in the blind faith and sensory pleasures. Although emptiness is the real nature of all phenomena, our mind has a tendency to display the attractive or repulsive form of the reality. These 3,000 realms have been organized by the Buddha on the basis of all the sensory phenomena perceivable by the six sense bases. The connectivity of these six sense bases with aggregates and hindrances can be reconstructed as shown in Fig. 4.9.

Thus, the connectivity of the 3,000 realms established with the three divisions of Satipaṭṭhāna sutta namely, hindrances (nīvaraṇa), aggregates (khanda) and sense bases (āyatana) are clearly perceivable to every individual without any external aid or means. These 3,000 realms may be called as 3,000 dhamma as these phenomena of frequent occurrences can be seen and perceived on the frame of the body and mind of oneself. These 3,000 phenomena may also be referred to as 3,000 Dhammakkhandha and for what reasons? It is because the Buddha, during the framework construction of the four Noble truths

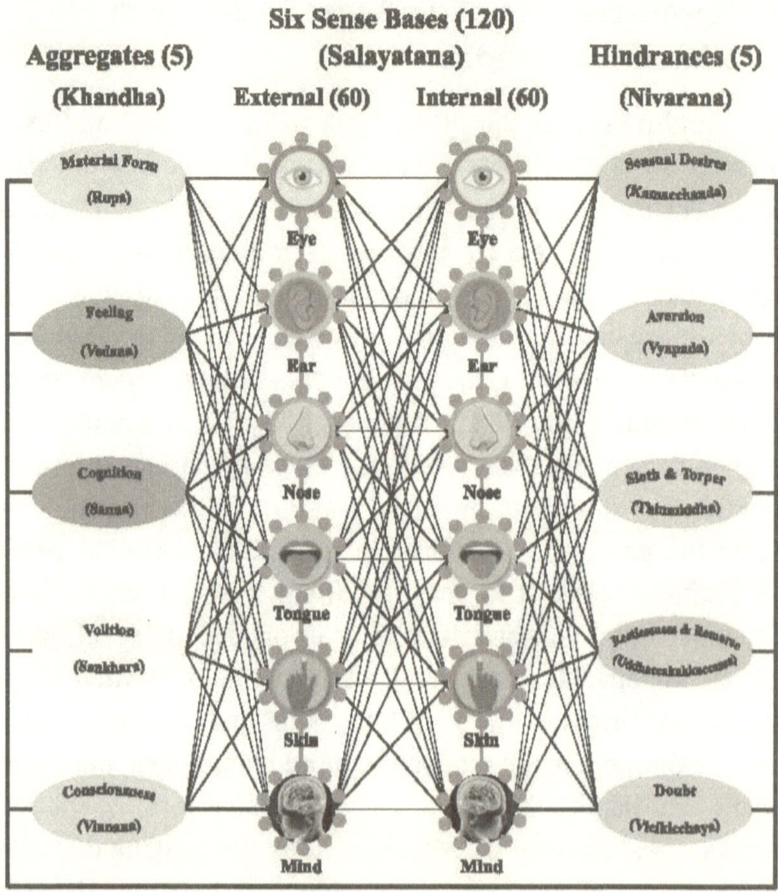

Fig. 4.9: Reconstruction of 3,000 realms with Hindrances, Aggregates and six Sense bases.

and the four foundations of mindfulness established that the mental and physical aggregates of Nama-rupa constitutes the realm of bare khandha. They are bare khandha as they do not have the ability to initiate the phenomena of attraction or aversion without the connectivity of the sense bases. Simultaneously, division of the six sense bases (āyatana) constitutes the realms of the worlds of the six-sense based Dhamma. When the bare khandha comes in contact with the sense bases, then and there itself it causes the initiation of the attraction or aversion towards the phenomena depending upon the pleasant or unpleasant sensation of the feeling produced by the contact. Thus, the contact of these five bare khandha with the six sense bases initiates and establishes 3,000 Dhamma aggregates (upadankhandha) which can be referred to as the 3,000 Dhammakkhandha. The Buddha establishes in the first Noble truth of suffering that the five upadankhandha constitutes the whole world of suffering. In other words, 3,000 Dhammakkhandha are synonymous to the 3,000 Dhamma aggregates (upadankkhandha) of the suffering.

84,000 Dhammakkhandha

Psycho-cosmic Topography of Enlightenment

"The purpose of meditation is to purify the mind. The development of a pure mind results in real happiness, real peace, real harmony, real liberation."

– S. N. Goenka

This chapter of 84,000 Dhammakkhandha has been separated from the chapter of 3000 Dhammakkhandha, mainly for two reasons. Firstly, the author wanted to establish the simile of the 3,000 Dhammakkhandha with that of the 3,000 realms. The need of the detailed elaboration of 3,000 Dhammakkhandha was necessary in the similar modalities used for presenting the details of the 3,000 realms in chapter three. Secondly, the author wanted to segregate the two main divisions of Dhammānupassanā i.e. Factors of enlightenment and Four noble truths, showing their integral importance to establish 84,000 Dhammakkhandha as the only way for the cultivation of wisdom and enlightenment as revealed by the Buddha in the Mahāsatipaṭṭhānā sutta [34].

While observing the relativity of the 3,000 dhammakkhandha with that of 3,000 realms we have considered first three divisions of the Dhammānupassanā i.e. hindrances (nīvaraṇa), khandha (aggregates) and sense bases (āyatana). The multiplying these factors with each other amounts to 3,000 dhammakkhandha which are the 3,000 phenomena that we perceive in our external and internal worlds.

Although we can perceive the reality with these 3,000 phenomena, these are not enough to grasp the true nature of reality of all the phenomena unless it is observed with the support of the seven factors of enlightenment (bojjhaṅga) and the four Noble truths (ariya sacca). Without inclusiveness of these last two divisions, the perception of reality would not be able to bear the fruits of the mindfulness, wisdom and enlightenment. Therefore, we would like to elaborate these last two divisions in detail to ascertain its role in the process of the perception of reality. Now let us elaborate these two divisions of Dhammānupassanā to establish their fundamental role in the cultivation of mindfulness, wisdom and enlightenment.

5.1   Factors of Enlightenment (Bojjhaṅga Dhamma)

The term Bojjhaṅga (Bodhi+aṅga) denotes the factors of enlightenment, or the factors for insight, wisdom. The Buddha says, "Just as, monks, in a peaked house all rafters whatsoever go together to the peak, slope to the peak, join in the peak, and of them all the peak is reckoned chief: even so, monks, the monk who cultivates and makes much of the seven factors of wisdom, slopes to Nibbana, inclines to Nibbana, tends to Nibbana."

The seven Bojjhaṅga are:

1.   Awareness (Sati),

2.   Investigation of Dhamma (Dhammavicaya),

3.   Effort (Vīriya),

4.   Rapture (Pīti),

5.   Tranquility (Passaddhi),

6.   Concentration (Samādhi) and

7.   Equanimity (Upekkhā)

In Satipaṭṭhānā Sutta, the Buddha explains as to how the factors of the enlightenments are developed and perfected in the mind of meditators:

"Idha, bhikkhave, bhikkhu santam vā ajjhattam satisambojjhangam 'atthi me ajjhattam (satisambojjhangam, dhammavicayasambojjhangam, vīriyasambojjhangam, pītisambojjhangam, passaddhisambojjhangam, samādhisambojjhangam or upekkhāsambojjhangam)' ti pajānāti, asantam vā ajjhattam satisambojjhangam ... upekkhāsambojjhangam 'natthi me ajjhattam satisambojjhango' ti pajānāti, yathā ca anuppannassa satisambojjhangassa...

upekkhāsambojjhangam uppādo hoti tam ca pajānāti, yathā ca uppannassa satisambojjhangassa ...upekkhāsambojjhangam bhāvanāya pāripūrī hoti ta capajānāti".

"Here, monks, a monk understands properly that, when the factor of enlightenment (awareness, investigation of Dhamma, effort, rapture, tranquility, concentration or equanimity), is present within him, "The factor of enlightenment, is present in me." He understands properly that, when the factor of enlightenment, is absent from him, "The factor of enlightenment (awareness ... equanimity), is absent from me." He understands properly, how the factor of enlightenment (awareness ... equanimity), that has not yet arisen in him, comes to arise. He understands properly, how the factor of enlightenment (awareness ... equanimity), that has now arisen, is developed and perfected".

It is only with developed insights that these factors come into existence. It means when one experiences the arising and passing away of all mental and material phenomena (udaya-vyaya jhāna) through right mindfulness, these seven factors arise.

Whenever these factors leading to realization or knowing appearance and disappearance, the investigation of Dhamma enlightenment factor will arise, and thus, the first stage, second, third and fourth stage of enlightenment may be attained.

Mindfulness (Sati): Sati, often translated as "mindfulness," is a first and foremost factor of the enlightenment in the practice of Buddhism.

Sati refers to a mental faculty that involves awareness, attentiveness, and remembering. It involves being fully present in the moment and having a clear, non-judgmental awareness of one's thoughts, feelings, sensations, and actions. It plays a crucial role in the Noble eightfold path as Right mindfulness (samma sati) which is a core guideline for ethical and mental development.

The practice of mindfulness meditation is a central component of Buddhist meditation techniques. Practitioners focus their attention on the present moment, often using an anchor such as the breath, bodily sensations, or a specific object of meditation. Through sustained mindfulness practice, individuals cultivate insight into the nature of reality and the impermanent, unsatisfactory, and selfless nature of all phenomena.

Mindfulness helps individuals recognize the impermanence of all experiences and phenomena. This insight is fundamental to Buddhist teachings and is a key aspect of achieving enlightenment. By observing the arising and passing away of thoughts, emotions, and sensations, practitioners come to understand the transient nature of existence.

The ultimate goal of Buddhism is to overcome suffering (dukkha) and attain liberation from the cycle of birth and death (samsara). Sati plays a critical tool in this process because it allows individuals to become acutely aware of the causes of suffering, particularly attachment and clinging to impermanent things.

Through the development of mindfulness, practitioners can gain profound insights into the nature of reality and the self. These insights can lead to a transformative experience known as enlightenment (nibbana), in which one breaks free from the cycle of suffering and attains a state of lasting peace and wisdom.

Investigation of Dhamma (Dhammavicaya): Dhammavicaya is a second factors of enlightenment in Buddhism. It plays a significant role in the path to awakening and enlightenment. Dhammavicaya is often translated as "investigation of Dhamma" or "analysis of phenomena." It involves a deep and systematic investigation of the Dhamma and also extends to the investigation of mental and physical phenomena, including one's own experiences and the nature of reality.

Investigation of phenomena is closely associated with wisdom (paññā) and is instrumental in the development of insight (vipassana). It is through the systematic analysis and investigation of the Dhamma and the nature of reality that practitioners gain a deeper understanding of the four Noble truths, three characteristics of existence i.e. impermanence, suffering, non-self, and other essential Buddhist concepts.

Ignorance (avijja) is considered the root cause of suffering in Buddhism. Through the practice of such investigation, practitioners confront and dispel ignorance by directly observing the impermanence, unsatisfactoriness, and selflessness of all phenomena. This insight leads to a deep transformation of one's understanding and helps break the cycle of suffering. As practitioners continue to investigate the nature of reality and the Dhamma, they may have profound insights that lead to liberation from the cycle of birth and death. These insights can culminate in the attainment of enlightenment, where one experiences lasting peace, wisdom, and freedom from suffering.

Efforts (Vīriya): Vīriya, often translated as "effort" or "energy," makes a third factor of enlightenment in Buddhism. It plays a significant role in the path to awakening and enlightenment. Vīriya refers to the diligent and persistent effort and energy applied to various aspects of Buddhist practice. It involves the sustained application of mental and physical energy in the pursuit of wholesome and virtuous actions, as well as the development of meditation and mindfulness.

Viriya is essential in overcoming laziness, lethargy, and procrastination which are obstacles on the spiritual path. It involves a resolute commitment to practicing the Buddha's teachings and making progress on the path to enlightenment.

While viriya emphasizes effort, it is also important to practice it in a balanced and sustainable manner. Overexertion and burnout should be avoided. The energy applied should be directed skillfully toward the right practices, whether it's meditation, ethical conduct, or studying the Dhamma. It is crucial in the cultivation of virtues such as generosity, morality (sila), and compassion and also employed in the development of mindfulness (sati) and concentration (samadhi), which are integral components of meditation practice.

In the context of meditation, vīriya involves the consistent effort to maintain one's focus and awareness. Meditators must apply sustained energy to observe the mind, its thoughts, emotions, and sensations, and to return to their chosen meditation object whenever distractions arise. For this purpose, vīriya is instrumental in overcoming the five hindrances (nivarana) in meditation: sensual desire, ill-will, sloth and torpor, restlessness and worry, and doubt. Diligent effort is necessary to subdue these hindrances and progress in meditation.

Thus, through the cultivation of viriya, practitioners make progress on the path to enlightenment. The diligent effort applied over time leads to the purification of the mind, the development of wisdom, and ultimately, the attainment of liberation from suffering and the cycle of birth and death.

Rapture (Pīti): Pīti, often translated as "rapture" or "joyful interest," makes fourth factor of enlightenment in Buddhism. It plays a significant role in the path to awakening and enlightenment.

Pīti refers to a strong sense of joy, enthusiasm or rapture that arises in the mind during meditation and other spiritual practices. It is a pleasurable and uplifting mental state that is characterized by a sense of inner delight and happiness.

Pīti is particularly relevant in meditation practices as it encourages meditators to continue their practice with enthusiasm and energy. When meditators experience joy and rapture during their practice, they experience the practical proving of the Dhamma over one's body and mind that keep them to stay focused and motivated. It is also effective in countering mental hindrances such as sloth and torpor (drowsiness), restlessness and worry, and doubt. When the mind is filled with joy and rapture, it becomes naturally concentrated, and distractions are less likely to arise.

As practitioners progress in their meditation and spiritual development, pīti can deepen and become more refined. It is often associated with initial breakthroughs in meditation, marking the beginning of a deeper understanding of the mind and the path to enlightenment. In Buddhist practice, it's important for pīti to be balanced and not turn into attachment or craving. Practitioners should cultivate mindfulness (sati) alongside pīti to observe the impermanent nature of this joyful state and not become overly attached to it, as it is not an end in itself but a step along the path to enlightenment. As practitioners continue their practice, they use the joy and enthusiasm generated by pīti to further develop concentration, mindfulness, and insight.

Ultimately, pīti, along with other factors of enlightenment, contributes to the purification of the mind and the development of wisdom. As practitioners progress, they may experience deeper states of joy and insight, leading them toward the ultimate goal of liberation from suffering and the cycle of birth and death.

Tranquility (Passaddhi): Passaddhi, often translated as "tranquility" or "calm," makes fifth factor of enlightenment in Buddhism. It plays a crucial role in the path to awakening and enlightenment.

Passaddhi refers to a state of inner calm, serenity, and tranquility that arises in the mind of a practitioner during meditation and spiritual practice. It is characterized by a deep sense of peace and stillness.

This serenity is particularly relevant in meditation practices, where it signifies a deep level of mental calm and relaxation. It is the result of the practitioner's ability to let go of distractions, agitation, and restlessness and to cultivate a focused, tranquil state of mind.

It also serves as an antidote to mental hindrances such as restlessness and worry. When the mind is calm and tranquil, it becomes less prone to distraction and more capable of sustained concentration.

Tranquility of the mind is an essential condition for the development of insight. A calm and focused mind is better able to investigate the nature of reality, including the impermanence, unsatisfactoriness, and selflessness of all phenomena. While passaddhi is a state of calm, it should be balanced with mindfulness and alertness. It is not a passive or dull state but rather a dynamic calmness that allows for clear awareness and insight. While the serenity of the mind deepens and consummates, it cultivates equanimity and non-reactivity alongside passaddhi. As practitioners progress on the path, their experience of passaddhi can become increasingly profound and transformative. Passaddhi, when cultivated in conjunction with other factors of enlightenment, contributes to the purification of the mind and the development of wisdom. It supports the practitioner on the journey to liberation from suffering and the cycle of birth and death.

Concentration (Samādhi): Samādhi generally translated as "concentration" or "meditative absorption," is a sixth factor of enlightenment in Buddhism. It is also eighth and last foundation pillar of the Noble eightfold path (Samma samādhi). At both the places it plays a central role in the path to awakening and ultimate liberation.

Samādhi refers to a state of deep and one-pointed concentration of the mind. It involves a profound level of mental stillness, focus, and absorption, often leading to a heightened sense of awareness and inner tranquility.

Samādhi is particularly crucial in meditation practices as it involves the unification of the mind, where all distractions and wandering thoughts are set aside, and the practitioner's attention is fully absorbed in the chosen object of meditation.

Together, with Piti and Passaddhi, it creates a balanced state of mental calm, joy, and unwavering focus during meditation. Samādhi is instrumental in overcoming the five hindrances that obstruct progress in meditation. In the context of meditation, samādhi is often described in terms of the four jhanas. These are progressively deeper states of meditative absorption characterized by heightened mental clarity and equanimity. The jhanas are considered stages of Samadhi and are the stepping stones towards enlightenment.

While samādhi itself is a powerful mental state, it is not an end in itself but a means to an end. The deep concentration achieved in samādhi facilitates the development of insight and wisdom. Insight arises when the meditator investigates the nature of reality and gains a deep understanding of the three characteristics of existence. Samādhi, when cultivated in conjunction with other factors of enlightenment, leads to the purification of the mind and the development of wisdom. Ultimately, it paves the way for the practitioner to attain liberation from suffering and the cycle of birth and death and to realize enlightenment or nibbana.

Equanimity (Upekkhā): Upekkhā synonymous to "equanimity" is the seventh and a last factor of enlightenment in Buddhism. It plays a crucial role in the path to awakening and enlightenment.

Upekkhā refers to a state of mental balance, impartiality, and equanimity. It is characterized by a calm and steady attitude in the face of both pleasant and unpleasant experiences, free from attachment or aversion.

Equanimity extends beyond meditation practice and is essential in everyday life. It involves responding to life's ups and downs with a balanced and non-reactive mind, neither clinging to nor pushing away experiences. It is particularly effective in counteracting the mental defilements of attachment and aversion. It helps practitioners maintain a sense of inner peace and detachment, which allows them to respond to situations wisely rather than emotionally.

In meditation, upekkhā plays a vital role in maintaining concentration and mindfulness. It prevents the mind from being disturbed by distracting thoughts or emotions, facilitating deep states of samādhi. Like other factors of enlightenment, it not only supports the development of insight and wisdom during meditation but reigns in the mind as the beacon on the path of righteousness. By maintaining equanimity, meditators can observe the impermanent, unsatisfactory, and selfless nature of all phenomena without clinging or aversion.

Upekkhā, with other factors of enlightenment, contributes to the purification of the mind and the development of wisdom. It is an essential quality for realization of the four Noble truths of suffering, its cause, its cessation and a path leading the cessation of suffering. This realization of the causal genesis brings about the liberation from suffering and the cycle of birth and death and for realizing enlightenment.

Upekkhā is also one of the "four Brahmaviharas" in Buddhist practice. Alongside loving-kindness (metta), compassion (karuna), and sympathetic joy (mudita), upekkhā represents an attitude of boundless goodwill and impartiality toward all worldly phenomena.

Bojjhaṅga bhāvanā is the cultivation of seven factors that aimed in the attainment of enlightenment in oneself. It is through the cultivation and fulfillment of these seven factors of enlightenment in oneself, the practitioner can become free of defilements. For this, one's consciousness has to be focused on the four-fold satipaṭṭhāna. Bojjhaṅga Dhamma does not cultivate in oneself without establishing one's consciousness in the four-fold satipaṭṭhāna.

The seven factors of Enlightenment have been well expounded, cultivated and fully developed by the Blessed One. These factors of Enlightenment are conducive to perfect understanding, to full realization and to enlightenment." Bojjhaṅga has been expounded by the Blessed One as the consolidated discourse on three similar events experienced by Ven. Mahakassapa, Ven. Mahamoggallana and the Buddha himself in Khandha saṃyutta, Sutta 45 (SN 45.8). When these three were afflicted with disease, and were seriously ill, the magical power of recitation of the Bojjhaṅga sutta, each of them recovered from affliction and illness. On one occasion, the Blessed One while expounding the importance of the seven Bojjhaṅga dhamma's at Pipphali cave near Rajagaha, spoke to the Mahakassapa:

"Kassapa, these seven factors of enlightenment are well expounded by me and are cultivated and fully developed by the Blessed One. They conduce to perfect understanding, to full realization (of the four Noble truths) and to Nibbana. What are the seven?"

"Mindfulness (sati), the factor of enlightenment, Kassapa, is well expounded by the Blessed One, and is cultivated and fully developed by me. It conduces to perfect understanding, to full realization and to Nibbana."

"Investigation of the Dhamma (dhammavicaya), the factor of enlightenment, Kassapa, is well expounded by the Blessed One, and is cultivated and fully developed by me. It conduces to perfect understanding, to full realization and to Nibbana."

"Persevering effort (vīriya), the factor of enlightenment, Kassapa, is well expounded by the Blessed One, and is cultivated and fully developed by me. It conduces to perfect understanding, to full realization and to Nibbana."

"Rapture (pīti), the factor of enlightenment, Kassapa, is well expounded by the Blessed One, and is cultivated and fully developed by me. It conduces to perfect understanding, to full realization and to Nibbana."

"Calm (passadhi), the factor of enlightenment, Kassapa, is well expounded by me, and is cultivated and fully developed by me. It conduces to perfect understanding, to full realization and to Nibbana."

"Concentration (samādhi), the factor of enlightenment, Kassapa, is well expounded by the Blessed One, and is cultivated and fully developed by me. It conduces to perfect understanding, to full realization and to Nibbana."

"Equanimity (upekkhā), the factor of enlightenment, Kassapa, is well expounded by the Blessed One, when cultivated and fully developed by me. It conduces to perfect understanding, to full realization and to Nibbana."

"These seven factors of enlightenment, Kassapa, are well expounded by the Blessed One and are cultivated and fully developed by me. They conduce to perfect understanding, to full realization and to Nibbana."

5.2   Noble Truths (Ariya-Sacca Dhamma)

The four Noble truths (ariya-sacca) serve as a concise summary of all Buddhist teachings, encapsulating the vast array of doctrines within the threefold canon. "I teach suffering, its origin, cessation, and the path-this is my only teaching," the Buddha stated during his first sermon in the Dhammacakkappavattana sutta over 2,550 years ago [42].

The Buddha is often compared to a physician. In the first two Noble Truths he diagnosed the problem (suffering) and identified its cause. The third Noble Truth is the realization that there is a cure. The fourth Noble Truth, in which the Buddha set out the Eightfold Path, is the prescription, the way to achieve a release from suffering.

The Nobel Truth of Suffering (Dukkhā): In the first truth of suffering (*Dukkhā*), the Buddha teaches that everything that happens in the world of mind and matter, all is suffering. The Buddha has given a very profound and clear definition as to what shall be referred to as the suffering which is as follows:

"Jāti pi dukkhā, jarā pi dukkhā, (byādhi pi dukkhā) maraam pi dukkham, sokaparidevadukkhadomanassupāyāsā pi dukkhā, appiyehi sampayogo pi dukkho, piyehi vippayogo pi dukkho, yampiccham na labhati tam pi dukkham, sankhittena pañcupādānakkhandhā dukkhā".

"Birth is suffering, old age is suffering, (sickness is suffering), death is suffering, sorrow, lamentation, pain, grief and distress are suffering, the association with something that one does not like is suffering, the disassociation with something that one does like is suffering, not to get what one desires is suffering; in short, the clinging to the five aggregates is suffering".

The Nobel Truth of Origin of Suffering (Dukkhā Samudaya): The origin or cause of suffering is the second Noble truth expounded by the Buddha that teaches that all suffering, and all rebirth, is produced by craving *(tanhā)*. The Buddha has given a very profound and clear teaching of the arising of suffering as follows:

And what, monks, is the Noble truth of the Arising of Suffering?

"Yāyaṃ taṇhā ponobbhavikā nandīrāgasahagatā tatratatrābhinandinī, seyyathidaṃ, kāmataṇhā bhavataṇhā vibhavataṇhā".

"It is this craving that occurs again and again and is bound up with pleasure and lust and finds delight now here, now there. That is, the craving for sensual pleasures, the craving for repeated rebirth and the craving for annihilation".

But where does this craving, monks, arise and where does it get established?

"Yam loke piyarūpam sātarūpam etthesā tanhā uppajjamānā uppajjati, ettha nivisamānā nivisati".

"Wherever in the world [of mind and matter] there is something enticing and pleasurable, here this craving arises and gets established".

Here at this point the Buddha opens up the whole world of the mind and matter as the cause of suffering. It is necessary at this juncture to go through the lines of the section of the Noble Truth of suffering expounded by the Buddha in Mahāsātipaṭṭhāna sutta (Sacca: Dukkhā

Samudaya pabba). The Buddha takes human bodily experience of the mind and matter through the whole world of six sense bases (Saḷāyatana) which is enticing and pleasurable and where this craving arises and gets established again and again.

Kiñca loke piyarūpam sātarūpam?

But what in the world [of mind and matter] is enticing and pleasurable?

"Cakkhu loke piyarūpam sātarūpam, etthesā tanhā uppajjamānā uppajjati, ettha nivisamānā nivisati. Sotam loke piyarūpam sātarūpam, etthesā tanhā uppajjamānā uppajjati, ettha nivisamānā nivisati. Ghānam loke piyarūpam sātarūpam, etthesā tanhā uppajjamānā uppajjati, ettha nivisamānā nivisati. Jivhā loke piyarūpam sātarūpam, etthesā tanhā uppajjamānā uppajjati, ettha nivisamānā nivisati. Kayo loke piyarūpam sātarūpam, etthesā tanhā uppajjamānā uppajjati, ettha nivisamānā nivisati. Mano loke piyarūpam sātarūpam, etthesā tanhā uppajjamānā uppajjati, ettha nivisamānā nivisati."

"The eye in the world [of mind and matter] is enticing and pleasurable; there this craving arises and gets established. The ear ... is enticing and pleasurable; there this craving arises and gets established. The nose ... is enticing and pleasurable; there this craving arises and gets established. The tongue ... is enticing and pleasurable; there this craving arises and gets established. The body... is enticing and pleasurable; there this craving arises and gets established. The mind in the world [of mind and matter] is enticing and pleasurable; there this craving arises and gets established."

In the line of the above sequence all the worlds [of mind and matter] that are enticing and pleasurable; there this craving arises and gets established. Here this sequence is counted with one set of the external sense bases as the total sixty worlds of mind and matter. When we again repeat it with the another set of the internal sense bases, again we get a similar set of total sixty worlds of mind and matter. Thus, this sixty external and sixty internal worlds of mind and matter makes the total 120 worlds of mind and matter, as the cause of the suffering.

1. The eye (Cakkhu loke) in the world [of mind and matter] is enticing and pleasurable; there this craving arises and gets established.

2. The ear (Sotaṃ loke) ... is enticing and pleasurable; there this craving arises and gets established.

3. The nose (Ghānaṃ loke) ... is enticing and pleasurable; there this craving arises and gets established.

4. The tongue (Jivhā loke) ... is enticing and pleasurable; there this craving arises and gets established.

5. The body (Kayo loke) ... is enticing and pleasurable; there this craving arises and gets established.

6. The mind (Mano loke) ... is enticing and pleasurable; there this craving arises and gets established.

7. Visible objects, material forms (Rūpā loke) in the world [of mind and matter], are enticing and pleasurable; there this craving arises and gets established.

8. Sounds (Saddā loke) ... are enticing and pleasurable; there this craving arises and gets established.

9. Smells (Gandhā loke) ... are enticing and pleasurable; there this craving arises and gets established.

10. Tastes (Rasā loke) ... are enticing and pleasurable; there this craving arises and gets established.

11. Touch (Phoṭṭhabbā loke) ... is enticing and pleasurable; there this craving arises and gets established.

12. The contents of the mind (Dhammā loke) ... are enticing and pleasurable; there this craving arises and gets established.

13. The eye consciousness (Cakkhuviññāṇaṃ loke) in the world [of mind and matter] is enticing and pleasurable; there this craving arises and gets established.

14. The ear consciousness (Sotaviññāṇaṃ loke) ... is enticing and pleasurable; there this craving arises and gets established.

15. The nose consciousness (Ghānaviññāṇaṃloke) ... is enticing and pleasurable; there this craving arises and gets established.

16. The tongue consciousness (Jivhāviññāṇaṃ loke) ... is enticing and pleasurable; there this craving arises and gets established.

17. The body consciousness (Kāyaviññāṇaṃ loke) ... is enticing and pleasurable; there this craving arises and gets established.

18. The mind consciousness (Manoviññāṇaṃ loke) ... is enticing and pleasurable; there this craving arises and gets established.

19. The eye contact (Cakkhusamphasso loke) in the world [of mind and matter] is enticing and pleasurable; there this craving arises and gets established.

20. The ear-contact (Sotasamphasso loke) ... is enticing and pleasurable; there this craving arises and gets established.

21. The nose-contact (Ghānasamphasso loke) ... is enticing and pleasurable; there this craving arises and gets established.

22. The tongue-contact (Jivhāsamphasso loke) ... is enticing and pleasurable; there this craving arises and gets established.

23. The body-contact (Kāyasamphasso loke) ... is enticing and pleasurable; there this craving arises and gets established.

24. The mind-contact (Manosamphasso loke) ... is enticing and pleasurable; there this craving arises and gets established.

25. The sensation arising from the eye-contact (Cakkhusamphassajā vedanā loke) in the world [of mind and matter] is enticing and pleasurable; there this craving arises and gets established.

26. The sensation arising from the ear-contact (Sotasamphassajā vedanā loke) ... is enticing and pleasurable; there this craving arises and gets established.

27. The sensation arising from the nose-contact (Ghānasamphassajā vedanā loke) ... is enticing and pleasurable; there this craving arises and gets established.

28. The sensation arising from the tongue-contact (Jivhāsamphassajā vedanā loke) ... is enticing and pleasurable; there this craving arises and gets established.

29. The sensation arising from the body-contact (Kāyasamphassajā vedanā loke) ... is enticing and pleasurable; there this craving arises and gets established.

30. The sensation arising from the mind-contact (Manosamphassajā vedanā loke) ... is enticing and pleasurable; there this craving arises and gets established.

31. The perception of visible objects, of material forms (Rūpasaññā loke), in the world [of mind and matter] is enticing and pleasurable; there this craving arises and gets established.

32. The perception of sounds (Saddasaññā loke) ... is enticing and pleasurable; there this craving arises and gets established.

33. The perception of smells (Gandhasaññā loke) ... is enticing and pleasurable; there this craving arises and gets established.

34. The perception of tastes (Rasasaññā loke) ... is enticing and pleasurable; there this craving arises and gets established.

35. The perception of touch (Phoṭṭhabbasaññā loke) ... is enticing and pleasurable; there this craving arises and gets established.

36. The perception of mental contents (Dhammasaññā loke) ... is enticing and pleasurable; there this craving arises and gets established.

37. The mental reaction to visible objects (Rūpasañcetanā loke) in the world [of mind and matter] is enticing and pleasurable; there this craving arises and gets established.

38. The mental reaction to sounds (Saddasañcetanā loke) is enticing and pleasurable; there this craving arises and gets established.

39. The mental reaction to smells (Gandhasañcetanā loke) is enticing and pleasurable; there this craving arises and gets established.

40. The mental reaction to tastes (Rasasañcetanā loke) ... is enticing and pleasurable; there this craving arises and gets established.

41. The mental reaction to touch (Phoṭṭhabbasañcetanā loke) ... is enticing and pleasurable; there this craving arises and gets established.

42. The mental reaction to mind objects, mental contents (Dhammasañcetanā loke) ... is enticing and pleasurable; there this craving arises and gets established.

43. The craving after visible objects (Rūpataṇhā loke) in the world [of mind and matter] is enticing and pleasurable; there this craving arises and gets established.

44. The craving after sounds (Saddataṇhā loke) ... is enticing and pleasurable; there this craving arises and gets established.

45. The craving after smells (Gandhataṇhā loke) ... is enticing and pleasurable; there this craving arises and gets established.

46. The craving after tastes (Rasataṇhā loke) ... is enticing and pleasurable; there this craving arises and gets established.

47. The craving after touch (Phoṭṭhabbataṇhā loke) ... is enticing and pleasurable; there this craving arises and gets established.

48. The craving after mind objects, mental contents (Dhammataṇhā loke) ... is enticing and pleasurable; there this craving arises and gets established.

49. The thought conception of visible objects (Rūpavitakko loke) in the world [of mind and matter] is enticing and pleasurable; there this craving arises and gets established.

50. The thought conception of sounds (Saddavitakko loke) ... is enticing and pleasurable; there this craving arises and gets established.

51. The thought conception of smells (Gandhavitakko loke) ... is enticing and pleasurable; there this craving arises and gets established.

52. The thought conception of tastes (Rasavitakko loke) ... is enticing and pleasurable; there this craving arises and gets established.

53. The thought conception of touch (Phoṭṭhabbavitakko loke) ... is enticing and pleasurable; there this craving arises and gets established.

54. The thought conception of mind objects, mental contents (Dhammavitakko loke) ... is enticing and pleasurable; there this craving arises and gets established.

55. The rolling in thoughts of visible objects (Rūpavicāro loke) in the world [of mind and matter] is enticing and pleasurable; there this craving arises and gets established.

56. The rolling in thoughts of sounds (Saddavicāro loke) ... is enticing and pleasurable; there this craving arises and gets established.

57. The rolling in thoughts of smells (Gandhavicāro loke) ... is enticing and pleasurable; there this craving arises and gets established.

58. The rolling in thoughts of tastes (Rasavicāro loke) ... is enticing and pleasurable; there this craving arises and gets established.

59. The rolling in thoughts of touch (Phoṭṭhabbavicāro loke) ... is enticing and pleasurable; there this craving arises and gets established.

60. The rolling in thoughts of mind objects, mental contents (Dhammavicāro loke) … is enticing and pleasurable; there this craving arises and gets established. This, monks, is the Noble Truth of the Arising of Suffering.

In this way, the Buddha enhances our understanding of consciousness in the second Noble truth-the arising of suffering-through a critical examination of the six sense bases. This analysis weaves together all ten worlds, revealing an intricate tapestry of experiences related to the truth of suffering's emergence in both inner (60) and outer (60) realms of the sensory world.

Noble Truth of the Cessation of Suffering (Dukkha Nirodha): The Extinction or cessation of suffering is the third Noble truth expounded by the Buddha in sequence which teaches that if all suffering, and all rebirth, is produced by craving *(tanhā)*, it can be extinguished by cessation of craving. The Buddha, with his supreme understanding of the law of nature, has explained this Cessation of suffering with the least yet the most expressive set of word as follows:

"Yo tassāyeva tanhāya asesavirāganirodho cāgo patinissaggo mutti anālayo".

"It is the complete fading away and cessation of this very craving, forsaking it and giving it up; the liberation from it, leaving no place for it".

"But where may this craving, monks, be eradicated; where may it be extinguished"?

"Yam loke piyarūpam sātarūpam, etthesā tanhā pahīyamānā pahīyati, ettha nirujjhamānā nirujjhati".

"Wherever in the world [of mind and matter] there is something enticing and pleasurable: there this craving may be eradicated and extinguished".

"But what in the world [of mind and matter] is enticing and pleasurable"?

Here at this point the Buddha once again opens up the whole world of the mind and matter that works for the cessation of suffering. Once again, we should go through the lines of the section of the Noble Truths of cessation of suffering expounded by the Buddha in Mahāsatipaṭṭhānā sutta (Saccha Pabba: Dukkha nirodha). Here again the Buddha takes human bodily experience of the mind and matter through the whole world of six sense bases (Saḷāyatana) which is enticing and pleasurable and where this craving gets eradicated and extinguished.

Kiñca loke piyarūpaṃ sātarūpaṃ?

"But what in the world [of mind and matter] is enticing and pleasurable?

> *"Cakkhu loke piyarūpam sātarūpam, etthesā tanhā pahīyamānā pahīyati, ettha nirujjhamānā nirujjhati. Sotam loke piyarūpam sātarūpam, etthesā tanhā pahīyamānā pahīyati, ettha nirujjhamānā nirujjhati. Ghānam loke piyarūpam sātarūpam, etthesā tanhā pahīyamānā pahīyati, ettha nirujjhamānā nirujjhati. Jivhā loke piyarūpam sātarūpam, etthesā tanhā pahīyamānā pahīyati, ettha nirujjhamānā nirujjhati. Kāyo loke piyarūpam sātarūpam, etthesā tanhā pahīyamānā pahīyati, ettha nirujjhamānā nirujjhati. Mano loke piyarūpam sātarūpam, etthesā tanhā pahīyamānā pahīyati, ettha nirujjhamānā nirujjhati"*

"The eye in the world [of mind and matter] is enticing and pleasurable; there this craving may be eradicated and extinguished. The ear ... is enticing and pleasurable; there this craving may be eradicated and extinguished. The nose ... is enticing and pleasurable; there this craving may be eradicated and extinguished. The tongue ... is enticing and pleasurable; there this craving may be eradicated and extinguished. The body ... is enticing and pleasurable; there this craving may be eradicated and extinguished. The mind in the world [of mind and matter] is enticing and pleasurable; there this craving may be eradicated and extinguished."

In the line of the above sequence all the worlds [of mind and matter] that are enticing and pleasurable; there this craving may be eradicated and extinguished. Here this sequence is counted with one set of the external sense bases as the total sixty worlds of mind and matter. When we again repeat it with the another set of the internal sense bases, again we get a similar set of total sixty worlds of mind and matter. Thus, this sixty external and sixty internal worlds of mind and matter makes the total 120 worlds of mind and matter, as the cessation of the suffering.

1. The eye in the world [of mind and matter] (Cakkhu loke) is enticing and pleasurable; there this craving may be eradicated and extinguished.

2. The ear (Sotaṃ loke) ... is enticing and pleasurable; there this craving may be eradicated and extinguished.

3. The nose (Ghānaṃ loke) ... is enticing and pleasurable; there this cravingmay be eradicated and extinguished.

4. The tongue (Jivhā loke) ... is enticing and pleasurable; there this craving may be eradicated and extinguished.

5. The body (Kayo loke) ... is enticing and pleasurable; there this craving may be eradicated and extinguished.

6. The mind (Mano loke) ... is enticing and pleasurable; there this craving may be eradicated and extinguished.

7. The objects of sight, the material forms in the world [of mind and matter] (Rūpā loke), are enticing and pleasurable; there this craving may be eradicated and extinguished.

8. The sounds (Saddā loke) ... are enticing and pleasurable; there this craving may be eradicated and extinguished.

9. The smells (Gandhā loke) ... are enticing and pleasurable; there this craving may be eradicated and extinguished.

10. The tastes (Rasā loke) ... are enticing and pleasurable; there this craving may be eradicated and extinguished.

11. The touch (Phoṭṭhabbā loke) ... is enticing and pleasurable; there this craving may be eradicated and extinguished.

12. The contents of the mind (Dhammā loke) ... are enticing and pleasurable; there this craving may be eradicated and extinguished.

13. The eye-consciousness (Cakkhuviññāṇaṃ loke) in the world [of mind and matter] is enticing and pleasurable; there this craving may be eradicated and extinguished.

14. The ear-consciousness (Sotaviññāṇaṃ loke) ... is enticing and pleasurable; there this craving may be eradicated and extinguished.

15. The nose-consciousness (Ghānaviññāṇaṃ loke) ... is enticing and pleasurable; there this craving may be eradicated and extinguished.

16. The tongue-consciousness (Jivhāviññāṇaṃ loke) ... is enticing and pleasurable; there this craving may be eradicated and extinguished.

17. The body-consciousness (Kāyaviññāṇaṃ loke) ... is enticing and pleasurable; there this craving may be eradicated and extinguished.

18. The mind-consciousness (Manoviññāṇaṃ loke) ... is enticing and pleasurable; there this craving may be eradicated and extinguished.

19. The eye-contact (Cakkhusamphasso loke) in the world [of mind and matter] is enticing and pleasurable; there this craving may be eradicated and extinguished.

20. The ear-contact (Sotasamphasso loke) ... is enticing and pleasurable; there this craving may be eradicated and extinguished.

21. The nose-contact (Ghānasamphasso loke) ... is enticing and pleasurable; there this craving may be eradicated and extinguished.

22. The tongue-contact (Jivhāsamphasso loke) ... is enticing and pleasurable; there this craving may be eradicated and extinguished.

23. The body-contact (Kāyasamphasso loke) … is enticing and pleasurable; there this craving may be eradicated and extinguished.

24. The mind-contact (Manosamphasso loke) … is enticing and pleasurable; there this craving may be eradicated and extinguished.

25. The sensation that arises from the eye contact (Cakkhusamphassajā vedanā loke) in the world [of mind and matter] is enticing and pleasurable; there this craving may be eradicated and extinguished.

26. The sensation that arises from the ear contact (Sotasamphassajā vedanā loke) … is enticing and pleasurable; there this craving may be eradicated and extinguished.

27. The sensation that arises from the nose contact (Ghānasamphassajā vedanā loke) … is enticing and pleasurable; there this craving may be eradicated and extinguished.

28. The sensation that arises from the tongue contact (Jivhāsamphassajā vedanā loke) … is enticing and pleasurable; there this craving may be eradicated and extinguished.

29. The sensation that arises from the body contact (Kāyasamphassajā vedanā loke) … is enticing and pleasurable; there this craving may be eradicated and extinguished.

30. The sensation that arises from the mind contact (Manosamphassajā vedanā loke) … is enticing and pleasurable; there this craving may be eradicated and extinguished.

31. The perception of visible objects (Rūpasaññā loke) in the world [of mind and matter] is enticing and pleasurable; there this craving may be eradicated and extinguished.

32. The perception of sounds (Saddasaññā loke) … is enticing and pleasurable; there this craving may be eradicated and extinguished.

33. The perception of smells (Gandhasaññā loke) … is enticing and pleasurable; there this craving may be eradicated and extinguished.

34. The perception of tastes (Rasasaññā loke) ... is enticing and pleasurable; there this craving may be eradicated and extinguished.

35. The perception of touch (Phoṭṭhabbasaññā loke) ... is enticing and pleasurable; there this craving may be eradicated and extinguished.

36. The perception of mental contents (Dhammasaññā loke) ... is enticing and pleasurable; there this craving may be eradicated and extinguished.

37. The mental reaction towards visible objects (Rūpasañcetanā loke) in the world [of mind and matter] is enticing and pleasurable; there this craving may be eradicated and extinguished.

38. The mental reaction towards sounds (Saddasañcetanā loke) ... is enticing and pleasurable; there this craving may be eradicated and extinguished.

39. The mental reaction towards smells (Gandhasañcetanā loke) ... is enticing and pleasurable; there this craving may be eradicated and extinguished.

40. The mental reaction towards tastes (Rasasañcetanā loke) ... is enticing and pleasurable; there this craving may be eradicated and extinguished.

41. The mental reaction towards touch (Phoṭṭhabbasañcetanā loke) ... is enticing and pleasurable; there this craving may be eradicated and extinguished.

42. The mental reaction towards mental contents (Dhammasañcetanā loke) ... is enticing and pleasurable; there this craving may be eradicated and extinguished.

43. The craving after visible objects (Rūpataṇhā loke) in the world [of mind and matter] is enticing and pleasurable; there this craving may be eradicated and extinguished.

44. The craving after sounds (Saddataṇhā loke... is enticing and pleasurable; there this craving may be eradicated and extinguished.

45. The craving after smells (Gandhataṇhā loke) ... is enticing and pleasurable; there this craving may be eradicated and extinguished.

46. The craving after tastes (Rasataṇhā loke) ... is enticing and pleasurable; there this craving may be eradicated and extinguished.

47. The craving after touch (Phoṭṭhabbataṇhā loke) ... is enticing and pleasurable; there this craving may be eradicated and extinguished.

48. The craving after mind objects, mental contents (Dhammataṇhā loke) ... is enticing and pleasurable; there this craving may be eradicated and extinguished.

49. The thought conception of visible objects (Rūpavitakko loke) in the world [of mind and matter] is enticing and pleasurable; there this craving may be eradicated and extinguished.

50. The thought conception of sounds (Saddavitakko loke) ... is enticing and pleasurable; there this craving may be eradicated and extinguished.

51. The thought conception of smells (Gandhavitakko loke) ... is enticing and pleasurable; there this craving may be eradicated and extinguished.

52. The thought conception of tastes (Rasavitakko loke) ... is enticing and pleasurable; there this craving may be eradicated and extinguished.

53. The thought conception of touch (Phoṭṭhabbavitakko loke) ... is enticing and pleasurable; there this craving may be eradicated and extinguished.

54. The thought conception of mental contents (Dhammavitakko loke) ... is enticing and pleasurable; there this craving may be eradicated and extinguished.

55. The rolling in thoughts of visible objects (Rūpavicāro loke) in the world [of mind and matter] is enticing and pleasurable; there this craving may be eradicated and extinguished.

56. The rolling in thoughts of sounds (Saddavicāro loke) ... is enticing and pleasurable; there this craving may be eradicated and extinguished.

57. The rolling in thoughts of smells (Gandhavicāro loke) ... is enticing and pleasurable; there this craving may be eradicated and extinguished.

58. The rolling in thoughts of tastes (Rasavicāro loke) ... is enticing and pleasurable; there this craving may be eradicated and extinguished.

59. The rolling in thoughts of touch (Phoṭṭhabbavicāro loke) ... is enticing and pleasurable; there this craving may be eradicated and extinguished.

60. The rolling in thoughts of mental contents (Dhammavicāro loke) in the world [of mind and matter] is enticing and pleasurable; there this craving may be eradicated and extinguished.

In this way, the Buddha enhances our understanding of consciousness in the third Noble truth-the cessation of suffering-by critically examining the six sense bases. This exploration links all ten worlds, unveiling a rich tapestry of experiences related to the cessation of suffering in both internal (60) and external (60) realms of the sensory worlds.

The Nobel Truth of the Path leading to the Cessation of Suffering (Dukkhā Nirodhagamini Patipada): The path leading to the cessation of suffering is the fourth and last Noble truth expounded by the Buddha. The eightfold path is also called the Middle way as it avoids both indulgence and severe asceticism, neither of which the Buddha had found helpful in his search for enlightenment.

"Ayameva ariyo atthangiko maggo, seyyathidam, sammāditthi, sammāsankappo, sammāvācā, sammākammanto, sammā-ājīvo, sammāvāyāmo, sammāsati, sammāsamādhi".

"It is this, the Noble eightfold path, namely: right understanding, right thought, right speech, right action, right livelihood, right effort, right awareness and right concentration".

The Eightfold path (Atthangika magga) consists of

1. Right understanding (sammā-ditthi),

2. Right thought (sammā-sankappo),

3. Right speech (sammā-vācā),

4. Right action (sammā-kammanto),

5. Right livelihood (sammā-ajivo),

6. Right effort (sammā-vāyāmo),

7. Right awareness (sammā-sati) and

8. Right concentration (sammā-samādhi).

Its first two Right thought and Right speech constitute Wisdom (paññā). Other three i.e. Right speech, Right action and Right livelihood constitutes Morality (sīla) while the last three i.e. Right effort, Right mindfulness and Right concentration constitutes Concentration (samādhi).

In the Buddha's first sermon, the Dhammacakkappavattana Sutta [42], it is said that the first Nobel truth (Dukkhā) is to be fully critically understood (parinneya tabbā); the second Nobel truth (dukkhā smudaya-craving) to be abandoned (pahā tabbā); the third Nobel truth (dukkhā nirodha-nibbāna) to be realized (sacchhīka tabbā) and the fourth Nobel truth (attangiko maggo) to be cultivated (bhāve tabbā).

"The truth of suffering is to be compared with a disease, the truth of the origin of suffering with the cause of the disease, the truth of extinction of suffering with the cure of the disease, the truth of the path with the medicine".

5.3   Calculations of the 84,000 Dhammakkhandha

We have discussed the importance of the other two integral segments of the Dhammanupassana i.e. factors of enlightenment (bojjhaṅga) and Noble truths (sacca) as expounded by the Buddha in the Mahāsatipaṭṭhānā sutta. We have also acknowledged the inter-connectivity of the 3,000 Dhammakkhandha in the previous chapter. Cluster of Dukkha triplet consisting three factors of Nīvaraṇa pabba [5] x Khanda pabba [5] x Āyatana pabba [60+60=120] makes the total sum of the 3,000 Dhammakkhandha as illustrated in Fig. 4.8 and 4.9.

If we connect the 3,000 Dhammakkhandha with the seven factors of the enlightenment and four factors of the Noble truth, the sum total of the result comes to 84,000 Dhammakkhandha.

Various factors of the Dhammanupassana used for the calculation of 84,000 dhammakkhandha are Nīvaraṇa-Khandha-Āyatana- Bojjhaṅga-Saccha. These factors have been summarized as follows:

I. Nīvaraṇa Pabba [5]: Kāmacchanda, Vyāpādo, Thin- Middha, Udducca- Kukkucca, Vicikicchā

II. Khanda Pabba [5]: Rūpa, Vedanā, Saññā, Saṅkhārā, Viññāṇa

III. Āyatana Pabba: External and Internal world of sense bases (Āyatana) Loke (12x10=120): Cakku, Sotam, Ghanam, Jivha, Kayo, and Mano loke

    1. Cakkhu Āyatana Loke (20): Cakkhu, Cakkhu viññāṇaṃ, Rūpa, Cakkhu samphasso, Rupasamphassajā vedanā, Rūpa saññā, Rūpa sañcetanā, Rūpa taṇhā, Rūpa vitakko and Rūpa vicāro loke.

2. Sotam Āyatana Loke (20): Sotam, Sota viññāṇaṃ, Sadda, Sota samphasso, Saddasamphassajā vedanā, Sadda saññā, Sadda sañcetanā, Sadda taṇhā, Sadda vitakko and Sadda vicāro loke.

3. Ghanam Āyatana Loke (20): Ghanam, Ghana viññāṇaṃ, Gandha, Ghana samphasso, Ghana samphassajā vedanā Gandha saññā, Gandha sañcetanā, Gandha taṇhā, Gandha vitakko and Gandha vicāro loke.

4. Jivha Āyatana Loke (20): Jivha, Jivha viññāṇaṃ, Rasa, Jivha samphasso, Jivhasamphassajā vedanā, Rasa saññā, Rasa sañcetanā, Rasa taṇhā, Rasa vitakko and Rasa vicāro loke.

5. Kayo Āyatana Loke (20): Kayo, Kaya viññāṇaṃ, Photthabba, Kayo samphasso, Kayosamphassajā vedanā, Photthabba saññā, Photthabba sañcetanā, Photthabba taṇhā, Photthabba vitakko and Photthabba vicāro loke.

6. Mano Āyatana Loke (20): Mano, Mano viññāṇaṃ, Dhammā, Mano samphasso, Manosamphassajā vedanā, Dhammā saññā, Dhammā sañcetanā, Dhammā taṇhā Mano vitakko and Mano vicāro loke.

IV. Bojjhaṅga-Seven Factors of the enlightenment: Seven factors of the enlightenment Bojjhaṅga [7], namely Sati, Dhammavicaya, Vīriya, Pīti, Passaddhi, Samādhi, Upekkhā further join to the cluster of Dhammakkhandha triplet of Khanda- Āyatana - Nīvaraṇa to make the total sum of 21000 dhammakkhandha.

V. Sacca-Four Nobel Truths: The four Nobel truths of Dukkha, Dukkha Samudayo, Dukkha Nirodho, Dukkhanirodhagāminī patipadā further get attached to the quartet of the Khanda-Āyatana - Nīvaraṇa -Bojjhaṅga to make the total sum of 84,000 dhammakkhandha as illustrated in Fig. 5.1 and Table 5.1.

Nīvaraṇa [5] x Khanda [5] x Āyatana [60+60=120] x Bojjhaṅga (7) x Sacca (4) = [5] x [5] x [120] x [7] x [4] = 84,000 Dhammakkhandha.

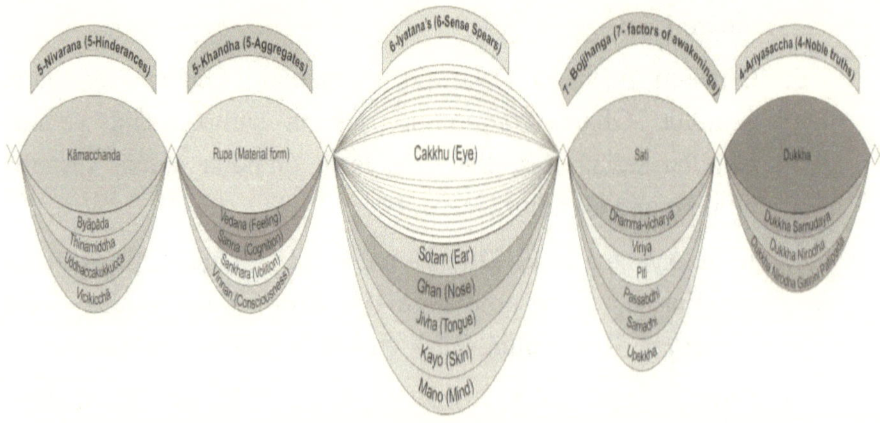

Fig. 5.1: Presentation of Connectivity of Nīvaraṇa-Khandha-Āyatana-Bojjhaṅga-Sacca Dhammakkhandha.

5.4 Interconnectivity of the 84,000 Dhammakkhandha

In the previous chapter we have constructed the base of 3,000 Dhammakkhandha depicted in Fig. 4.8. This figure is now further reconstructed by adding the divisions of the bojjhaṅga and saccha to it to establish its righteous base of 84,000 dhammakkhandha of Dhamma aggregates. As soon as we add up the seven factors of enlightenment and the four factors of the four Noble truths to 3,000 dhamma aggregates, its sum total goes to 84,000 Dhamma aggregates, the magic figure that has mesmerized as well as illusioned millions of the wayfarers on the path of enlightenment. The interconnectivity of the five divisions of the contemplation of the mind contents (Dhammanupassana) in 84,000 Dhammakkhandha has been illustrated in Fig. 5.2, 5.3 and 5.4.

Table 5.1: Sequence of Khandha, Āyatana, Nīvaraṇa, Bojjhaṅga and Sacca.

Nīvarana (5)	Khandha (5)	Āyatana Loke		Bojjhaṅga (7)	Sacca (4)
		Internal Āyatana Loke (6x10=60)	External Āyatana Loke (6x10=60)		
Kamcchando	*Rūpā*	Cakkhu loke	Cakkhu loke	Sati	Dukkkā
		Sotaṃ loke	Sotaṃ loke		
		Ghānaṃ loke	Ghānaṃ loke		
		Jivhā loke	Jivhā loke	Dhamma-vicaya	
		Kayo loke	Kayo loke		
		Mano loke	Mano loke		
Vyapado	Vedana	Cakkhu loke	Cakkhu loke		Dukkhā Samudaya
		Sotaṃ loke	Sotaṃ loke		
		Ghānaṃ loke	Ghānaṃ loke		
		Jivhā loke	Jivhā loke	Viriya	
		Kayo loke	Kayo loke		
		Mano loke	Mano loke		
Thin- Middha	Saññā	Cakkhu loke	Cakkhu loke		Dukkhā Nirodha
		Sotaṃ loke	Sotaṃ loke		
		Ghānaṃ loke	Ghānaṃ loke		
		Jivhā loke	Jivhā loke	Piti	
		Kayo loke	Kayo loke		
		Mano loke	Mano loke		
Uddhacca-Kukkucca	Saṅkhārā	Cakkhu loke	Cakkhu loke		
		Sotaṃ loke	Sotaṃ loke		
		Ghānaṃ loke	Ghānaṃ loke		
		Jivhā loke	Jivhā loke	Passaddhi	Dukkhā Nirodha Gamini Patipada
		Kayo loke	Kayo loke		
		Mano loke	Mano loke		
Vicikiccha	*Viññāna*	Cakkhu loke	Cakkhu loke	Samādhi	
		Sotaṃ loke	Sotaṃ loke		
		Ghānaṃ loke	Ghānaṃ loke		
		Jivhā loke	Jivhā loke	Upekkhā	
		Kayo loke	Kayo loke		
		Mano loke	Mano loke		

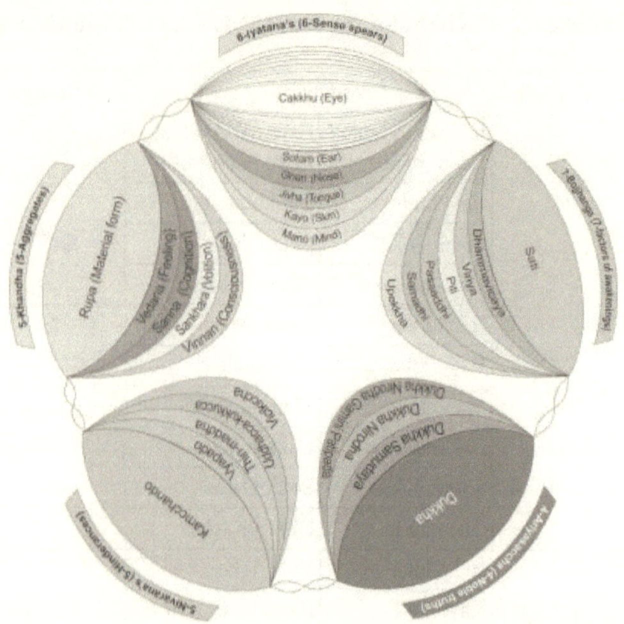

Fig. 5.2: Presentation of circular-connectivity of Nīvarana-Khandha- Āyatana-Bojjhaṅga-Sacca Dhammakkhandha.

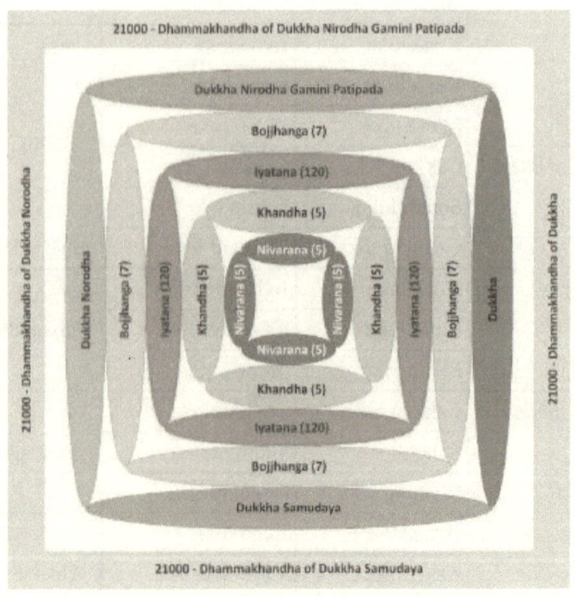

Fig. 5.3: Presentation of the square-connectivity of the 84,000 Dhammakkhandha.

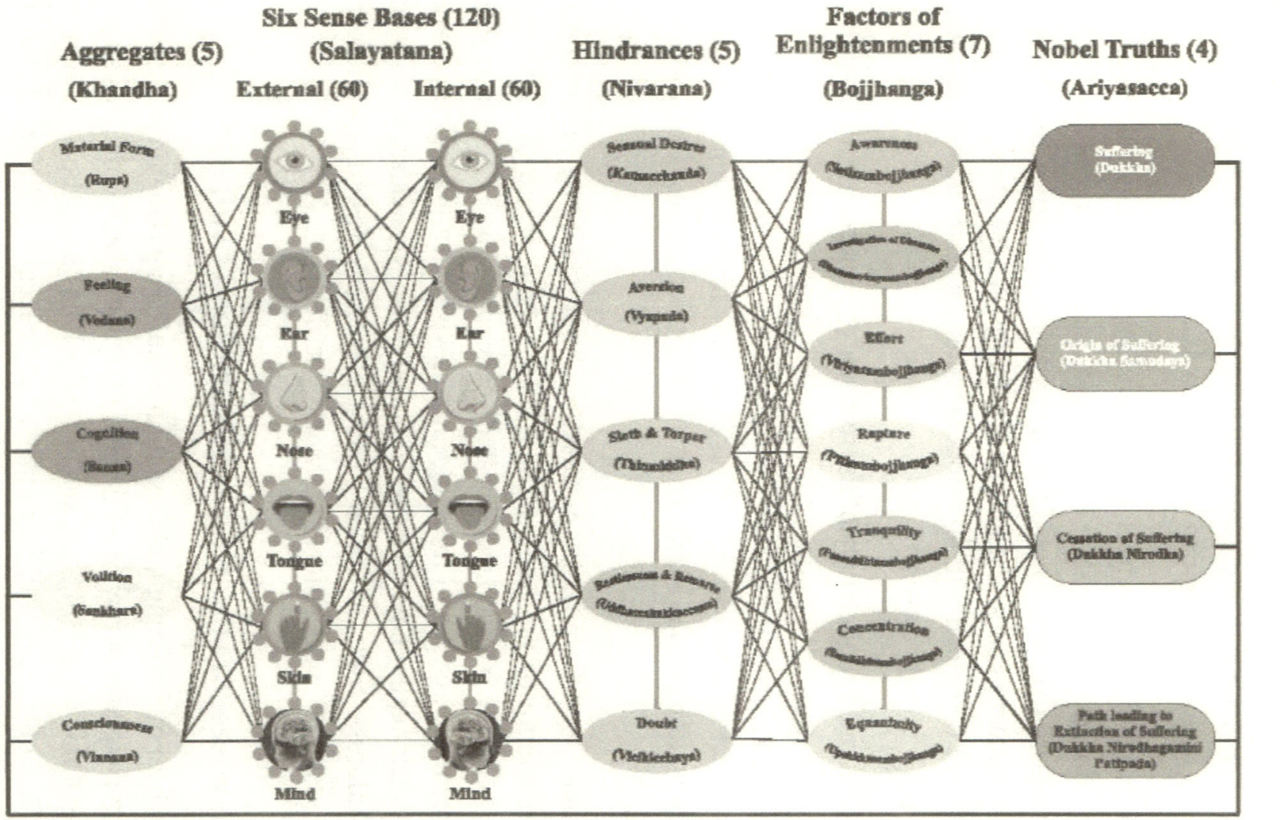

Fig. 5.4: Presentation of inter-connectivity of Nīvaraṇa-Khandha- Āyatana- Bojjhaṅga-Sacca Dhammakkhandha

Mindfulness fosters a discerning awareness that allows practitioners to grasp all aspects of Dhamma at once, transcending both time and space. This deep insight captures the entirety of existence, unveiling the complex connections among phenomena.

In this heightened awareness, temporal and spatial limits fade, enabling recognition of 3,000 realms and beyond, including the 84,000 worlds made up of five hindrances, five aggregates, 120 sense bases, seven enlightenment factors, and four Noble Truths. All the elements of these worlds are contained within a singular moment of thought, illustrating the mind's infinite capacity.

This integrated connectivity of the five sets of mindfulness of Dhamma, highlights the interrelation between the five hindrances and their solutions, the emptiness of the five aggregates, the function of six sense bases in perception, the cultivation of seven enlightenment factors, and the realization of four Noble Truths within the framework of body and mind.

Through this immediate process, practitioners gain a profound understanding of the transient and insubstantial nature of all things, along with the interconnectedness of existence. They come to realize the liberating essence of mindfulness and wisdom, allowing perception of ultimate reality beyond material constraints. Consequently, elevated mindfulness reshapes their comprehension, fostering wisdom, compassion, and liberation from worldly suffering.

5.5 Wheel of Suffering and Cessation of Suffering

The wheel of Suffering and Cessation of suffering (Dhammakkhandha chakka) explains herewith all the 84,000 Dhammkakhandha in a single spoke of this wheel (Fig. 5.5 and 5.6) which has been shown to remain in a flux of change and impermanence (anicca), suffering (dukkhā), unsubstantiality (anatta) and arising and passing away (uppad-vaya) on the 12 nidanas of the dependant origination (paticcasamutpadā).

This wheel has the moment anticlock wise to take a seeker of Nibbana from starting point of ignorance (avijjā) to the end point of cessation of suffering (*...jara maranan...nirodho hotiti*). As mentioned above, a single spoke of this wheel speaks of all the 84,000 Dhammakkhandha interconnected together like the bogies of the train. From its periphery it starts with the upādānakkhandha (5 aggregates) amalgamated with the āyatana (12-Sense bases). The place of these 12 sense bases have been just at the middle where the six internal and six external sense spears further divides in 10 'loke' [(Here the part of the mind involved in the experience of the feeling (vedanā) and causing further reaction or nonreaction towards the sensed object is called as 'loke')].

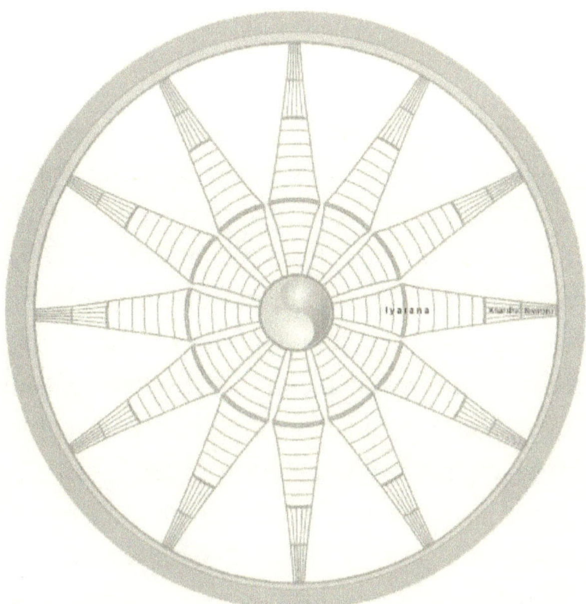

Fig. 5.5: Wheel of Suffering (Dukkha Chakka)

The word 'loke' which comes repeatedly in the Mahāsatipaṭṭhānā sutta is the plural of the term 'lok' which is commonly used in most of the Indian languages for denoting the world, worldly things or common mass (public) in general sense. Each of the sense bases (for instant -

Cakkhu, 10 'loke' becomes cakkhu loke, cakkhu-viññāṇa loke, rūpa loke, cakkhu-rūpa samphasso loke, cakkhu sampajja-vedana loke, rupa-saññā loke, rūpa-sancetana loke, rūpa-taṇha loke, rūpa-vitakko loke and rūpa-vicaro loke as illustrated in Table-5.1 and Fig. 5.1. Just like this example of cakkhu, other remaining five internal and five external sense spears such as hearing (sotam), smell (ghanam), tongue (jivha), skin (kayo) and mind (mano) makes the total 120 'Loke' in this nearly middle part of the spoke of the wheel. The part of the sense bases then has the further connection with the five hinderances [(pancha-nivarana of sensual desire (kamcchando), ill-will (vyapado), sloth and torpor (thin-middha), restlessness and remorse (uddhacca-kukkucca) and skeptical doubt (vicikiccha)]. Pancha-upadam khandha takes a central stage of the wheel of suffering as the Buddha declare in the first Noble truth of suffering.

The wheel of suffering (Dukkhā chakka) as illustrated in Fig. 5.5 has only these three parts. This wheel of suffering moves clockwise almost in the direction of the flow of the gushing river of suffering that flows on from one Sansara to another, from one birth to another birth almost unceasingly without any effort by the sufferer towards the cessation of suffering. It should not be understood from the ongoing explanation that the faculties of the seven factors of awakening (bojjhaṅga) and the faculties of fathoming four Noble truths are absent or not present in the common nescience lot (puthajjana). It can only be said that these faculties are either at the state of dormancy or very weakly developed or put to use towards the critical analysis of the day-to-day experiences of the world without attraction or aversion towards it as long as the enquiring mind comes in contact with the Dhamma through a noble friend (kalyanmitta) who really seeks his as well as his fellow beings' release form the Dukkha as illustrated in the wheel of cessation of suffering (Fig. 5.6).

Fig. 5.6: Wheel of Cessation of Suffering (Dhammakkhandha Chakka)

Prediction of the Buddha on satipaṭṭhānā: The Buddha expressed at the end of the Mahāsatipaṭṭhānā sutta that the practice of these four foundations will bring one of two results: Arahatship in this life, or state of Non-returner. The results will come in 7 years, 6 years, 5 years, 4 years, 3 years, 2 years, 1 year, 7 months, 6 months, 5 months, 4 months, 3 months, 2 months, 1 month, ½ month or 1 week.

As we have discussed and analyzed various components of the 3,000 realms for their objectivity, fulfilments of the objectives, limitations of the human mind, and various challenges faced by the meditator, we shall analyze the components of the 3,000-84,000 dhammakkhandha with the same instrument of scrutiny.

5.6   Objectives of 84,000 Dhammakkhandha

The Buddha predicted that the practice of mindfulness of the four foundations will bring one of two results: Arahatship in this life, or state of Non-returner. We have extrapolated that the five divisions of

Dhammanupassana constitutes 84,000 Dhammakkhanda. Therefore, the principal objective of perception of 84,000 Dhammakkhandha is not only cultivation of wisdom but also its consummation in to the incorporable enlightenment.

If all human beings have the ability to perceive three thousand realm or Dhammakkhandha, then he or she is even better equipped to do so by evolving the seven factors of enlightenment within to perceive the four noble truths. By putting himself or herself on the middle path, treading over the path with mindfulness, such person can be expected to realize the ultimate liberation from suffering, the goal of the 3,000 realms.

Cultivation of mindfulness is a crucial factor in progressing on the path towards rūpa jhana, arūpa jhana, and ultimately, enlightenment. Here are the steps involved:

1. Establishing mindfulness: The first step is to establish mindfulness by bringing one's attention to the present moment and observing one's thoughts, feelings, and bodily sensations without judgment.

2. Concentration: Once mindfulness is established, the meditator needs to develop concentration by focusing on a single object, such as the breath. This helps to still the mind and reduce distractions.

3. First jhana: With continued practice, the meditator may enter the first jhana, characterized by intense joy and happiness, and a one-pointed concentration on the chosen object of meditation.

4. Second jhana: The meditator then progresses to the second jhana, characterized by a deep sense of tranquility and equanimity, as well as a heightened concentration.

5. Third and fourth jhanas: The meditator then progresses to the third and fourth jhanas, characterized by even deeper states of equanimity and concentration.

6. Arūpa jhanas: After achieving the fourth jhana, the meditator can progress to the arūpa jhanas, which are states of meditation focused on formless objects such as infinite space, infinite consciousness, nothingness, and neither perception nor non-perception.

7. Enlightenment: Through continued practice and cultivation of mindfulness, the meditator can ultimately attain enlightenment, which is characterized by a deep understanding of the nature of reality and the cessation of suffering.

Although Ichinen sanzen philosophy is to help individuals understand and cultivate this potential for enlightenment within themselves and also believe that it is achieved through the practice of mindfulness and the cultivation of compassion and wisdom. By focusing on the present moment and cultivating a sense of compassion and understanding for all beings, one can begin to realize the interconnectedness of all things and the ultimate nature of reality but the progressive path of the enlightenment is not planned. Buddhism's ultimate goal has always been to enable people to attain freedom from suffering, or enlightenment.

5.7 Limitations of Human mind

Having analyzed various factors of the 3,000 realms with the tools of the Buddha's charter of enquiry, the same yardstick of truth is applicable here herein for 84,000 Dhamma aggregates. Since the propagation of Buddhism, the dhamma has been practiced in India and all over the world, by Theravada, Mahayana Buddhists and also by the meditators of the Vipassana and Zen. It has been practiced with poise and equanimity by both Buddhists as well as non-Buddhists. It has been found to be equally beneficial to all those who embraced it followed the directives of the discipline and walked over the path ardently and steadfastly with complete mindfulness. So it is obvious to reveal the fact that dhamma is observed on the body and mind, here and now. There has not been a limitation of the human mind to grasp the facts associated with the 84,000 dhamma aggregates.

Critical and impartial mindfulness of our own body, feelings, mind and mental contents is all about the path of the Dhamma, middle way of the Tathagata, the Buddha. All the external and internal conditions, criteria and phenomena that are subjected to clear perception of reality by support system of our own sense organs. No external faculty or the sensory system can be relied in by the seeker of truth on the path of cultivation of insight and wisdom.

There would definitely be the practical possibilities to understand the technical aspects of the path without walking over it. There would also be people coming from different ideologies to develop faith and clear understanding in Buddhism, which may or may not be an obstacle for the initiator. However, and as far as the practical obstacles for the perception of reality through 84,000 dhamma aggregates is concerned, there could not be any difficulty as long as the six sense bases (āyatana) of the observer are stainless and the mind is clear and free from doubts. Dhamma gives its fruits here and now. It can be sensed, perceived and experienced by the wise for themselves within the framework of their body and mind. Since the time of the Buddha, millions have trodden the path and many of them have reached their fulfilment of the goal of liberation and enlightenment.

5.8 Challenges

Clear understanding and perception of the factorial design of the 84,000 Dhammakkhandha within the framework of the body and mind is in fact a normal process of the contact, sensation of feeling, perception and cognition of the things with the sense organs. It is a part of our all-daily routine activities and we all are quite accustomed to this natural process of perception. In the language of biological science, we may call it the work of the sensory nervous system.

The cause and effect of all the routine and common perceptible phenomena of the sense bases can be clearly understood by breaking the world of the consciousness in its ultimate fragments. Of course, it cannot be done by the modern scientific instrumentation. Each and every phenomenon of all the six sense bases which occurs in a blink of an eye, in a single thought moment, seems to be a unique, unbreakable and permanent phenomenon. The Buddha teaches the suffering humanity to see the impermanence of all the dhamma by separating them sequentially in the chain of ten separate incidences. Then one can see and perceive that this is the world of the eye (chakku loke), this is world of the eye consciousness (chakku viññāṇa loke), this is the world of the visible form (rūpa loke), this is the world of the eye contact (cakkhu samphasso loke), this is the world of the sensation of feeling arising from the visible form (cakkhusamphassajā vedanā loke), this is the world of the perception of the visible form (rūpa saññā loke), this is the world of the mental reaction to visible form (rūpa sañcetanā loke), this is the world of craving of the visible form (rūpa taṇhā loke), this is the world of thought conception of visible form (rupa vitakko loke), and this is the world of rolling thought associated with the visible form (rūpa vicāro loke).

In this way when the sequential incidences of the compounded eye consciousness is broken down in its individual reality, one could be able to perceive that the actual reality of the phenomena of the world of eye as a sense bases is very feeble and impermanent, in the continuous process of arising and passing away without any stop in between two sequential occurrences. This clear understanding of reality of the conditioned phenomena further unravels that the enticing and pleasurable craving arises and establishes here in this mind for the continuity of the world of becoming. This becomes the base of the cause of the suffering (Dukka-samudaya). After this clear understanding about the housing of the craving, the mind further unravels the reality of the conditioned phenomena that the enticing and pleasurable craving is eradicated and extinguished here in the mind, for the discontinuation of the world of becoming without any external influence. This clear understanding works as a base for the cessation of the suffering (Dukkha-nirodha).

This clear understanding of the impermanence of all the phenomena of the physical and mental worlds. These all-conditioned phenomena of the physical and mental worlds can be perceived in a single thought moment within the framework of the body and mind by every human being.

This reality of all conditioned phenomena is very much naked truth visible to everybody. The major challenge is to learn to see and perceive this naked truth. The human mind prefers to lives in such type of compartment where all the doors of the six sense bases are tightly closed to the reality of the conditioned world. The incessant feeding of the craving with all types of enticing and pleasurable hindrances works as a thick dark cloud that obstruct the light of insight to reach the ignorant mind to see the naked reality of the worldly phenomena with clear understanding. Therefore, the ignorance (avijja) is called as the root cause of the craving. Once rays of the insight reach in the house filled with darkness since aeons, it illuminates the whole world of reality and opens up the universe of the supreme enlightenment.

Chapter 6

3000 Realms & 84,000 Dhammakkhandha

Relativity for Cultivation of Insight

"I praise that perfect Buddha, the Supreme philosopher, who taught us relativity; free of cessation and creation, without annihilation and permanence, with no coming and no going, not a unity nor a plurality, fabrications quieted, the supreme bliss."

– Nagarjuna

The figures like 3,000 Realms or 84,000 Dhammakkhandha evolved with a very strong base of the Buddha's teachings. These figures are the indicators of the dhamma in relationship to the cultivation of insight and wisdom with the critical understanding of the variety of the worldly phenomena. Throughout the Canon, we find that the Buddha had been very critical in his analytical and statistical expressions. The figures like three Jewels (Ratana), four Noble truths (Ariyasacca), five aggregates (Upādānakkhandha), seven factors of enlightenment (bojjhaṅga), Noble eightfold path (Ariyo athaṅgiko maggo), eight ethical code of conducts (Sila), ten mindfulness (anussati), twelve reason of causal genesis (paticcasamuppada), thirty-two bodily impurities (patikul-manasikara), fourty subjects of meditation (kammatthana), eighty-nine consciousness (chitta) so on and so forth. All these and many other figures set out by the Buddha were critically well explored and evaluated by the Buddha himself and his monks during the Dhamma discourses. There had never been any confusion about these figures.

Tipitaka was introduced in Sri Lanka by Ven. Mahindra Mahathera in the 3rd Century BCE. [43] It is a very extensive and important treatise as well as doctrinal foundation of Theravada Buddhism. Tipitaka is the collection of primary Pali texts which was written down in the reign of King Vattagāmini (1st century BCE) in Sri Lanka, at the fourth Buddhist council. In the Tipitaka, we can find only two places where the reference of number 84,000 appears as a numerical extent of the Buddha's complete teachings. Firstly, it appears in the Theragāthā text that belongs to the Sutta Pitaka, of the Tipitaka and secondly in the Aṭṭhakathā which covers the commentaries on the Pali Buddhist canon that provide much information on the society, culture, and religious history of ancient India and Sri Lanka.

However, there is no reference directly from the Buddha about the 84,000 dhamma or Dhammakkhandha as the total discourses of his teachings. The first and foremost reference is the Pali canon itself that refers to the 84,000 Dhamma comes from the Theragāthā.

6.1   Theravada and 84,000 Dhammakkhandha

Theragāthā: In Sutta Pitaka, Khuddaka Nikaya, Theragāthā: Gāthā-1027, there appears the statement of the Ven. Ananda in the form of following Gāthā:

"Dvasīti Buddhato Gaïhaü Dve Sahassàni Bhikkhuto Caturàsitisahassàni Ye Me Dhammà Pavatinno"

"82,000 (Teachings) from the Buddha I have received; 2,000 more from his disciples; Now 84,000 teachings are familiar to me."

If we look at the above original Pali text, only these numbers are mentioned in it, together with "Dhamma" meaning "teachings" in this context. The word "Dhammakkhandha" does not appear at all [44]. In this context, the focus of this question as per Ven. Anand's declaration goes to the complete discourses of the Buddha in the Canon. Ven.

Ananda's statement in Theragatha has been extrapolated and correlated with the number of total discourses of the Buddha during his 45 years of preachings. This matter had generated much curiosity and enthusiasm in this magic figure of 84,000, to count out the total discourses given by the Buddha and some of his senior monks. The references of the Attakatha provide the analytical statistic of the 84,000 discourses of the Buddha as per the Canon.

Ven. Ananda's statement in Theragatha, would be perfectly true to have total 84,000 discourses of the Buddha and other monks. However, the Theravada records put to rigorous scrutiny and analysis by many Buddhists thinkers and writers, the outcome of the scrutiny could not resolve the issue with full proof. It is also a matter of debate, whether all the discourses of the Buddha given in his preaching's for 45 long years have really been recorded in its completeness or there had been additions and deletions in them during the period of time.

Authors analysis of the four foundations of mindfulness from the Mahasatipaṭṭhānā sutta unravels the concept of 84,000 Dhammakkhandha reffered to as the only way for the cultivation of the wisdom and enlightenment (Ekayano maggo). Dhammakkhandha, concept goes in alignment with the Buddhist phenomenology, and perfectly support the perception of clear understanding of the reality. It assures the seeker of truth that there is no prerequisite of the complete knowledge in the form of 84,000 Dhamma teachings spread throughout Tipitaka for the attainment of wisdom and enlightenment. This practical relativity of the 84,000 Dhammakkhandha provides the vision for clear observation of the interplay of hindrances, aggregates, and sense bases. The way with which it brings the wondering mind on the middle way and evolve it with the support of factors of enlightenment to see the Noble truths, filling the mind up to the brim with equanimity is motivating. Its progressive front to open the gates at every stage of jhana to a higher and higher stage from mundane to supermundane jhanas and paths leading to the liberation from suffering is peerless. This relativity of the path with respect to attainment of its aim and objective is very clearly put forth by the Buddha in the only path of Satipaṭṭhānā, four foundations of mindfulness.

Aṭṭhakathā: The Aṭṭhakathā or 'Commentary' means the "explanation of the meaning". The aṭṭhakathas can be mentioned as exegetical treatises on the texts of the Pali canon. When Pali Tipitaka was introduced in Sri Lanka in the 3rd Century BCE, we do not find any atthakathas or other abhidhammic works of that period. It was the time of Buddhaghosa, who visited Sri Lanka in the first-half of the fifth century AD, was no doubt by far the greatest commentator and the author of the most important commentaries [45]. Buddhaghosa justifies the belief that the three pitakas are the words of the Buddha himself. His fourteen alleged commentaries on the Tipitaka have been available. His commentaries on the Dīghā Nikāya especially on the Mahaparinibbana sutta has been known as Sumanagalavilāsinī. According to Commentary to the Dīghanikāya, Sumanagalavilāsinī, Buddha's precepts consist of 84,000 categories of the Dhamma in Buddhist Scriptures. They are divided into 3 categories, as follows:

1. Vinaya-pitaka (a scripture of monastic discipline) consists of 21,000 Dhamma.

2. Suttanta-pitaka (a scripture of discourse) consists of 21,000 Dhamma.

3. Abhidhamma-pitaka (the Higher Doctrine) consists of 42,000 Dhamma.

This above division of the 84,000 dhamma in three baskets as indicated in the atthakathā cannot be validated due to various issues associated with the measures to be applied for counting of the Dhamma. The matter in this way remained invalidated till the period of the King Ashoka.

6.2   King Ashoka and 84,000 Dhammakhandha

When the Third Buddhist Council was held 235 years after Mahaparinibbana of the Buddha, King Ashoka asked the Arahat Ven. Moggaliputta Tissa Mahathero, Head of the Sangha, about the numerical extent of the Buddha's Teachings to which the Mahathera answered that it consists of 84,000 Dhammakkhandha (Aggregates of Dhamma). In veneration to the Buddha's Teachings, King Ashoka ordered his ministers to build 84,000 monasteries and stupas all over his empire. The Mahathera obtained the Buddha's relics from Rajagaha and let the emperor enshrine them in the stupas that he had built.

This relation corresponds to the similar account, in the Mahāvaṃsa, of Aśoka's construction of 84,000 monasteries (vihāras): Mahavâmsa records Ven. Moggaliputta Tissa as the spiritual teacher of the King Ashoka and his son Ven. Mahinda, and also as the one who presided over the Third Buddhist Council at Patliputta [46]. Mahavâmsa mentioned letter writing in at least six places. In one of them it says that King Asoka received letters from 84,000 centers "On every side from the 84,000 cities came letters on one day with the news "The Viharas are completed". Then he proclaimed that there will be a festival for seven days' time".

One of the most surprising matters is that the terminology, "84,000 Dhamma" used in the Tripitaka and Aṭṭhakathā has been referred to as "84,000 Dhammakkhandha," in most of the records associated with the legend of King Ashoka. However, no proper explanation has been in support of the validation of the 84,000 Dhammakkhandha, in any of the written records. Author is of the opinion that during the period of over 200 years after the Mahaparinibbana of the Buddha, there would have been much detailed analysis of this magic figure 84,000. As the worldly phenomena (Dhamma) coexists in association with the external physical world (khandha), it would have been an obvious reason to add a word "khandha' with Dhamma to refer all worldly phenomena as "Dhammakkhandha".

Beyond doubt, we can establish the relativity of the 84,000 Dhammakkhandha envisioned in the legend of Ashoka with the four foundations of mindfulness expounded in Mahāsatipaṭṭhānā sutta for the cultivation of the happiness, peace and enlightenment.

6.3   Mahayana and 84,000 Dhammakkhandha

Mahayana Buddhism is not a single group but a collection of Buddhist traditions: Zen Buddhism, Pure Land Buddhism, and Tibetan Buddhism are all forms of Mahayana Buddhism. In these and other sects of Buddhism there are beliefs that the Buddha taught many skillful means or paths. In Buddhism, these are typically described with the vehicle, path or doors metaphors. 84,000 doors to enlightenment have emerged through such Zen Buddhist, mystical Buddhist, intellectual Buddhist, devotional Buddhist and hipster Buddhist as many doors, one destination. We should try to unravel the reasons behind these beliefs to explore the relative evolution of the figure 84,000 in these sects to correlate them with the 84,000 Dhamma or Dhammakkhanda of the Theravada Buddhism.

84,000 Hooks in Zen Buddhism: Zen Buddhism relates the 84,000 Dhammakkhandha (Dharma aggregates) of the Theravada tradition with the consciousness of mind of 84,000 hooks. Each and every teaching served as a reminder to cut a certain hook to that artificial consciousness that belonged to the false self (anatta). Zen Buddhism describe it as a mind of 84,000 sharp hooks, walking through a very tight corridor (your present consciousness field) of an impermeable, buoyant material or prime- subset that best could be described as soft and stick-friendly bark tissue.

Upon its surface, your hooks, all in number more than you can ever keep count of, at any given moment, and all created by your every desire since beginning less time of countless births you cannot recall in your ordinary state of mind-numbness. Every such hook was and still is born out of ignorance through your mind's constant division of itself into form (to some), sensation (to others), thought and memory (to most), makes you become stuck on that bark tissue-like wall of samsara, causing an experience of interdependent origin to your mind and hence a spiritual friction, which is anything but true Dharma and the blissful completeness of noble wisdom and perfect freedom found in the latter [47].

In other more radical sects, like the Zen Buddhist sect especially by the Chan Masters of the Tang and Sung Era, it was strongly advised to cut off all hooks in one swift cut hence allowing the freed mind, to ascend to its true level of being self-aware as mind only, instantly curing the illusion of being the lower reflection of itself, or the no- self, which Mara had tricked it into hooking on.

There are of course many other sects in Buddhism that through the millennia have approached the dilemma of the mind of 84,000 hooks, but that is for you to find out if you desire to explore those options, of finding a way to completely unhook yourself from the body consciousness of ignorance and suffering.

We can certainly relate the mind of 84,000 hooks with the 84,000 dhammakkhandha as it exactly befits an interplay of mind and matter in the intricate psycho-cosmic topography of the wisdom and enlightenment. However, we cannot practically exercise the concept of mind of 84,000 hooks with the simultaneously evolved topography of the 3,000 realms of the Nichiren Buddhism.

6.4 Sarvastivada and 84,000 Dhammakkhandha

Dharmaskandha ("Dhamma aggregates") is the second text of the Sarvastivadin Abhidhamma which focuses on Sarvastivadin doctrines, especially concerning the stages of the Arahat's progress. Dharmaskandha means "collection of dhammas". It was supposed to be composed by Ven. Sariputra (according to the Tibetan sources) or Ven. Mahamoggalayana (according to Chinese sources). It begins with a matika as a summary of the topics, showing its antiquity, as these were supposedly only assigned by the Buddha himself. It presents 21 subjects, the first 15 of which concern with the practice of the spiritual path, and the realization of its fruits. The 16th subject deals with "various other issues" while subjects 17 to 20 deal with the enumeration of the ayatanas, dhatus and khandhas as encompassing "all dhammas". Here it should be noted that the dhamma associated with the ayatanas, dhatus and khandha are reffered to as all dhamma which supports the consideration of the dhammakkhanda. The 21st subject deals with regards to dependent origination.

Sarvastivada Abhidhamma consider all the factors which have been considered as important for framing the concept of the 84,000 Dhammakkhandha. Therefore, Sarvastivada seems to be much more accurate for the calculation of the dhammakkhandha as compared to the Theravada and Mahayana approach.

6.5 Buddhist Meditation: 84,000 Iterations

The Pali Canon includes references to many different types of meditation. Sarah Shaw collects many of these texts in her book, Buddhist Meditation: An Anthology of Texts from the canon (London: Routledge, 2006) [48]. One of the best-known of these is the Metta meditation, in which one projects feelings of love and compassion to the six directions, consisting of the four horizontal directions (east, west, north and south) plus above and below (zenith and nadir). This meditation is frequently mentioned in the canon. However, the author in her discussion takes an integral approach to the topic of Buddhist meditation, for, if there are 84,000 iterations of something, then there must be an underlying unity of which there are 84,000 iterations. That unity is mindfulness, the essence of meditation. In taking this approach to Buddhist meditation using Shaw's translations, aided by the comprehensive understanding of the canon.

"84,000 iterations," is a very important concept in the Buddhist meditation. It is associated with the through and clear understanding of the physical body (rūpa) and its mental phenomena of feeling (vedanā), perception (saññā), mental formation (saṅkhārā), and consciousness (viññāṇa). During the meditation the sharp and penetrating mind passes through all the 84,000 dhmmakkhandha within the framework of the body and mind. This en passage of the mind makes it possible to see and clearly perceive the 84,000 worldly phenomena to understand the four Noble truths.

If we correlate "3,000 iterations," as per the concept of Ichinen sanzen, this enrouting of the mind with 3,000 realms would not develop clear understanding of the reality, due to the absence of the factors of enlightenment and Noble truths.

6.6   Nichiren Buddhism and 3,000 Realms

We have seen that there has been a dilemma of the mind of 84,000 hooks in the Zen Buddhist practice. On the line of the above discussion regarding the inclusiveness of the magical figure 84,000 Dhamma or 84,000 Dhammakkhandha in various sects of Buddhism, 3,000 realms of Nichiren Buddhism talks about the factorial framework and explain all the factors that encompasses 3,000 realms. This opens up the wider enquiry for establishing the relativity of 3,000 realms with 84,000 Dhammakkhandha, since most of the issues associated with Buddhist phenomenology have been very seriously deliberated and established in various sects of Buddhism.

The Buddhist principle of "Ichinen sanzen" and its philosophical framework based on Nichiren Buddhism, expresses why and how it is possible for ordinary human beings to attain Buddhahood amid the realities of daily life. Ven. Nichiren's "The Doctrine of three thousand realms in a single moment of life," has been described by him as the heart and core of the Buddha's teachings and established a practice to enable all people to experience the state of Buddhahood in their daily lives. The practice of chanting "Nam-myoho- renge- kyo" with faith in our inherent Buddha nature actualizes the principle of three thousand realms in a single moment of life in the life of the practitioner. Ven. Nichiren believed the Lotus sutra as an important scripture in Mahayana Buddhism, and one of the Buddha's vital teachings, holding the key to happiness. The Lotus sutra clarifies that the world of Buddhahood, as with the other nine worlds, is equally inherent in the lives of all people and thus is a potential open to all within this lifetime. It also clarifies that the true aspect is inseparable from all phenomena, and that all phenomena, just as they are, are in themselves the true aspect.

The common thread that the author finds in all the major sects of Buddhism is that all of them affirm the magic figure 84,000 in the form of dhamma, Dhammakkhandha or the Dhamma hooks as we have seen. Nichiren Buddhism deviates in this matter to establish the notion of 3,000 realms by using the variables of the ten worlds, ten factors and three realms. It has also deviated remarkably from the established Buddhist phenomenology where the basic conceptual and practical framework of the Dhamma is almost invisible.

The author wished to expand and delineate the view of all these historical records with more satisfactory analysis. In his book, 84,000 Dhammakkhandha of Buddhism [35], he has fixed the narrative of thesis, antithesis as follows:

Thesis: "The 84,000 Dhammakkhandha of Buddhism accounts to the total number of discourses of the Buddha".

Antithesis: "The 84,000 Dhammakkhandha of Buddhism does not account to the total number of discourses of the Buddha".

Further, to resolve this conflict between the thesis and antithesis, the author has proposed the synthesis by reconciling their common truths, and evolving a new proposition which is as follows:

Synthesis: "There must be something else in Buddha's teachings that accounts to the 84,000 Dhammakkhandha of Buddhism".

With this new preposition, the author has found five key factors of Dhammakkhandha in the Buddha's very important foundational discourse of Mahāsatipaṭṭhānā sutta associated with the four foundations of Mindfulness. The Buddha has completely expanded the mind-matter phenomenology in the foundation of the mind content i.e. Dhammanupassana, where he opened the realm of the mind contents and it's all respective Dhamma along with physical variables of the khandha. Author's synthesis of this psycho-cosmic topography of the Dhammakkhandha reveals the interconnectedness of all the dhamma with the khandha. It practically works for the transformation of the mind for the realization of the wisdom and enlightenment.

6.7   Relativity of 84,000 Dhammakkhandha for cultivation of Insight

The Buddha advises the Kalamas to "know for themselves" and to "investigate" rather than accepting things on faith or authority. This emphasis on experiential knowledge is consistent with the Buddha's emphasis on the importance of personal practice and the cultivation of inner wisdom.

84,000 Dhammakkhandha is the practical field of the body and mind of an individual for the cultivation of wisdom. It stands upon the real worldly experiences of the six sense bases (dhamma) constanly coming in contact with the mental and physical aggregates (khandha) and there is no place for any imaginary mental conception. Our worldly experiences are nothing but the things we see with the eyes, hear with the ears, smell with the nose, taste with the tongue, touch with the skin and know with the mind. These six-sense based worldly experiences develop the hindrances that distract the mind's ability to clearly see the true nature of the reality. The first hindrance of sensory desires brings about affection towards the material world. On the contrary second hindrance of ill-will causes much anguish and aversion. Third hindrance of the sloth and torpor at times fills us with discouragement, frustration, boredom, indifference, hopelessness, resistance and works for giving up. With the fourth hindrance, restlessness and worry, restlessness brings about an inability to focus and the mind recoils from being directed. Worry, other half of the fourth hindrance develops the agitated feeling of regret for what one has done and not done in the past. The fifth hindrance, doubt, so easily distract the meditator by disturbing inner questions about the path and practice.

Steadfast seeker of truth works ardently, patiently, and persistently with calm and quite mind on all these fetters and finds a way just like a small stream of water move ahead in spite of the obstacles in its way. Perceiver employs the good faculty of the mind to open up and activate the dormant factors of the enlightenment for assistance not to fight but to clearly understand the nature of hindrances. These factors of insight in turn develops an enthusiasm, energy and force to clearly see and perceive the reality of all the worldly phenomena. 84,000 Dhammakkhandha thus open up and reveal the interconnectivity of all the phenomena and transform the mind for the realization of the enlightenment.

Jhana is a state of meditative absorption that can lead to a deep perception of reality. Through the practice of jhana, an individual can develop heightened concentration, mindfulness, and insight, which can enable them to perceive reality in a more direct and immediate way. Some practical possibilities in the perception of reality through jhana, provides specific beneficial effects for the development of concentration, mindfulness and insight as follows:

1. Heightened concentration: Jhana can help to develop a deep and sustained level of concentration that allows an individual to focus their attention on a single object or task for extended periods of time. This can lead to a greater understanding of the nature of reality by enabling the individual to observe phenomena in a more detailed and nuanced way.

2. Increased mindfulness: Jhana can also help to develop a greater sense of mindfulness, or awareness of the present moment. This can help individuals to become more attuned to their own thoughts and emotions, as well as to the world around them, which can lead to a more accurate perception of reality.

3. Greater insight: Through the practice of jhana, an individual can develop a deeper understanding of the nature of reality and the interconnectedness of all things. This can lead to a greater sense of empathy and compassion, as well as a more profound appreciation of the beauty and complexity of the world.

Overall, the practice of jhana can help individuals to develop a more direct and immediate perception of reality, which can lead to a greater sense of inner peace, happiness, and well-being. However, it is important to note that the practice of jhana requires discipline, patience, and commitment, and may not be suitable for everyone.

Chapter 7

Science of Happiness, Peace & Enlightenment

Cognitive Scientology

*"If there is any religion that could correspond to the need of
Modern sciences, it would be Buddhism"*

– Albert Einstein

Subjective well-being is used as the scientific term for happiness and life satisfaction-positive thinking and feeling that our life is going well, not burdensome. Negative feelings are undesirable and unpleasant feelings such as depression, anger, and worry that people tend to avoid if they can. Scientists rely primarily on self-report surveys to assess the happiness of individuals. People's levels of subjective well-being are influenced by both internal factors, such as personality and outlook, and external factors, such as the society in which they live. Some of the major determinants of subjective well- being are a person's inborn temperament, the quality of their social relationships, the societies they live in, and their ability to meet their basic needs. In certain cases, people adapt to conditions so that over time their prevailing circumstances may not influence their happiness as much as one might predict they would. It has been observed that individuals with subjective well-being are happy people, have healthier life, have better social relationships, and are more productive at work. On the other hand, people without subjective well-being are chronically stressed, depressed, or angry.

Thus, happiness does not just feel good, but it is good for people and for those around them [49].

There is a very specific reason for keeping the sequence of the happiness, peace and enlightenment in the title of this chapter. Buddhism has a particular focus on happiness that comes from the decisions we make about how to live our life, and the types of thoughts we think and how we regulate our emotions. In the practice of jhana the appearance of these refined states of the mind occurs till the four rupa jhana in the sequence of exuberant joy, delight, happiness and peace with equanimity. Then in the further absorption in the arupa jhana ends in the liberation from the suffering. This progressive stages of the jhana and its attainments can be scientifically correlated and validated. Neurological point of view, the pleasure and happiness seem to be an interplay of the chemicals that we call neurotransmitters. It is worthwhile to understand a role of these happy chemicals in joys and woes of the suffering humanity.

7.1 Human Brain and Mind: Relativity

We have seen the activity of the brain and mind as a coordinator and also as a supreme sensory organ that brings about the coordination of other sensory organs. As we are now entering in the area of the neurological science, it is necessary to understand the relativity of the brain's activity with respect to the experiences of the mind.

The relationship between the brain and the mind is a complex and ongoing area of study in the field of neuroscience and psychology. Modern psychology can measure and gives a visual display of the amount, level, or contents of something. It has no access to gauge the intensity of the very subtle human expressions of delight, happiness, peace, friendliness, compassion, sympathetic joy, and equanimity which streams out as the rewards of the righteousness. While our understanding is far from complete, I can provide a brief overview of the neurology of the brain and how it relates to the activity of the mind.

The Brain's structure: The brain is a highly intricate organ composed of billions of neurons (nerve cells) and supporting cells called glia. It is divided into several major regions, including the cerebrum, cerebellum, brainstem, and various subcortical structures. The cerebrum, which makes up the bulk of the brain, is responsible for higher cognitive functions, such as thinking, memory, perception, and consciousness.

Neurons and Synapses: Neurons are the basic building blocks of the brain. They communicate with each other through electrical and chemical signals. Neurons are connected via synapses, which are tiny gaps where information is transmitted from one neuron to another. Neurons use neurotransmitters to transmit signals across synapses. These neurotransmitters play a crucial role in shaping our thoughts and emotions.

Neural Networks: The brain functions through complex neural networks, where groups of neurons work together to perform specific tasks or processes. Networks are responsible for various mental functions, such as language processing, motor coordination, and emotional regulation.

The Mind: The mind encompasses all mental processes and activities, including thoughts, emotions, perceptions, memories, and consciousness. While the brain provides the biological substrate for the mind, the mind itself is considered a product of the brain's activity. The relationship between brain activity and conscious experience is a topic of ongoing research and debate.

Consciousness: Consciousness is a state of awareness and subjective experience. It is considered one of the most complex aspects of the mind. The exact mechanisms underlying consciousness are not fully understood, and it remains a topic of philosophical and scientific inquiry.

Cognitive Functions: Various regions of the brain are associated with specific cognitive functions. For example, the frontal lobes are involved in decision-making and executive functions, while the hippocampus is crucial for memory formation. Cognitive functions arise from the coordinated activity of multiple brain regions working together.

Plasticity: The brain exhibits plasticity, which means it can adapt and reorganize in response to experiences, learning, and injury. This plasticity enables learning and recovery from brain injuries but also means that the mind can be shaped by environmental influences.

Thus, the brain is the physical organ responsible for generating the mind's activities. The relationship between the activity of brain and experiences of the mind is intricate and multifaceted. Neuroscientists continue to explore this complex interplay to gain a deeper understanding of how the brain gives rise to the mind.

7.2   Consciousness of Reality

Complete mindfulness of 84,000 Dhammakkhandha cultivated through four foundations of mindfulness, expounded by the Buddha; "3,000 realms in a single thought moment," a hallmark of Nichiren Buddhism, or 84,000 hooks of Zen meditation invariably speaks about the complete awareness and clear understanding of the human mind. Therefore, real nature of consciousness and its understanding is a subject matter of applied Buddhism. It is necessary to discuss this issue of human awareness at this juncture. The notion of one tenth consciousness of normal human mind is raised by many philosophers and researchers. This ten percent consciousness is also believed as a myth by many people. Whatever may be the truth, this ten percent myth is firmly rooted in many popular cultures of the society, despite many efforts to debunk it. The origin of the "Ten percent" myth is unclear, but some people attribute it to a misunderstanding of a statement in an article by William James [50]. The quote is as follows:

"Most of us feel as if we lived habitually with a sort of cloud weighing on us, below our highest notch of clearness in discernment, sureness in reasoning, or firmness in deciding. Compared with what we ought to be, we are only half awake. Our fires are damped; our drafts are checked. We are making use of only a small part of our possible mental and physical resources."

There are a plethora of articles debunking this myth both in popular media and from neuroscientists. Neuroscientists now have tools for creating images and tracking the activity of living, functioning brains. Although instruments like Positron Emission Tomography (PET) scans and functional Magnetic Resonance Imaging (fMRI) have revolutionized our understanding of brain function but these techniques have not been able to assess the real topography of this notion. The entire brain is constantly active, even in periods of sleep: regulating, monitoring, sensing, interpreting, reasoning, planning, and acting. It has been observed that even people with degenerative neural disorders such as Alzheimer's and Parkinson's disease still use more than 10% of their brains.

We are definitely using more that 10 percent of our brain during our daily routine activities. However, instead of exposing the hollowness of the James statement, we should try to explore our lacking associated with the understanding of the worldly realms. The facts pointed out by James in his article about the utilization of the small part of the brain, opens up many layers of the human consciousness associated with the clear understanding of the worldly phenomena. It is necessary to know and understand as to what is expected in the notion of complete i.e. hundred percent consciousness because with that yard stick only, we can correlate the use of the brain. In such circumstances, we also need the standard scale of consciousness to prove or disapprove James's statement.

I definitely find much truth in the James statement in his article. He points out that we are below our highest notch of clearness in discernment, sureness in reasoning, or firmness in deciding, due to which we are only partly awake as compared with what we ought to be. If we are partly awake, we should see towards the human beings who are known to be fully awakened one in the history of human civilization. If we are below our highest notch of clearness in discernment, we must try to delve in the depth of mindfulness of the worldly phenomena. If our mind is wavering regarding the sureness in reasoning, or is in duality over the firmness in decision making, we should take a support of the causal analysis and dependent origination.

7.3   Hypothesis of Ten-steps Mindfulness Model

The Buddha, the Awakened One, after attainment of enlightenment delivered his first sermon in which he preached the four Noble truths: suffering, its cause, its cessation and the middle way for cessation from suffering. The Buddha, while expounding the causal genesis in second and third Noble truth of suffering, preached the establishment of mindfulness for the clear perception of the worldly phenomena. We have discussed this aspect in details in the previous chapters. This ten-world linked mindfulness of worldly phenomena and its activity domain has been illustrated in Table-7.1.

Out of the above ten-step realms of mindfulness, only one of them exists in the external world and that is the world of external physical objects (Rūpa khandha). Rest all the other nine realms exists in the mind and work internally. Mostly, we react instantly as soon as our sense organ establishes contact with the external sense object. Such immediate reflections to the external aggregates are considered raw, immature and vulgar by the wise. This instant reaction against the stimulus is devoid of mindfulness and wisdom. Most of the instant reflections against the contact are in the form of affection or aversion makes such individuals only one tenth conscious of the reality as an individual is only using one realm information out of the ten-realms mediated mindfulness. Such individual is not able to see the real nature of the phenomena, since he is not able to contemplate upon the other linking chains of the consciousness which are very important for

Table 7.1: Ten-steps mindfulness of worldly phenomena and its activity domains.

S.N.	World of Sense bases	Activity domain
1.	World of six Sense organs (Ayatana) (cakkhu, sotaṃ, ghānaṃ, jivhā, kayo, mano)	Internal
2.	World of six Sense objects (rupā, saddā, gandhā, rasā, phoṭṭhabbhā, dhammā)	External and internal
3.	World of Consciousness of six sense organ (viññanā)	Internal
4.	World of Contact of six sense organ with object (samphasso)	Internal
5.	World of Sensation of the sense object (samphassaja vedanā)	Internal
6.	World of Perception (saññā)	Internal
7.	World of Mental reaction towards object (sañchetanā)	Internal
8.	World of Craving towards object (taṇhā)	Internal
9.	World of Thought conception of object (vitakko)	Internal
10.	World of Rolling in thoughts of object (vicāro)	Internal

further analysis of the information received through the contact of the sense object.

The circumspection of all the facets of mindfulness is necessary to understand the real nature of the worldly phenomena. This circumspect analysis of each and every passing phenomenon breaks up the myth of the so believed permanent and substantial nature of reality. Clear understanding of the reality is supported by the factors of enlightenment to understand the universal truths of suffering. Let us explore the relative cognitive scientology of the human mind by the Buddha's 10-step process of consciousness building.

7.4 Worlds of Cognitive Scientology of Mind

The ten-step mindfulness process is a very critical and complex process of human mind. The work domain and expertise of each section of the ten-step chain of cognitive awareness is very well coordinated by the mind without any internal or external interference. In this process, Truth of suffering, helps in understanding nature of suffering; Truth of origin of suffering, helps in recognizing role of craving; Truth of cessation of suffering, helps to the practical attainment of cessation of suffering; and the Truth of the path helps the seeker to cultivate the Noble eightfold path. In the Noble Eightfold path, Right understanding comprehend the four Noble truths; Right intention cultivate renunciation, loving-kindness, and non-violence; Right speech, Right action and Right livelihood establishes a strong moral base required for the understanding of the truth in its essence. Right efforts bring about the vigour. Right mindfulness and Right concentration develop mental clarity and focus to cultivate wisdom (paññā) by understanding the true nature of phenomena as impermanent, suffering, and non-self. The specific role of all the ten serially, intricately chained worlds in the ten-world mediated cognitive scientology of human mind is explained as follows:

1. *Role of Six sense organs in the 10-step cognitive process of mind:* Six sense organs (salāyatana) namely eye (cakkhu), ear (sotam), nose (ghānam), tongue (jivhā), body (kayo) and mind (mano) perform the key functions of receiving and processing sensory information, conditioning consciousness and perception, influence feelings, intentions, and actions. It coordinates by interacting with other sense bases and mental factors. Practically these sense organs help to develop mindfulness of sense bases and helps to recognize impermanence. Understanding sense bases' role in consciousness helps detach oneself from cravings. Cultivating awareness of sense bases supports to develop wisdom.

2. *Role of Sense objects in the 10-step cognitive process of mind:* Sense objects (visaya) are visible forms (rupā), sounds (saddā), smells (gandhā), tastes (rasā), tactile sensations (phoṭṭhabbhā) and mental phenomena (dhamma). These sense objects stimulate sense bases, condition consciousness and perception, influence feelings, intentions, and actions. They also interact with other sense objects and mental factors. During these interactions they help in understanding impermanence of the sense objects, suffering that is caused by attachment to sense objects and non-self (anatta) as they lacs their inherent existence. Practically they help to meditate on sense objects to develop mindfulness, observe sense objects' impermanence and cultivate detachment from sense objects.

3. *Role of Consciousness in the 10-step cognitive process of mind:* Consciousness (viññanā) of all six sense organs play a very important role in developing awareness of sense objects. Consciousness rises from contact between sense organ and object conditions perception, feelings, and intentions. It further recognizes sense objects, conditions perception and feelings, influences intentions and actions. It also interacts with other mental factors. In this process it helps in understanding the impermanence of constantly changing consciousness, its nature of suffering and its lack of inherent existence.

Mind (citta) also referred to as viññanā is also a part of the mind that develops discriminating awareness and discriminates between objects. Ālaya-viññāna (Storehouse consciousness) stores all the impressions in the mind.

4. *Role of Contact in the 10-step cognitive process of mind:* Contact (sampassa) is an intersection of sense organ, sense object, and consciousness that preliminarily conditions feelings, perception, and intentions. It marks the beginning of the cognitive process. Contact connects sense organ and sense object,

triggers consciousness and feelings, influences perception and intentions and interacts with other mental factors. It develops the understanding of impermanence due to constantly changing contact, its nature of suffering and its lack of inherent existence. Practically it meditates on contact to develop mindfulness, observe contact's impermanence and cultivate detachment from contact.

5. *Role of Feelings arising from contact in the 10-step cognitive process of mind:* Feelings arising from contact (sampassaja vedanā) is categorised as pleasant (sukha), unpleasant (dukkha) or neutral (adukkhamasukha). It arises from contact between sense organ and object. It conditions perception, intention, and craving, influences emotional response and attachment and interacts with other mental factors. It develops the understanding of impermanence due to constantly changing feelings, its nature of suffering and its lack of inherent existence. Practically it meditates on mindfulness of feelings, observe its impermanence and cultivate detachment from feelings.

6. *Role of Perception in the 10-step cognitive process of mind:* This step of perception (saññā) is important as it is associated with the interpretation of feelings and sensations. It is also involved in the process of recognition and labelling of experiences. It conditions intention, craving, and action. As it interprets feelings and sensations, while doing so it also influences intention and craving, conditions action and behaviour and interacts with other mental factors. It develops the understanding of impermanence due to constantly changing perception, its nature of suffering and its lack of inherent existence. Practically it meditates on perception to develop mindfulness, observe its impermanence and cultivate detachment from perception.

7. *Role of Intention/volition in the 10-step cognitive process of mind:* Intention/volition (sañchetanā) is the step of taking decision to act

or react, actuation of the direction of thought and action (kamma). It conditions craving and action. Volition determines direction of thought and action that influences craving and attachment, conditions action and its consequences. It also interacts with other mental factors. It develops the understanding of impermanence due to constantly changing intention, its nature of suffering and its lack of inherent existence. Practically it recognizes impermanence of intentions to develop mindfulness of volition and cultivate detachment from volition.

It is necessary for the practitioner to understand the distinction between saññā and sañchetanā. As described above, saññā means perception or idea while sañchetanā means volition, intention, or conscious decision. saññā focuses on recognition and categorization, while sañchetanā involves intentional direction. saññā is more automatic, whereas sañchetanā is deliberate. In the context of generation of kamma, saññā contributes to the formation of attachment (upadana) and ignorance (avijja) whereas sañchetanā plays a crucial role in developing wholesome (kusala) or unwholesome (akusala) actions.

8. *Role of Craving in the 10-step cognitive process of mind:* Craving (taṇhā) is a desire for pleasure or existence, attachment to sense objects that conditions suffering and rebirth. Craving arises from intention and perception, fuels ignorance and attachment. It interacts with other mental factors for conditioning of suffering and rebirth. It develops the understanding of impermanence due to constant change of craving, its nature of suffering and its lack of inherent existence. Practically it recognizes impermanence of craving, develop mindfulness of craving and cultivate detachment from sensuality craving (kama-taṇhā), existence craving (bhava-taṇhā) and non-existence craving (vibhava-taṇhā).

9. *Role of Thought/conceptualization in the 10-step cognitive process of mind:* Thought/conceptualization (vitakko) is the thinking and

conceptualization of experiences that conditions reflection and action. Role of such thought is to interpret and conceptualize experiences, condition reflection and action. It interacts with other mental factors and fuels craving and attachment. It develops the understanding of impermanence due to constant change of thoughts, misconception that leads to suffering and its lack of inherent existence. Practically it recognizes impermanence of thoughts, develop mindfulness of thoughts and cultivate detachment from thoughts and conceptualization. During mindfulness meditation meditator observes thoughts without attachment and cultivate wisdom.

10. *Role of Discursive thinking/reflection in the 10-step cognitive process of mind:* Discursive thinking/reflection (vicāro) is reflection and rumination on thoughts, mental examination and investigation. It conditions action and decision-making. Role of such reflection is to examine and investigate thoughts, conditioning action and decision-making. It keeps on interacting with other mental factors and fuelling craving and attachment. It develops the understanding of impermanence due to constant change of reflection, mis-reflection that leads to suffering and its lack of inherent existence. Practically it recognizes impermanence of reflection, develop mindfulness of discursive thoughts and cultivate detachment from discursive thinking. During mindfulness meditation, meditator meditate on discursive thoughts to develop mindfulness to observe reflection's impermanence and cultivate detachment from reflection.

Every passing phenomenon thus observed through this deca-world scrutiny mode, establishes the clear understanding of the reality as impermanent and unsubstantial phenomena. The mind with such clear understanding can delve into the causal genesis of all the physical and mental activities. It is expected that such individuals with clear understanding of reality may evolve their consciousness to the higher class of the Noble ones, either completely liberated or on the path of liberation from the suffering.

The author would like propose herewith his hypothesis of "Ten-world mediated mindfulness of the worldly phenomena as a mode to establish mindfulness and clear understanding of the reality. Beyond doubt, this is the objective with which we are trying to discuss the subject matter of the present book. The author firmly believes that this model of evaluating the human consciousness on the basis of the causal genesis is a base for establishing mindfulness, cultivating wisdom and enlightenment.

7.5   Rewards and Pleasures

Neuroscience studies showed that some part of brain (e.g. amygdala, hipocamp and limbic system) and neurotransmitters (e.g. dopamine, serotonin, norepinephrine and endorphin) play a role in control of happiness. A few studies pointed to the role of cortisol and adrenaline (adrenal gland) and oxytocin (pituitary gland) in controlling happiness. Physical health and typology also concluded in most related studies to have a significant role in happiness [51].

Robert Lustig, author of "The Hacking of the American Mind: The science behind the corporate takeover of our bodies and brains" explains the key differences between pleasure and happiness and discuss the basic brain mechanisms [52]. Pleasures and rewards are synonymous. Happiness and contentment are synonymous. We all need rewards to get up in the morning, go to work, make a living etc. Reward is central to the survival of species. Most people are confused and fail to differentiate these two concepts namely, pleasure and happiness. With the specific and in deft scrutiny of these concepts, we can notably and clearly identify seven differences in order to understand its real nature.

1. Pleasure is very subtle, a short termed like a meal. Happiness is long termed like a lifetime treasure.

2. Pleasure is visceral; you can feel it in your body. Happiness is ethereal, you can feel it through mental contents.

3. Pleasure is taken Casino. Happiness is given like habitat for humanity.

4. Pleasure is achievable alone like a personal enjoyment of an ice-cream. Happiness is achieved in social groups like the birthday party.

5. Pleasure is achievable with material substances. Happiness is hardly achievable with material welfare.

6. Extremes of pleasures, whether it be through material welfare or behavioural satisfaction tends to addictiveness. In such individuals there is a lack of control over thoughts, urges, and impulses associated with activities. Such behavioural activities that are done in excess, significantly impact one's life in a negative way. There is '...aholic' of every one of those addictions like shopaholic, sexaholic, alcoholic, chocoholic etc. There is no such thing as being addicted to too much happiness.

7. Lastly and perhaps most important for this discussion point we can consummately certify in neurological terminology that pleasure is dopamine and happiness is serotonin.

So, with these two different neurotransmitters, dopamine and serotonin, altogether two different areas of the brain, two different regulatory pathways. two different mechanisms of actions, two different drivers and two different mental perception works.

In his book "Atomic Habits" James Clear [53] has explained the habit formation in the same way as a process that involves four stages:

1. Cue: A trigger or prompt that sets off the habit. This can be a specific time of day, a location, or an emotional state.

2. Craving: The motivation or desire behind the habit. This is the reason why you want to perform the habit.

3. Response: The behaviour or action taken in response to the cue and craving.

4. Reward: The benefit or payoff of the behaviour, which reinforces the habit.

Clear also explains that to change a habit, you need to address each of these stages:

- To break a bad habit, identify the cue and find alternative responses that don't lead to the unwanted behaviour.
- To build a good habit, create an implementation intention that specifies when and where you will perform the new behaviour.

So then, how does it matter? What we should be afraid of? Why should we care? The answer to this question may be an eye opener for all of us.

7.6   Dopamine verses Serotonin

Researchers have observed that positive and negative moods affected by brain chemical in several ways. Two of the most important neuro-transmitters that involved in mood are dopamine and serotonin. Positive mood and negative mood mediated by dopamine and serotonin levels. Perhaps the most influential neurochemical theory of positive mood is presented by Ashby et al. [54]. The two main elements of their theory are that: (i) positive mood is associated with (but not necessarily caused by) increased levels of dopamine in the brain and (ii) some of the changes in cognition observed in positive mood are due to the increased dopamine levels associated with positive mood. Another neurochemical agent that associated with emotional states is serotonin (5-hydoxy tryptamine). Serotonin is a neurotransmitter that mediates satisfaction, happiness and optimism.

Dopamine is the learning neurotransmitter. It is the positive reinforcement. It is the transmitter that says, this feels good, I want more. Serotonin is the opposite to dopamine. It's the neurotransmitter that says, this feels good, I don't want or need anymore. People sometimes refer to dopamine and serotonin as the "happy hormones" due to the role they play in regulating mood and emotion. However, dopamine and serotonin are clearly two different things. And the problem is, if you don't know the difference, then you are basically subject to continuing to try to reward yourself, ad nauseum.

It is very important at this juncture to check out the intricate role of these two important neurotransmitters in our pleasures and rewards visa vis, happiness and contentment. Dopamine is an excitatory neurotransmitter that binds to its receptor to excite the next neuron. This is synaptic receptor activation. Neurons like to be activated, they don't like to be bludgeoned. Chronic overstimulation of any neuron in the body leads to neuronal cell death. It is because neurons are so metabolically taxing that if you just keep it up and keep it up, that neuron is basically going to exhaust and die. Therefore, the post synaptic neuron that has the dopamine receptors on it, it has a fail-safe. It has a protective mechanism, in order not to be overwhelmed. By doing so, it down- regulates the dopamine receptor. How it affects the brain? Even though you have lots of lagan's, lots of dopamine molecules, you have fewer receptors, which means there is less chance that any molecule will find the receptor. In human terms it means that if you need more and more to get less and less. That is the phenomenon we call tolerance. So, dopamine lead to tolerance. When those neurons actually do start to die, that is called addiction.

Now serotonin, other neurotransmitter is not accepted, its inhibitory in its activity. If it inhibits the next neuron, do you need to down-regulate the receptor? No, because you are not going to the neurons, not going to die as it is not getting overexcited. So, there is no such thing as overdosing of too much happiness. But there is one thing that down-regulate serotonin, that is dopamine. So, the more pleasure you seek, the unhappier you get. If you cannot differentiate between pleasure and happiness and you are led astray by your coveted substance. You may get happy by taking that substance without a thought of the future consequences. If you want your reward here and now, and there is no ability to cognitively inhibit that feeling of award, that then drives the dopamine even faster. You are sadly mistaken. This need of reward ultimately injures someone, something or hurt or embarrass someone and will do a number on you. It's doing a number on all the human beings submerged in the ocean of life and death.

7.7 Lizard Brain

There is also a third component to this pathway that is absolutely essential and it is cortisol. Cortisol is a stress hormone. With the point of view of this discussion, it works on the prefrontal cortex of the brain, a part right behind our forehead, above our eyes. The prefrontal cortex is the part of the brain that keeps you from doing stupid things. If you have a dysfunctional prefrontal cortex, you cannot see the future. You only live for the moment. Prefrontal dysfunction is what turns the human into a lizard. Ultimately that leads to neuronal cell death. So, as the combination of dopamine and cortisol, that leads to addiction. So, the reward is good, plus stress is not. We all are now so chronically stressed and the chronic stress makes you want reward, because of this lizard brain and so it sets you for addiction. On the other side serotonin side chronic stress, also in cortisol, it does bind to its receptor to inhibit the next neuron. The problem is that the serotonin receptor is down-regulated by cortisol. This condition of lesser serotonin and fewer receptors, brings about depression. Addiction and depression both occurs, one due to dopamine and second due to lack of serotonin. We can say that the chronic stress belies both of these two major afflictions of human conditions. There is one reward system, that reward system which is pretty darn important. If you don't receive awards, you don't get out of bed, you actually lie in bed and die out of pleasure. It's just like those transgenic animals that are knocked out of reward system and those animals have no will to live.

We all fall victim to our own habits, whether good or bad. From smoking, eating unhealthy food, or exercising every morning before we go to work. We did not consciously make or form these habits in an instant, it takes time and mastering of the brain to actually make them develop into what we are accustomed to in our daily lives. It is not just coincidence. Whether we like it or not, our habits dictate our life in every aspect. These are both good and bad habits. Most of us have both. It's a matter of identifying the one's not serving us and eradicate them. The truth is though, most people rather live with it and just deal with it because they are comfortable. That's a life of pure mediocracy. It is a choice. Og Mandino propose that we must become slaves to the habits that serve us in a way to grow. Either way we're slaves to all our habits so why not pick the best ones, delete the crappy one's and replace them. All it takes is a small bit of willingness to accept the challenge of change. Some studies have said that it takes 21 days of doing something to make it a habit. However, it's not that easy when one enquires in this area of the cause and effect theory associated with the ultimate truths of the reality [55].

This concept of pleasure and happiness befits perfectly with the technique and concept of happiness and peace explained by the Buddha through the four foundations of mindfulness. In the Satipaṭṭhānā Sutta, the Buddha proposes a technique for overcoming the five impurities or hindrances. In this technique of four foundations of mindfulness: the body (kaya), feelings (vedana), states of mind (citta) and the mental objects (dhamma), the confrontation with the hindrances enters into a last foundation, the contemplation of mental objects (dhammanupassana), where it comes as the first exercise to counteract the hindrances.

7.8   Relativity with 2D, 3D, and Multidimensional Theories of Human Feelings

Human emotions have long fascinated scholars across various disciplines, including psychology, neuroscience, and philosophy.

Theories of human feelings can be categorized into two-dimensional, three-dimensional, and multidimensional frameworks. These models aim to articulate the complexities of emotional experiences and their implications for human behaviour. Two-dimensional (2D) theories often simplify emotional experiences into two primary axes: valence and arousal. Valence refers to the intrinsic attractiveness (positive valence) or averseness (negative valence) of an emotion, while arousal indicates the intensity of the emotional experience, ranging from calm to highly activated states. The Circumplex Model of Emotions, proposed by Russell (1980), exemplifies this approach [56]. In this model, emotions are represented in a circular arrangement with valence on one axis and arousal on the other, leading to a spectrum of emotional states from happiness to sadness and from calmness to excitement.

Three-dimensional (3D) theories expand upon the two-dimensional frameworks by introducing a third dimension to capture additional nuances in emotional experiences. The Plutchik Wheel of Emotions, proposes eight primary emotions (joy, trust, fear, surprise, sadness, disgust, anger, and anticipation) arranged in a wheel format. These primary emotions can blend to form more complex feelings, illustrating the dynamic interplay of emotions. This model can be visualized as three orthogonal axes representing valence, arousal, and an additional dimension reflecting intensity or complexity of emotions [57].

Multidimensional theories offer even more complexity, acknowledging that human feelings are not easily categorized into simple dimensions. The Component process model, proposed by Scherer (2001), argues that emotions arise from a combination of various components, including cognitive appraisal, physiological responses, and expressive behaviours. This model emphasizes the process of how emotions are elicited, experienced, and expressed, suggesting that emotions are dynamic and context-dependent [58]. Multifactorial models, such as the *Dimensional Theory of Emotion* developed by Watson and Tellegen, integrate various factors such as personality traits, situational context, and individual differences, providing a more holistic view of emotional experiences [59].

Understanding human emotions through two-dimensional, three-dimensional, and multidimensional frameworks provides a rich perspective on how feelings influence behaviour and interpersonal dynamics. Each model contributes unique insights, from basic emotional responses to the intricate interplay of various emotional components. Continued exploration of these theories can enhance our understanding of emotional well-being and inform therapeutic practices.

The Buddha's teachings on mindfulness, particularly through the four foundations of mindfulness (satipaṭṭhānā), provide profound insights into human feelings and their management. This analysis can be juxtaposed with modern theories of human feelings, including two-dimensional, three-dimensional, and multidimensional frameworks, to explore the intersections between ancient wisdom and contemporary psychological understanding. In particular, the second foundation-Mindfulness of feelings-provides direct insight into the nature of emotions, encouraging practitioners to observe feelings as they arise without attachment or aversion. Modern two-dimensional theories, such as Russell's Circumplex model of affect, categorize emotions based on valence (positive or negative) and arousal (high or low). The Buddha's mindfulness of feelings can be likened to this model, as it encourages practitioners to recognize and classify feelings into pleasant, unpleasant, and neutral categories. This aligns with the valence aspect of the circumplex model. However, the Buddha emphasizes a non-attachment to these feelings, viewing them as transient rather than fixed states, which diverges from a purely analytical approach that may seek to label or define emotional states.

Three-dimensional models, such as Plutchik's Wheel of Emotions, introduce complexity by including the intensity of emotions. The Buddha's approach acknowledges the varying intensities of feelings, as practitioners are encouraged to observe the depth of their emotional experiences and the subsequent reactions that arise. This parallels Plutchik's understanding of the complexity and interplay of primary emotions. While Plutchik's model focuses on the interaction of emotions, the Buddha's teachings prioritize understanding and detachment from these emotional states, fostering a mindset of equanimity rather than mere emotional analysis. Multidimensional theories, like the Component process model by Scherer, encompass a range of factors that contribute to emotional experiences, including cognitive appraisal, physiological responses, and social contexts. The four foundations of mindfulness resonate with this approach, as they encompass a holistic view of human experience-recognizing that feelings arise from a complex interplay of bodily sensations, mental states, and contextual factors. The Buddha's teachings emphasize the importance of insight into the impermanent and interdependent nature of emotions, advocating for awareness and understanding as a path to liberation. In Buddhist psychology, the analysis of feelings and mental states is crucial for understanding the nature of craving and attachment. The Buddha classified mental states (cittas) into various categories, notably the twentyfive shobhan (wholesome) and fourteen ashobhan (unwholesome) cittas. This classification helps practitioners recognize and cultivate positive mental states while counteracting negative ones, ultimately leading to greater peace and liberation from suffering. This focus on transformative awareness contrasts with the more analytical stance of some multidimensional theories that may not emphasize the spiritual or transformative aspects of emotional understanding. This approach underscores the transformative potential of mindfulness and ethical living in addressing the root causes of craving, ultimately guiding individuals toward enlightenment.

7.9 Relativity with Mathematics and Computation Sciences

The integration of spirituality, mathematics, and the binary concept of computation sciences reveals a rich tapestry of connections between abstract, philosophical ideas and practical, scientific methods. Spirituality and mathematics both seek to uncover deeper truths about existence, albeit through different lenses. The binary system in computation provides a foundational framework for processing information, which can metaphorically resonate with spiritual and philosophical themes of duality and unity. Exploring these domains together offers a more nuanced understanding of how human thought, both abstract and concrete, attempts to grapple with the mysteries of reality and existence.

The Buddha's concept of root cause and end of suffering seems to be closely related to the binary concept of 0 and 1 which is indeed a fundamental principle in computational science, and it has far-reaching parallels in the natural world and human experience. Nothing is '0' and Something is '1' in the physical world. In the physical realm, "nothing" can represent the absence of matter, energy, or space, while "something" represents their presence.

In other words, Existence and Non-Existence may be related to Zero and Non-Zero States. In physics, zero can represent a state of equilibrium, while non-zero states indicate motion, energy, or change.

Nothing (0) and Something (1) in human experience is the Absence and Presence. "Nothing" can symbolize the absence of a person, idea, or experience, while "something" represents their presence. It may also be associated with Emptiness and Fulfilment. Emptiness or void can be seen as "nothing," while fulfilment, purpose, or meaning can be seen as "something."

This binary concept may also be truly related to the philosophical and spiritual parallels as Being and Non-Being or Creation and Destruction. Philosophers have long debated the nature of existence (being) and non-existence (non-being), mirroring the 0 and 1 dichotomy. This dichotomy reminds us that even in the absence of something (0), there is always the potential for creation, existence, and meaning (1).

By exploring these connections, we can see how the binary concept of 0 and 1, existence and non-existence, is deeply intertwined with the theory of matter and antimatter, revealing profound insights into the nature of reality, existence, and the human experience. Matter is represented by 1, symbolizing existence, being, and presence while Antimatter is represented by -1, symbolizing the negation of existence, non-being, and absence. Matter (1) emerges from the void (0), symbolizing existence arising from non-existence. Annihilation on the contrary symbolizes the Nonexistence where matter (1) and antimatter (-1) collide, returning to the void (0), symbolizing existence returning to non-existence. These concepts may have profound philosophical implications. The binary concept of 0 and 1 reflects the ontological debate between existence and non-existence, being and non-being. It questions the entire cosmological matter-antimatter dichotomy mirrors as to how existence arose from the void. The interplay between matter and antimatter represents the dynamic relationship between existence and non-existence, highlighting the impermanence of reality [60, 61, 62].

The Buddha has explored this binary concept for understanding the cause of suffering (Dukkha samudaya) and the cessation of suffering (Dukkha nirodha). The Buddha explain this interplay of the Dhammakkhandha as enticing and pleasurable, providing the fertile ground for the craving to arise and establish in the mind as the existential domain of something. It can be coded as one (1). The Buddha further use the same enticing and pleasurable interplay of Dhammakkhandha by understanding impermanent and unsubstantial nature of all the material world, abandoning them all to realize the cessation of suffering. It may be coded as zero (0). The Buddha critically define cessation of suffering by using the word *"Yo tassāyeva tanhāya asesavirāganirodho cāgo patinissaggo mutti anālayo"*. "It is the complete fading away and cessation of this very craving, forsaking it and giving it up (cāgo patinissaggo); the liberation from it (mutti), leaving no place for it (*anālayo*)". This is the returning to the void (0), symbolizing existence returning to non-existence. It should be clearly understood that all these phenomena of the arising and passing away occurs with such unimaginable speed form zero (0) to one (1) and one (1) to zero (0) till the complete cessation of craving during the process of liberation from suffering.

7.10   Hindrances: Cause of Slavery

The Buddha says, hindrances are like a debt, a disease, imprisonment, slavery and a desert road, when they overpower the mind, a man can neither see his own good, the good of others, or the good of both, under their influences, he will do what he should not do and neglect what he ought to do. Hindrances corrupt the mind and weaken wisdom. They cause spiritual blindness and ignorance, destroy wisdom, lead to vexation and distract from the path of enlightenment. Hindrances are regarded as the heaps of demerits. Here the Buddha explains the Noble truth of the cause of suffering, he says, "...is enticing and pleasurable; when this craving arises, it arises here, when it establishes itself, it establishes itself here." *("...piyarūpaṃ sātarūpaṃ, etthesā taṇhā uppajjamānā uppajjati, ettha nivisamānā nivisati).* It is the same concept of the dopamine that blinds the aggravate prefrontal dysfunction leading to neuronal cell death and turns the human into a lizard.

Therefore, the abandonment of the hindrances marks the beginning of freedom. Here the inhibitory serotonin reigns. Freedom from the entanglement of the nasty hindrances, lustful passions and habits that ruin the life. While explaining the Noble truth of the eradication of suffering, the Buddha says, "...is enticing and pleasurable; when the craving eradicates, it eradicates here, when it extinguishes itself, it extinguishes itself here." *("...piyarūpaṃ sātarūpaṃ, etthesā taṇhā pahīyamānā pahīyati, ettha nirujjhamānā nirujjhati.).* With the hindrances abandoned, there is no limit to the possibilities for spiritual growth. It is for the full comprehension, entire understanding, destruction, elimination of these five impurities, that the Noble eightfold path should be cultivated.

7.11 Pursuit of Eternal Happiness and Peace

Pursuit of eternal happiness and peace had been a prime objective of the human endure since antiquity. Though human mind covets the eternal happiness and peace, he gets entangled in the conditioned phenomena of the pleasure and pain visa-vis attraction and aversion. Reason for this perception of a mirage as a reality is merely due to ignorance about the nature of reality.

Buddhism pursues happiness by using knowledge and practice to achieve mental equanimity. In Buddhist teachings, equanimity or peace of mind, is achieved by detaching oneself from the cycle of craving that produces suffering. So, by achieving a mental state where you can detach from all the passions, needs and wants of life, you free yourself and achieve a state of transcendent bliss and well-being. The Buddha encouraged his followers to pursue "tranquility" and "insight" as the mental qualities that would lead to the ultimate reality. As mentioned earlier, the Eightfold path as a whole is said to help one achieve these qualities. In particular, the areas of mental cultivation, which include right effort, right mindfulness and right concentration, are the mental skills and tools used for achieving eternal happiness. The Buddha felt that it was imperative to cultivate right mindfulness for all the aspects of life in order to see the things as they really are. He encouraged keen attention and awareness of all things through four foundations of mindfulness through concentration (sammā samādhi).

1. The first stage of concentration is one in which mental hindrances and unwholesome intensions disappear and a sense of bliss is achieved.

2. In the second stage, activities of the mind to doubt about the path and practice comes to an end and only delight or rupture remains.

3. In the third stage, bliss itself begins to disappear.

4. In the fourth stage of the jhana, all sensations including bliss disappears. It is replaced by a total peace of mind, which the

Buddha described as an eternal sense of happiness that streams out of the equanimity towards all the worldly phenomena.

Let us analyze how this eternal happiness and peace is achieved by the Buddhist practice of right concentration? Right concentration is intimately associated with the ethical practice. When an individual on the path of the middle way, practice the jhana, the seven factors of enlightenment are activated during the right and steadfast practice of jhana. The first three factors of enlightenment i.e. awareness (sati), investigation of the phenomena (dhammavicaya), and efforts (vīriya) are brought to the stage of fulfilment and perfection in the first stage of the jhana. With the strong force of the factors of enlightenment, the house of hindrances is completely shattered. During this demolition of the house of hindrances, first to burn up is the doubts (vicikkicchā) about the path and practice. The strong unwavering faith in the path and practice is also due the realization of the fruits of the path and practice.

This realization and fruition of the practice is very much necessary for all of us in all walks of life. We cannot believe on any unheard, unknown person, place of thing unless and until we witness and acknowledge it in reality. This is a very important boost to the mindfulness. Due to the cessation of the hindrances, the state of mind automated towards the fulfilment of the fourth factor of enlightenment i.e. delight or rupture (pīti). There cannot arise a real eternal delight in the mind of a person without the unwavering faith. Therefore, the second stage of jhana is the fulfilment and perfection of the rupture. As the mind steps in the next third absorption with one pointedness, the clear perception of the worldly phenomena starts seeing the faults of conditionality with the eternal delight. Disappearing delight gets replaced with the more refined state of happiness and bliss (sukha) in the third jhana. The pure one pointed mind looks towards this happiness as the conditioned phenomena subject to change. The further fulfilment and perfection of the other remaining three factors of enlightenment, i.e. tranquillity (passadhi), concentration (samādhi) and equanimity (upekkhā), the conditioned happiness and bliss ceases to replace it with perfect equanimity towards all worldly phenomena. In this way the four stages of the rūpa jhana refines the mind and prepare a base for the lasting eternal happiness and peace of the arūpa jhana.

Here, fulfilment and perfection of the embodiments of enlightenment- the final bliss, means the clear and complete understanding of the four noble truths i.e. suffering, its cause, its cessation and the path that leads to the cessation of suffering within the frame of one's own body and mind.

In Buddhism, the eternal nature of happiness and peace, often associated with enlightenment, is a fundamental concept that revolves around the cessation of suffering and the realization of ultimate truth. It teaches that it is possible to attain a state of profound and lasting happiness and peace through the clear understanding of the four Noble truths and practice of the Noble eightfold path based on ethical and mental guidelines. The happiness and peace of enlightenment are considered eternal because they are not subject to the fluctuations and impermanence of ordinary experiences. They are not dependent on external circumstances, possessions, or relationships. Instead, they arise from a deep understanding of the nature of reality and the mind, leading to the cessation of craving and attachment.

7.12   Science of Happiness, Peace and Enlightenment

With this basic interplay of the happy chemical in the human brain driven by the reward and pleasure, let us now enter inside the technique and science of the complete liberation from suffering, the Nibbana.

The Noble eightfold path constituted of the eight factors are right view, right intention, right speech, right action, right livelihood, right efforts, right mindfulness and right concentration. These eight factors are frequently divided into three broader disciplines: the group of moral discipline (sila), the group of concentration (samādhi) and the group of Wisdom (paññā). The moral discipline comprises the three factors of right speech, right action and right livelihood; discipline of concentration comprises of other three factors of right efforts, right mindfulness and right concentration while the discipline of wisdom is covered by the remaining two factors of right view and right intention. Training of each of these three disciplines, in dependence on its predecessor, provide the support for its successor. Moral training provides the foundation for concentration, concentration functions as the base for wisdom. Wisdom reaches its climax in the four paths and fruits which uproots the subtlest strata of impurities and release in final liberation from suffering.

The New Wisdom schools of China and Japan believes that there are many different paths to enlightenment, but the most important one for us is the path of jhana. Jhana is a practice of mind control by which we stop all thinking and seek to realize truth in its essence. It is a practice of 'stopping and realizing'. If we cease all discriminative thoughts, it will keep us from the further accumulation of error, while the practice of realizing will clear away delusions. Stopping is an entrance into the wonderful silence and peacefulness of potentiality, while realizing is an entrance into the riches of intuition and transcendental wisdom. If anybody thoroughly understands what has been said here about Jhana, he will appreciate that its practice is not an easy task. However, to clear away the misunderstandings, ignorance and hindrances and the guide towards enlightenment, I shall aid them with my own analysis with the view points of the conventional Buddhist perspectives and modern scientific reasoning. I shall try to correlate how in the first phases of the jhana suffuses the mind with the exuberant joy, rupture and happiness and how during the further phases of jhana this rupture and happiness culminates in the consummation of the peace, transcendental wisdom and incorporable enlightenment.

7.13 Role of Jhana in Happiness, Peace and Enlightenment

Jhana or the practice of meditation is central to Buddhism. The study of the scriptures produces intellectual understanding; only meditation on these principles as power latent in the mind, will produce the intuitive awareness of their validity. Secluded meditation has many virtues. All the Buddhas have own their insight and wisdom in a state of secluded meditation and they are the reason why the Buddhas have devoted themselves to it. There are in fact twenty-eight advantages to be gained from the jhana. The advantages are as follows:

Secluded meditation guards him who meditates, lengthens his life, gives him strength, and shut out faults; it removes ill fame, and leads to good repute, it drives out discontent, and makes for contentment; it removes fear and gives confidence; it removes sloth and generates vigor; it removes greed, hate and delusion; it slays pride, breaks up preoccupations, makes thoughts one-pointed, softens the mind, generates gladness, makes one venerable, gives rise to much profit, makes one worthy of homage, brings exuberant joy, causes delight, shows the one being of all conditioned things, abolishes rebirth in the world of becoming, and it bestows all the benefits of an ascetic life. These are the twenty-eight advantages of the jhana which induce the tathagata to practice it. And it is because Tathagata wishes to experience the calm and easeful delight of the jhana with this end in view. There are four reasons why Tathagata tend jhana: so that they may dwell at ease; on account of its faultless virtues; because it is the road to all holy states without exception; and because it has been praised, lauded, exalted and commended by all the Buddhas.

The importance of the jhanas in the Buddhist path to deliverance can readily be gauged from the frequency with which they are mentioned throughout the suttas. The jhanas figure prominently both in the Buddha's own experience and in his exhortations to disciples. While advocating the jhana and its benefits the Buddha points out stepwise progression of the monks to the bliss of jhanas. The Buddha says: There are Chunda, four pursuits of pleasure which leads to ultimate disenchantment, dispassion, cessation, peace, direct knowledge, enlightenment and nibbana (DN, 2:131-32). Which four? Here Chunda, secluded from sense pleasures, a bhikkhu enters and dwells in the first jhana… the second jhana… the third jhana… the fourth jhana [63].

The great Buddhist commentator, Ven. Buddhaghosha explains that jhana has the characteristic mark of contemplation and meditation of the object and the characteristics of the phenomena. The word jhana is also closely connected with the word samadhi, generally rendered as concentration or one pointedness of the mind.

The jhanas as the states of consciousness have the immediate aim of producing a progressive purification of the mind. It plays a precise role in a Buddhist spiritual discipline directed to final deliverance from suffering. The gradual attainments of stages of jhana are dynamic processes by which a mind is gradually purified of its taints. It starts with the elimination of defilements obstructing mental one- pointedness. These defilements are grouped together as the five hindrances (pancanivarana): Sensual desire (kāmcchanda), ill will (vyapāda), sloth and torpor (thinmiddha), restlessness and worry (uddhaccakukkucca) and doubt (vicikicchā).

There is an association of four important mental states of jhana as the constituting factors: applied and sustained thought (vitakka-vichāra), rupture (pīti), happiness (sukha), and one- pointedness of mind (ekaggata). Attainment of the higher jhanas is a process whereby the earlier grosser factor is successively eliminated and the subtler ones brought to greater prominence. In the case of the first jhana, the factors to be abandoned are the five hindrances.

Beyond the four jhanas lies another fourfold set of higher states which deepen the element of serenity developed in the jhanas. These attainments known as the immaterial states (arūpa jhana) as they correspond ontologically to the immaterial realms of existence.

Rūpa jhana and Arūpa jhana are meditative states described in the Buddhist traditional meditative practices especially in Vipassana meditation. According to the teachings, the practice of jhana can lead to a deep understanding of the nature of reality and the cessation of suffering.

7.14 Science of Jhana

The meditator who starts experiencing the benefits of jhana can understand in depth and explain the changes that he or she has undergone in the inner self. Jhana brings about all the benefits depending upon the stages of the jhana. Mahasatipaṭṭhānā sutta arrange the contents of Sammāsamādhi into a fourfold system of the material (rūpa) jhana. The constitution of the fourfold system and its science can be presented as follows:

Material (Rūpa) Jhana: Rūpa jhana refers to the meditative absorption in which the practitioner focuses on a physical object or sensation, such as the body, bodily sensation, mind and mind objects. The practitioner gradually becomes more absorbed in the object of focus, and the mind becomes more and more tranquil and focused. There are four levels of rūpa jhana, each deeper than the previous one. Let us see how the meditative practice of Sammāsamādhi brings about the expected rewards of exuberant joy, delight, happiness, one pointedness and equanimity which can be validated scientifically with the yardsticks of the modern psychiatry. In the various progressive stages of the rūpa jhana, seven factors of enlightenment (bojjhaṅga) namely sati, dhammavicaya, vīriya, pīti, passaddhi, samādhi and upekkha plays a very important role for setting oneself on the path of jhana and its further progress [34].

The practice of Sammāsamādhi, also known as right concentration, can be understood as a science for the cultivation of happiness and peace towards the practical understanding of suffering.

The Buddha's teachings on Sammāsamādhi emphasize the importance of developing a stable and focused mind through the practice of jhana or meditation. By cultivating a calm and concentrated mind, we can gain insight into the nature of reality and the causes of suffering.

The practice of Sammāsamādhi involves developing the ability to focus one's attention on a single object, such as our own body, sensations, mind or phenomena, and maintaining that focus for an extended period of time. Through this practice, the meditator can develop the ability to observe their thoughts and emotions without being carried away by them. This ability to observe and detach from one's thoughts and emotions is a key aspect of cultivating happiness and peace.

The practice of Sammāsamādhi can be understood as a science because it involves a systematic and methodical approach to understanding the mind and its relationship to suffering. By observing the mind and its patterns, the meditator can gain insight into the causes of their own suffering and develop strategies for overcoming it. Thus, the practice of Sammāsamādhi is a practical approach to understanding suffering because it involves a direct and personal investigation into the nature of reality. Through this investigation, the meditator can develop a deep and experiential understanding of the impermanent and unsatisfactory nature of all things, which is the basis for the Buddhist concept of suffering. Through the systematic and methodical approach of meditation, the meditator can develop a stable and focused mind, gain insight into the causes of suffering, and cultivate a deep and experiential understanding of the nature of reality.

Indian spiritual traditions, believe in the eight groups of elementary particles (kalapas) as the major building blocks of the body.

Kalapas refer to the eight aspects of the body that are associated with the elemental forces of earth, water, fire, air, and ether. These kalapas are considered to be the primary vehicles of our experience of reality, and therefore, they are closely related to our understanding of the ultimate reality [62].

Science of First Jhana- Experience of Delight and Happiness: The concept of jhana, which is central to Buddhist meditation, can be understood as a state of deep concentration or absorption. The first jhana is considered the initial stage of jhana attainment, characterized by the absence of five hindrances: sensual desire, ill-will, sloth and torpor, restlessness and worry, and doubt.

First jhana consciousness (viññāṇa) with all critical scrutiny and analysis with initial application (vitakka) and sustained application (vichāra) experiences delight (pīti), happiness (sukha), and one pointedness (ekaggata). At this starting stage, consummation of first three factors of enlightenment i.e. mindfulness (sati), critical analysis (dhammavicaya) and efforts (viriya) is attained which leads to abolish the hindrances, establishing full faith in the practice of jhana and eigntfold path [64].

The attainment of the first jhana is not a mystical or supernatural experience but rather a physiological, biochemical, and psychological process that can be understood and studied scientifically.

From a physiological perspective, the attainment of the first jhana involves the activation of the parasympathetic nervous system and the suppression of the sympathetic nervous system. This shift in the autonomic nervous system leads to changes in heart rate, blood pressure, and breathing rate, which in turn can produce feelings of calmness and relaxation. We can also put it other way that as the truth and reality of impermanence and unsubstantiality of all the phenomena are practically experienced on the framework of individual body and mind. It gives the signal to the mind that the dhamma works as proclaimed.

It brings about the unwavering faith on the Buddha's proclamation and Dhamma's assurance which develops the exuberant joy, rupture and happiness in the first jhana.

Biochemically, the attainment of the first jhana is associated with the release of endorphins, which are natural painkillers that produce feelings of pleasure and well-being. Endorphins are also associated with the suppression of negative emotions such as anxiety and depression.

Psychologically, the attainment of the first jhana involves the development of concentration and mindfulness, which enable the meditator to focus their attention on a single object or sensation. This concentration and mindfulness lead to a reduction in the activity of the default mode network, a network of brain regions associated with self-referential thinking and mind-wandering.

Overall, the first jhana can be understood as a physiological, biochemical, and psychological process that involves the suppression of the hindrances and the development of concentration and mindfulness. This understanding of the first jhana aligns with modern scientific perspectives on meditation and provides a framework for further study and exploration.

Science of Second Jhana- Experience of Delight (Pīti): Continued practice of meditation, the meditator steps ahead during his practice in the second jhana to further establish the cultivation of happiness and peace towards the practical understanding of suffering, and the development of pīti or delight, through a scientific perspective.

Second jhana consciousness drops the initial application (vitakka), sustained application (vichāra) and gets suffused with the refined delight (pīti), happiness (sukha), and one pointedness. This occurs due to the consummation of the fourth factor of enlightenment i.e. delight or rupture (pīti).

The second jhana is a deeper stage of meditative absorption than the first jhana, characterized by the experience of pīti, a sense of rapture or delight. This experience of pīti is not a mystical or supernatural phenomenon but rather a physiological and psychological process that can be understood and studied scientifically.

From a physiological perspective, the experience of pīti in the second jhana is associated with the release of dopamine, a neurotransmitter that is associated with pleasure and reward. Dopamine is released in response to the meditator's focus on a single object or sensation, leading to feelings of delight and satisfaction.

Psychologically, the experience of pīti in the second jhana involves the development of a deeper sense of concentration and mindfulness. The meditator's ability to maintain a steady focus on a single object or sensation leads to a reduction in distracting thoughts and emotions, which can contribute to a sense of joy and well-being.

This experience of pīti in the second jhana continues the cultivation of happiness and peace towards the practical understanding of suffering because it helps to counteract negative emotions and attitudes that contribute to suffering, such as desire, aversion, and ignorance by creating their antidotes. By experiencing a sense of delight and satisfaction, the meditator is better able to develop positive attitudes towards themselves and others, and to cultivate a deeper sense of empathy and compassion.

Thus, the experience of pīti in the second jhana can be understood as a physiological and psychological process that continues the cultivation of happiness and peace towards the practical understanding of suffering. Through the release of dopamine and the development of concentration and mindfulness, the meditator can experience a sense of delight and satisfaction, which can help to counteract negative emotions and attitudes and contribute to a deeper sense of empathy and compassion.

Science of Third Jhana- Experience of Happiness (Sukha): Samma Samadhi, Right concentration in the attainment of the third jhana replaces the sense of delight with the better and more refined reward and experience of happiness, sukha, which is responsible for the understanding of suffering and the four Noble truths, from a scientific perspective.

Third jhana consciousness drops even refined exuberent joy (pīti). It experiences only happiness (sukha) and one pointedness. The third Jhana is a deeper stage of meditative absorption than the second Jhana, characterized by the experience of Sukha, a sense of bliss or happiness. This experience of Sukha is not a mystical or supernatural phenomenon but rather a physiological and psychological process that can be understood and studied scientifically.

From a physiological perspective, the experience of sukha, bliss or happiness in the third jhana is associated with the release of serotonin and endorphins, types of neurotransmitters that are associated with pleasure and pain relief. Endorphins are released in response to the meditator's continued focus and concentration, leading to feelings of happiness and contentment.

Psychologically, the experience of sukha in the third jhana involves a deepening of concentration and mindfulness. The meditator's ability to maintain a steady focus on a single object or sensation leads to a reduction in distracting thoughts and emotions, which can contribute to a sense of peace and well-being.

This experience of Happiness (Sukha-vihari) in the third jhana is responsible for the understanding of suffering and the four Noble truths because it provides a direct experience of the impermanent and unsatisfactory nature of all things. By experiencing a deep sense of happiness and contentment, the meditator becomes more aware of the transitory nature of these positive states and the potential for suffering that arises when they inevitably fade away.

The experience of sukha in the third jhana helps to develop a deep sense of equanimity and detachment from both positive and negative experiences. This detachment can contribute to a more profound understanding of the four Noble truths and the nature of suffering.

Here also the experience of happiness in the third jhana can be understood as a physiological and psychological process that brings the reward and experience of happiness, responsible for the understanding of suffering and the four Noble truths. Through the release of endorphins and the deepening of concentration and mindfulness, the meditator can experience a sense of happiness and contentment, which can lead to a deeper understanding of the impermanent and unsubstantial nature of all worldly things. The meditator even experience that the sense of the happiness that arises is also impermanent, conditioned and having no substance, this positive states of happiness also inevitably fade away.

Science of Fourth Jhana- Experience of Peaceful Equanimity (Upekkhā): Samma samadhi in the attainment of the fourth and the last Rupa jhana brings the best and most refined reward and experience of ekaggata and upekkhā, which are responsible for the understanding of suffering and the four Noble truths from a scientific perspective.

With the consummation of the last three factors of enlightenment i.e. peace (passadi), samadhi (jhana), and equanimity (upekkhā), meditator experiences in the stage of its fourth jhana consciousness drops down the happiness and experiences only equanimity and one pointedness (ekaggata) devoid of the slightest stain of happiness and unhappiness.

The fourth jhana is the deepest and most refined stage of meditative absorption of the Rupa jhana, characterized by the experience of ekaggata and upekkhā. Ekaggata refers to one-pointedness of mind, while upekkhā refers to equanimity or impartiality. Together, these qualities provide the meditator with a deep sense of concentration, tranquility, and detachment.

From a physiological perspective, the experience of ekaggata and upekkhā in the fourth jhana is associated with changes in brain activity. Studies have shown that experienced meditators exhibit increased activity in the prefrontal cortex, a region of the brain associated with attention and concentration. This increased activity is thought to reflect the meditator's ability to maintain a steady focus on a single object or sensation, leading to a deep sense of one- pointedness of mind.

Psychologically, the experience of ekaggata and upekkhā in the fourth Rupa jhana involves a deepening of concentration and detachment. The meditator's ability to maintain a steady focus on a single object or sensation leads to a reduction in distracting thoughts and emotions, which can contribute to a sense of equanimity or impartiality giving the sense of neither pleasant nor unpleasant sensations which is also responsible for the understanding of suffering and the four Noble truths because it provides a direct experience of the nature of reality through direct experience a deep sense of concentration, tranquility, and detachment within the frame work of the body and mind. The summary of the Rupa jhanas is presented in Table 7.2.

Thus, till the attainment of the fourth jhana all the factors of enlightenment reach to its fulfilment to cultivate the insight and wisdom which further leads to much more refined immaterial stages of the arupa jhana. Once the fourth jhana is reached. The jhana factors remain constant. In the higher ascent of the immaterial attainments there is no further elimination of jhana factors [64].

Immaterial (Arūpa) Jhana: Arūpa jhana, on the other hand, refers to the meditative absorption in which the practitioner focuses on an object that is not physical, such as the concept of infinite space, infinite consciousness, nothingness, or neither perception nor non-perception. Arūpa jhana also continue in its attainments, four levels of arūpa jhana,

Table 7.2: Summary of the Rupa jhanas

Jhanas	Factors abandoned	Factors acquired/ intensified	Remarks
First Jhana	Five hindrances Sloth & torpor, Doubts, Ill will/Aversion, Restlessness. Greed/sensual pleasures	Five Jhana factors Applied thought, Sustained thought, Rupture, Happiness. One pointedness and of the mind	Five hindrances are opposed to the five jhana factors. Characterized by rupture and happiness born of seclusion Commentaries lists one pointedness as a feature of first jhana, others omit it.
Second Jhana	Applied thought Sustained thought	Rupture Happiness One pointedness of the mind	Disappearance of applied and sustained thought. Characterized by delight and happiness born out of concentration.
Third Jhana	Rupture	Subtle happiness One pointedness of the mind	Rupture fades, revealing a quite subtle, and pervasive happiness. Characterized by the mindfulness and equanimity.
Fourth Jhana	Happiness	One pointedness of the mind Equanimity	Happiness is replaced by equanimity. Mindfulness is purified by equanimity.

each deeper than the previous one providing the experiences in the nature of suffering and cessation of suffering.

According to the teachings, the practice of rūpa jhana can lead to the attainment of arūpa jhana. The practitioner begins by focusing on a physical object, such as the breath, and gradually develops deeper levels of concentration and mindfulness. As the mind becomes more tranquil and focused, the practitioner can then shift their focus to a non-physical object, such as the concept of infinite space, and enter the first level of arūpa jhana.

Through continued practice, the practitioner can develop deeper levels of concentration and mindfulness, leading to the attainment of deeper levels of arūpa jhana. According to the teachings, the practice of jhana can lead to the deepening of insight into the nature of reality and the cessation of suffering [64, 66].

In the arūpa jhana, practitioner steps ahead from the rūpa jhana based on the physical-internal and/or external objects to his or her focuses on a non-physical objects such as the concept of infinite space, infinite consciousness, nothingness, or neither perception nor non- perception. According to the teachings, the attainment of arūpa jhana can lead to a deeper understanding of the nature of impermanence, suffering and unsubstantial nature of all conditioned things of the world. The summary of the arūpa jhanas is presented in Table 7.3.

Science of the Base of Infinite Space-Experience of Infinite Space (Ākāsanañchāyatana): In the first level of arūpa jhana, the practitioner focuses on the concept of infinite space. This means that the mind has let go of its attachment to physical objects and sensations and is now focused on the infinite expanse of space. The practitioner experiences a sense of boundlessness and spaciousness, and the mind becomes increasingly tranquil and focused.

It is important to note that while the experience of arupa jhanas, including infinite space, has been described in great detail in traditional Buddhist texts, there is limited scientific research on these states of consciousness.

Table 7.3: Summary of the Arūpa jhanas

Immaterial jhanas (Arupa jhanas)	Factors abandoned	Factors acquired/ intensified	Remarks
Fifth Jhana Infinite space (Ākāsananchāyatana)	Materiality of the rūpa khandha	Mastery over 4th jhana & concentration on space	Entered when one experience infinite space.
Sixth Jhana Infinite consciousness (Viññaṇanchāyatana)	Citta- cetasika Vinnana khandha	Mastery over 1st auppa & concentration on consciousness	Entered when one experience infinite cosciousness.
Seventh Jhana Nothingness (Ākiñchaññāyatana)	Base of cosciousness	Mastery over 2nd auppa & concentration on neither space nor consciousness	Entered when one experience infinite nothingness.
Eighth Jhana (neither perception nor nonperception) (Nevsaññanasaññ-āyatana)	Base of nothingness	Mastery over the base of nothingness	Entered when one experiences neither perception nor nonperception.
Ninth Jhana Nirodhasamapatti	Validation of Cessation of suffering	Cessation of the feeling and perception	Entered when on experiences complete cessation of feeling and perception

There are some aspects of the experience of infinite space that can be understood from a scientific perspective. Firstly, it is known that the brain processes spatial information using a network of regions located in the parietal cortex. Studies have shown that when people visualize or imagine spatial dimensions, there is increased activation in these regions of the brain. It is possible that during the experience of infinite space, the brain's parietal network is particularly active, leading to a perception of boundlessness and expansiveness. Additionally, research has suggested that the experience of meditation can lead to changes in brain structure and function. Studies have shown that long-term meditation practice can increase gray matter volume in regions of the brain associated with attention, emotion regulation, and self- awareness. It is possible that the deep concentration and focus required to achieve the arūpa jhanas, including infinite space, may lead to similar changes in the brain.

The state of boundless space can be correlated with "Bhanga jhana," the meditative state of dissolution, in that both involve transcending the perception of solidity and form. In this state, rupa khandha completely scatters away into its elementary kasina matter of earth, water, fire, air, blue, yellow, red and white to develop a perception of the breaking apart of phenomena. The mind transcends all physical boundaries, experiencing infinite spaciousness. Both states reflect a shift from attachment to form toward a deeper realization of impermanence and the unconditioned.

Science of the Base of Boundless Consciousness- Experience of infinite consciousness (Viññaṇaṅchāyatana): In the second arūpppa of the arūpa jhanas, the practitioner experience of Infinite Space. During the experience of boundless consciousness, the practitioner perceives that consciousness extends infinitely in all directions, and there is no limit to its expanse. A meditator reaches the state of boundless consciousness by systematically breaking down the aggregates of consciousness (vedana, sanna, sankhara, and vinnana) through insight meditation, observing their impermanent, unsatisfactory, and selfless nature. By recognizing the dissolution of these aggregates, the mind detaches from conditioned phenomena and transcends limited identification with them. This leads to the realization of boundless consciousness, where awareness expands beyond the confines of individual experience into a limitless, unconditioned state. However, there is some scientific evidence that can shed light on the neural correlates of meditative states similar to the experience of boundless consciousness. Functional MRI (fMRI) studies have shown that experienced meditators have increased activity in the default mode network (DMN) of the brain during meditation. The DMN is a network of brain regions involved in self-referential thought and introspection. The experience of boundless consciousness, which involves a sense of infinite and boundless consciousness, may be related to increased activity in the DMN.

Science of Base of Nothingness-Experience of Nothingness (Ākiñchaññāyatan): Ākiñchaññāyatan the arūppa of the formless jhanas, which is the attainment of the states of deep concentration and mental absorption. In this state, the mind becomes completely empty of all mental objects and is free from any sense of self or identity.

The practice of Ākiñchaññāyatan involves letting go of all thoughts and mental concepts, and focusing on the emptiness and nothingness of the mind. The meditator must cultivate a strong and unwavering concentration, and allow the mind to become completely still and free from all mental distractions. The practice of ākiñchaññāyatan is not meant to be a goal in itself, but rather a stepping stone towards the ultimate goal of enlightenment. He suggests that by cultivating this state of nothingness, the meditator can gain a deeper understanding of the impermanence and emptiness of all phenomena, and can ultimately attain liberation from suffering [66]. A meditator experiences nothingness by transcending the perception of boundless consciousness and focusing on the absence of all phenomena. This state arises when the mind lets go of all objects, forms, and even the sense of spaciousness, realizing the profound emptiness of existence. It is a refined meditative attainment where awareness rests in the subtle perception of "nothingness" as the ultimate object.

Overall, the Science of base of nothingness (Ākiñchaññāyatan) is a practice of deep concentration and mental absorption that can lead to a profound understanding of the nature of reality and the ultimate goal of enlightenment in Buddhist teachings.

Science of the Base of Neither Perception nor Non-perception: Experience of Neither Perception nor Non-perception (Nevsaññanasaññāyatana): The practice of Arūpa jhana meditation brings about the attainment of fourth arūpa is known as the "Neither perception nor non- perception" or Nevsaññanasaññāyatana.

A meditator experiences the state of neither perception nor non-perception by transcending even the subtle perception of nothingness, reaching a state where ordinary perception ceases but a faint residual awareness remains. This state is characterized by the absence of gross mental activity, yet it is not complete unconsciousness, as a subtle, refined awareness persists. It represents the pinnacle of formless meditative attainments, where the mind approaches the limits of conditioned experience.

In this state, the mind is completely withdrawn from all external and internal stimuli, including sensory perceptions, thoughts, and emotions. The mind is so still and quiet that it is difficult to discern any mental activity. However, there is still some degree of awareness, as the meditator is able to recall the experience of this state of consciousness after emerging from it.

The Nevsaññanasaññāyatana is often seen as a precursor to the attainment of the highest level of jhana, which is known as the "Cessation of perception and feeling" or nirodha-samapatti. In this state, all mental activities cease completely, leading to a profound sense of peace and liberation from the cycle of birth and death.

Overall, the Nevsaññanasaññāyatana is considered to be a highly advanced state of meditation, which requires extensive practice and training under the guidance of a skilled teacher. It is regarded as an important milestone on the path to spiritual awakening and liberation in the Buddhist tradition [66].

The Buddha did not stop there, after the detailed description of the level to level explanation of the process of the culmination of ignorance to wisdom, from the grieving samsara to blissful nibbana. He explained the way by which the hindrances (nivarana) come to an end with the observation and understanding of the acquaintances of every phenomenon that arise after the contact of the sense organs with the aggregates. The complexity of this entire process of the practical interplay of internal and/or external sense organs (ayatana) with the aggregates (khandha) has been further resolved by the Buddha in the Mahāsatipaññhanā sutta that the factors of the enlightenment play a crucial and immensely beneficial role in the practical understanding of the real nature of suffering, it's cause, its cessation and the way that leads to the complete cessation of suffering.

The Buddha teaches that the human beings in whom ignorance (avijjā) and craving (taṇhā) remains present even in traces are subject to rebirth. The craving for existence lies at the hub of the wheel of becoming (bhavā) and sustaining its constant revolution.

The Buddha delve into depth of the wheel of becoming and discover kamma as the determinant of the place and conditions of rebirth. All the volitional actions-deeds, words and thoughts expressive of the deliberate intention constitute kammā. Unwholesome kammas (akusalakammā) are rooted in greed (lobha), hatred (dosa) and delusion (moha); while the wholesome kammas (kusalakammā) have their roots in non-greed, non-hatred and non-delusion. These unwholesome of wholesome kammās work has the capabilities of producing results (vipaka) in the future bringing about the suffering and failure or happiness and success as per the relativity of the kammā.

The Buddha has dug in the depth of the consciousness to discover all the elements of supportive and positive nature of human mind that works as the perfect antidotes to fight the negative attitudes of the mind while walking on the path of righteousness and liberation. The Buddha called these negative attitudes of the mind as unwholesome (14-akusala) and positive attitudes of mind as 25 wholesome (25- kusala). The role of these supportive elements of human attitude have been discussed in chapter-8 on adversaries and promoters of the happiness, peace and enlightenment.

7.15   Two Vehicles: Insight Jhana and Supermundane Path

The Buddha places wisdom at the head of all the spiritual faculties. It demonstrates understanding, search of truth, discernment, differentiation, erudition, proficiency, criticism, analysis, insight, intelligence, right views. Wisdom instrumental in attaining liberation is divided in two principal divisions: Insight-knowledge (vipassana nana) and the knowledge of supermundane paths (magga-nana). Insight knowledge takes the world (loke), of the conditioned formation (saṅkhārā) as its object. It is regarded as a mundane (lokiya) form of wisdom which brings about attainments of the four material and four immaterial jhanas.

The wisdom of the supermundane path is regarded as supermundane (lokuttara) as the insight further rises up from the mundane to supermundane to realize the four paths and their subsequent four fruitions. The four paths and fruitions are sotapañña, sotapatti phala, sakkatagami, sakkatagami phala, anagāmi, anagāmi phala, arahat and arahat phala on the progressive path of the attainment of transcendental enlightenment. Summary of the four supramundane paths has been illustrated in Table 7.4.

7.16   Role of Kalapa in Perception of Reality

Kalapa or Rupa-kalapa is the term in Buddhist phenomenology for the smallest unit of physical matter said to be about 1/46,656[th] the size of a particle of dust from a wheel of chariot. These kalapas are considered to be the primary vehicles of our experience of reality. The living body is made up of the ten inseparable elements which consists of the earth, water, heat, air, varna, gandha, rasa, oja, jivitendriya and bhavendriya first eight of these elements are referred to as atthakalapa [65].

Vibhanga is a text within the Buddhist Abhidhamma, which is a philosophical and psychological analysis of the nature of reality. Here is a brief overview of how these elements work in the Vibhanga:

Table 7.4: Summary of the four Supramundane paths (Lokuttaramagga)

Supramundane Paths	Factors eradicated	Immediate attainment	Remarks
First path & Fruit Stream entry (Sotapattimagga)	False views of personality (Sakkayaditthi) Doubt (Vicikiccha) Clinging to rites & rituals (Silabbata paramasa)	Sotapattiphala	The stream-enterer quits the level of a worlding (Puttujana) and become the first noble one. Fruit-Fourth noble person
Second path & Fruit Once-returner (Sakadagamimagga)	Attenuates sensual desires (Kamacchanda) Ill-will (Vyapada)	Sakadagamiphala	Path-third noble person Fruit-Fourth noble person
Third path & Fruit Non-retuner (Anagāmimagga)	Complete eradication of sensual desire (Kamacchanda) Complete eradication of Ill-will (Vyapada)	Anagamiphala	Path-Fifth noble person Fruit- Sixth noble person
Fourth path & Fruit Arahatship (Arahattamagga)	Desire for existence in the fine material world (Ruparaga) Desire for existence in the immaterial realm (Aruparaga) Conceit (Mana) Restlessness (Uddhacca) Ignorance (Avijja)	Arahattaphala	Path-Seventh noble person Fruit- Eighth noble person (Reaches the goal of complete liiberation
Phalasamapatti	Liberation from the cycle of birth and death.	Sets in Nibbana	Entered when on experiences complete cessation of perception and consciousness.

1. Earth (pathavi): In the Vibhanga, earth is described as the element that has the characteristic of solidity. It is one of the four primary elements that make up all material things.

2. Water (apo): Water is the element that has the characteristic of liquidity. It is also one of the four primary elements.

3. Heat (tejo): Heat is the element that has the characteristic of temperature. It is one of the four primary elements and is responsible for generating energy in the body.

4. Air (vayo): Air is the element that has the characteristic of motion. It is one of the four primary elements and is responsible for the movement of the body and the breath.

5. Complexion (varna): Varna refers to color or complexion. In the Vibhanga, it is described as an aspect of material form.

6. Olfaction (gandha): Gandha refers to odor or smell. It is also an aspect of material form.

7. Taste (rasa): Rasa refers to taste. It is another aspect of material form.

8. Vitality (oja): Oja is a substance that is generated in the body and is responsible for maintaining vitality and strength.

9. Life force (jivitendriya): Jivitendriya refers to the life faculty or the force that animates living beings. It is responsible for maintaining the continuity of life.

10. Sense of self (bhavendriya): Bhavendriya refers to the sense of existence or the awareness of being alive. It is responsible for the sense of self and the sense of continuity of existence.

In the Vibhanga, these elements are analyzed and explained in terms of their characteristics and functions. They are seen as fundamental aspects of reality and are important for understanding the nature of the self and the world. By understanding these elements and their interrelationships, one can gain insight into the nature of existence and the workings of the mind and body [65].

7.17 Role of Kasiṇa for entering Arupa Jhana

A kasiṇa is a tool or an external device representing a quality used as a support for developing concentration. Of the forty objects meditated upon as kammatthana, the first ten kammatthana grouped under ten kasiṇa are described as "things one can behold directly". They are:

1. Earth (pathavī kasiṇa)
2. Water (āpo kasiṇa)
3. Fire (tejo kasiṇa)
4. Air (vāyo kasiṇa)
5. Blue (nīla kasiṇa)
6. Yellow (pita kasiṇa)
7. Red (lohita kasiṇa)
8. White (odāta kasiṇa)
9. Space (ākāsa kasiṇa)
10. Consciousness (viññāṇa kasiṇa)

First four kasiṇa are constituted of the four great elements (elements) while the later four are the basic colour co-ordinates of the body organization. Ākāsa kasiṇa is the enclosed space while the viññāṇa kasiṇa is the element of consciousness. All these blends together very tightly to bring about the thresholds of the life in existence. Therefore, the contemplation of the kasiṇa provides a very strong support to the meditator who make a move from the rūpa jhana to arūpa jhana [66].

Kasiṇa jhana is a form of Buddhist meditation that involves focusing one's attention on a visual object, such as a colored disc or a flame, in order to achieve a state of deep concentration and mental absorption. This state of absorption can be used as a foundation for developing insight and wisdom into the true nature of reality.

The practice of kasiṇa jhana can help in understanding the true nature of reality by training the mind to become still and focused, and by helping to develop a more refined and subtle awareness of one's mental and physical states. Through this practice, one can come to see how the mind creates its own reality through the constant interplay of sensory inputs, mental formations, and perceptions. As one becomes more proficient in kasiṇa jhana, the mind becomes more adept at noticing the impermanent, unsatisfactory, and non-self nature of all phenomena. This awareness can lead to a deepening understanding of the Buddha's teachings on the four Noble truths and the three characteristics of existence.

Kasiṇa jhana help in the cultivation of wisdom by training the mind to see through the illusions and delusions that obscure our understanding of reality. As one becomes more proficient in kasiṇa jhana, one can come to see how the mind creates its own suffering through clinging to false ideas and perceptions. This can lead to a deeper understanding of the nature of suffering and the path to liberation from it. Overall, the practice of kasiṇa jhana can be a powerful tool for developing insight and wisdom into the true nature of reality, and for cultivating the mental qualities of concentration, mindfulness, and equanimity that are essential for the path of spiritual awakening.

7.18 Dependent Origination: Role in Spiritual Awakening

This universal science of spiritual awakening and freedom from the cycle of becoming has been explained scientifically by the Buddha as the outcome of the cause and effect in the paticcasamuppada also known as Dependent origination. Dependent origination is a fundamental concept in Buddhist philosophy that explains the interdependent nature of all phenomena. According to this concept, all phenomena arise and cease in dependence upon other phenomena. In the context of rebirth, Paticcasamuppada explains how the cycle of rebirth perpetuates itself. It states that the cycle of rebirth is caused by craving and ignorance, which lead to the formation of karmic actions (volitional activities). These karmic actions then produce the conditions for the arising of a new being in the next life. The twelve links of Paticcasamuppada describe the process of how this cycle of rebirth operates:

1. Ignorance (avijja): The lack of understanding of the true nature of reality.

2. Volitional activities (saṅkhārā): The karmic actions that arise from ignorance.

3. Consciousness (viññāṇaṃ): The awareness that arises in dependence upon the karmic actions.

4. Name and form (nama-rūpa): The mental and physical aspects that arise in dependence upon consciousness.

5. Six sense bases (salāyatana): The six sense organs (eyes, ears, nose, tongue, body, and mind) that arise in dependence upon name and form.

6. Contact (phassa): The meeting of sense organs with their respective objects.

7. Feeling (vedanā): The experience of pleasant, unpleasant, or neutral sensations that arise from contact.

8. Craving (taṇhā): The desire or attachment to the pleasant sensations and aversion to unpleasant sensations.

9. Clinging (upādāna): The attachment and grasping onto the objects of craving.

10. Becoming (bhava): The arising of a new existence based on the karmic actions produced by craving and clinging.

11. Birth (jati): The actual birth of a new being in a new existence.

12. Aging and death (jara-marana): The process of aging and eventual death that arises in dependence upon birth.

Thus, according to paticca samuppada, rebirth is a result of the interdependent nature of all phenomena, where the actions of one life lead to the conditions for the arising of a new life. This cycle of rebirth perpetuates itself until one break free from the cycle through the attainment of enlightenment and the cessation of craving and ignorance.

7.19 Development of Supernormal Knowledge (Abhiñña)

The meditator who masters the jhana reaching the higher levels and fulfils all the preliminary conditions, can direct his mind to the kinds of supernormal knowledge (Abhiññas) he wishes to attain. Abhiññas do not come as the automatic by-product of the jhana but require a prior resolution and determinate efforts on the part of meditators. There are six kinds of supernormal powers (Iddhis). Iddhis have sometimes been interpreted as miraculous powers. However, these powers do not derive from any divine source but from a psychic potency based upon a superior understanding of the inner and outer worlds dynamics. They operate completely within the framework of the law of cause and effect.

The first abhiñña-knowledge of supernormal powers (Iddhividhanana): When the meditators mind is thus purified and attained in imperturbability, he inclines his mind to the kinds of supernormal powers. Having being one, he becomes many; having been many, he becomes one; He appears and vanishes, He goes unhindered through walls, through enclosures, through mountains, as through open space. He dives in and out of the earth as though in water, He goes on unbroken water as though on earth. Seated cross- legged he travels in space like a winged bird. With his hand he touches and strokes the moon and sun so mighty and powerful. He wields bodily mastery even as far as the Bramma world. In this passage eight supernormal powers are expounded.

The second abhiñña-The divine ear-element (Dibbasotadhatu): The divine ear element is the ability to hear the sounds of deities as well as of human beings and to hear the sounds even from another world system as well as the sounds that are extremely nearby.

The third abiñña- the knowledge of others' minds (Cetopariya nana-paracittavijanana: This supernormal knowledge is the knowledge of others'minds, the ability to penetrate with one's own mind the mental states of others.

The fourth abhiñña- The knowledge of recollecting previous lives (Pubbanivasanussatinana): The knowledge of recollecting previous lives.

The fifth abhiñña-The divine eye (Dibbacakkhu): The knowledge of the passing away and rebirth of beings.

The sixth abhiñña- The knowledge of the destruction of the cankers (Asavakkhayanana): The knowledge of the destruction of the defilements of sensual desires (kamasava), craving of existence (bhavasava) and ignorance (avijjasava).

While the first five abhinnas are associated with the mundane direct knowledge and are regarded as the ornaments of the meditator, the sixth abhinna is regarded as its vital essence, the supreme goal of the entire practice of meditation [64].

7.20   Reflection on 3,000 Realms and 84,000 Dhammakkhandha

How far Ichinen sanzen philosophy perpetuate the understanding of root causes of ignorance and craving, role of sila, samadhi, paññā, rupa jhana, arupa jhana, kasina jhana, magga, paticca samuppada and the development of supernormal powers of abhinna is not clear? Although Ichinen sanzen focuses on the idea that all phenomena, including the Buddha nature and enlightenment, are present within a single moment of thought. As far as the thorough understanding of the root causes of ignorance and craving, Ichinen sanzen teaches that ignorance and craving arise from a fundamental delusion that causes us to view the world and ourselves as separate and distinct entities. This delusion creates a sense of attachment to our desires and aversions, leading to suffering.

In terms of the role of sīla, samadhi, and paññā, Ichinen sanzen emphasizes the importance of developing a strong ethical foundation (sīla) through observing the precepts, cultivating a focused and concentrated mind (samadhi), and cultivating wisdom (paññā) through deep contemplation and insight.

Ichinen sanzen does not specifically mention rūpa jhana, arūpa jhana, kasina jhana, magga, or paticca samuppada as necessary for the attainment of enlightenment. However, these concepts are all related to the development of concentration and insight, which are important components of Buddhist meditative practice.

Overall, while Ichinen sanzen has a unique perspective on the nature of reality and the path to enlightenment, it shares aggregates (khandha) as the common factor with the 84,000 dhammakkhandha. In the first Noble truth, the Buddha declares the suffering as the sole outcome of the five khandha i.e. rūpa, vedanā, saññā, saṅkhārā, viññāṇa. In that perspective, a factor of aggregate is enough for defining the first noble truth. However, many of the major foundational principles and practices of the practical and applied Buddhism have not been elaborated clearly in the philosophy of Ichinen sanzen.

Interestingly, it is important to elaborate here that the Blessed one has delivered the discourse on the arousing of mindfulness known as Satipaṭṭhānā Sutta two times. First known as Satipaṭṭhānā sutta [67] has been recorded in its brief version in Majjhima Nikaya-10 (MN- 10), and the second more expanded discourse known as Mahāsatipaṭṭhānā sutta is found to be recorded in Digha Nikaya-22 (DN-22). In the first brief version of Satipaṭṭhānā sutta, the Buddha has elaborated Dhammanupassana with only two divisions i.e. five hindrances (nivarana) and five aggregates (khanda) and ended the sutta. This seems to be due to the fact that the five aggregates (upadan-khandha) are the only root causes of the five hindrances which were elaborated while defining first noble truth of suffering. Since the perception of five aggregates of upadan-khandha is impossible without the six sense bases (āyatana), five aggregates automatically bring the six sense bases in action in the process of the perception of reality.

However, the Buddha might have understood the need of more expanded and elaborated version of the four foundations of mindfulness in this important sutta for crystal clear understanding of the reality of all the phenomena as it was propounded as the only way for the liberation from suffering. In this more elaborated version of Mahāsatipaṭṭhānā sutta, the Dhammanupassana has been fully explained in the five divisions namely, nivarana, khanda, āyatana, bojjhanga and saccha with all details without leaving anything whatsoever unresolved. It cannot be elucidated, whether the Buddha first presented the brief version and later the elaborated version of four foundations of mindfulness or vice-versa.

It can be justified by the fact that the experience of spontaneous enlightenment may be there to a serious meditator even with the absorption on the two divisions of hindrances and aggregates. As the factor of aggregates or khandha has been there in the 3,000 realms calculated in the concept of Ichinen sanzen, it would be enough for propelling the mind towards the path of liberation from suffering.

Thus, conclusively one can access the complete relativity and connectivity of all the factors of 84,000 Dhammakkhandha as a reality in the interplay of the dhamma and khandha in the physical and mental world. More and more people working on the meditative practices shall come, see and try to practically apply the factorial design of 84,000 Dhammakkhanda on their own framework of body and mind to explore the workability of all the perceptible dhamma, khandha and dhammakkhanda for the realization of truth.

Chapter 8

Happiness, Peace and Enlightenment

Promoters and Adversaries

---

*"Of all the religious founders worldwide, I hold the Buddha in the
highest regards. My reason says that the Buddha is the greatest
figure in the whole of the human history"*

– Bertrand Russell

Author was facing a dilemma of a situation over a thought of
compiling a separate chapter of "Promoters and Adversaries
of the happiness, peace and enlightenment". During all the long 45
years of the preachings, the Buddha only talked about his doctrine and
discipline in words and actions to free a man spiritually, to give the full
experience of the freedom form suffering. So, each and every teaching
of the Buddha is synonymous to dhamma that takes a man ahead on
the path of freedom and simultaneously while doing so, the Buddha
also makes his followers aware about the promoters and adversaries
on the path as the friends and enemies. Since the whole canon is full
with many such records and each word of the Buddha talks about the
freedom, how one should discriminate giving very particular factors
as adversaries or promoters of the path. This thought propelled me to
delve into the depth of this topic to enlist the friends and the enemies
on the path. Promoters support an individual walking over the path by
clearing all the oppositions and resistances on the path. On the contrary,
adversary is one that contends with, opposes, or resists an individual.
It is a blissful experience for an individual to walk, swim and even

fly over the mirage of the samsara to acknowledge the freedom from suffering, Nibbana. However, it is also wonderful to see the interplay of the promoters and adversaries in this whole progressive path. In this competition for predominance of samsara verses nibbana, it becomes confrontation of the ignorance-craving verses insight-enlightenment, where a competing person for and against the goal of Nibbana is oneself only.

Another compelling reason was to find the similarities and differences in Ichinen sanzen and Dhammakkhandha philosophy specially to understand the background support system to an individual on the path for the cultivation of insight and wisdom. In many a case, the readers outside the spear of Buddhism and even for many insiders too, the significant role played by these radiant friends and covetous enemies does not know. One feel that the phenomena has occurred due to his own mistakes. Of course, if mistake has occurred, it should be corrected. However, common ignorant man has no abilities to enter in the depth of the phenomena to explore the reality behind its real cause and effect. Hence, we should know about the actuating, motivating, supporting, forwarding and releasing factors of immeasurable potential for an individual in the entire internal and external universe.

For many such obvious reasons it was quite convincing to compile this chapter providing the lists of the promoters and adversaries to the readers. While enlisting the promoters and adversaries, it will be beyond my personal capabilities as well as the limitation of the book that I may miss some or many of these promoters and adversaries. It should not be understood that the promoters and adversaries noted here are the only friends and foes on the path of Dhamma. Human being is full of all types of positivities and negativities and for every positive attitude there is also a negative factor to counter it. Let us explore these vices which want a person to keep nose deep in samsarā and the virtues which support one to come up to the surface of the ocean of ignorance and open up an individual as a full bloomed lotus to see the reality and truth beyond the ocean of samsarā.

8.1   Absolute Equality: Dhamma for All

Dhamma set forth by the Buddha, is proclaimed as good in the beginning, good in the middle, good in the end, possessed of meaning and the letter, and complete in everything.

One of the most important universal features of the Dhamma is its Absolute equality. It's all-inclusiveness without any discrimination. It is this characteristic that has appealed the humanity beyond the borders of the countries and water tight compartments of the cultures. It has equally attracted sovereign rulers, philosophers, thinkers, scientists, poets, educated and uneducated, traders and peasants. In the case of ordination of the women to enter the Sangha and receive ordination, the Buddha initially refused his step-mother Ven. Mahapajapati Gotami. However, Ven. Ananda sat at the Buddha's side and argued on behalf of the ordination of women. The Buddha continued to refuse the request. Finally, Ananda asked if there was any reason women could not realize enlightenment and enter enlightenment like men. The Buddha admitted that there was no reason a woman could not be enlightened. "Women, having gone forth are able to realize the fruit of stream-attainment or the fruit of once-returning or the fruit of non-returning or arahatship," he said. The conventional conception of equality is narrow and restricted to political, economic and educational sectors, and equality between the two sexes, but none of them deals with the fundamental question of absolute equality. In view of the manifold differences of individuals in their family background (high or low), personal appearances (good looking or ugly), disposition (gentle nature or quick tempered), intellect (intelligent or dull), and health (strong or weak), fundamentally speaking, there can be no equality among mankind. However, such variations and differentiations are nothing but illusory phenomena of life. All mental phenomena, physical phenomena, combined physical and mental phenomena, as well as causes and effects are at par with each other. Not only between man and man, Buddha and Buddha, is there equality, but also between man and Buddha, man and woman, man and animals, man and dwellers of paradise and hells, man and ghosts; all of them are equal with each other. This basic principle and fountain-head of the Buddhism appeals all.

It can be understood form the principle of absolute equality of the Buddha's Dhamma that it is open for all human beings. It appeals and invite one and all to come and see to explore the hidden ultimate potential of enlightenment. It is this feature of equality that worked for the promotion of Buddhism. It has taken Buddhism from the middle land of the Indian subcontinent to all the corners of the world.

8.2 Scientific Outlook

The scientific outlook of Buddhism is characterized by a rational and empirical approach to understanding the nature of reality, the human mind, and the universe. While Buddhism is primarily a spiritual and philosophical tradition, it shares several key principles with scientific inquiry which has worked as a promoter of Dhamma among the various socio-cultural traditions. Here are some aspects of the scientific outlook within Buddhism:

1. Empiricism: Buddhism emphasizes the importance of direct personal experience and observation. It encourages individuals to explore the nature of reality through meditation and mindfulness practices, which involve carefully observing the workings of the mind and the world around us.

2. Interdependence: Buddhism teaches the concept of "dependent origination" or "interdependent co-arising," which suggests that all phenomena are interconnected and arise in dependence on other factors. This concept is akin to the scientific understanding of causality and the interconnectedness of natural processes.

3. Impermanence: Buddhism teaches that all things are impermanent and subject to change. This aligns with the scientific principle that the universe is in a constant state of flux and that nothing remains static.

4. Skepticism: Buddhism encourages a healthy dose of skepticism and critical thinking. Followers are encouraged to question and investigate their own beliefs and experiences, promoting a scientific spirit of inquiry.

5. Non-attachment: Buddhism advocates for non-attachment to material possessions and desires, emphasizing the importance of letting go of attachment to achieve a more objective and clear understanding of reality. This is similar to the scientific ideal of objectivity and impartiality in research.

6. Meditation and mindfulness: Buddhism places a strong emphasis on meditation and mindfulness practices as tools for gaining insight into the nature of the mind and reality. These practices have been studied scientifically for their potential benefits on mental well-being and cognitive processes.

7. Ethical framework: Buddhism provides a moral and ethical framework that encourages compassion, empathy, and the alleviation of suffering. This aligns with the scientific interest in understanding and promoting human well-being and the reduction of suffering.

It is important to note that while Buddhism and science share certain philosophical and methodological principles, they also have fundamental differences. Buddhism is a spiritual and metaphysical tradition that deals with questions of human existence, suffering, and liberation, whereas science primarily focuses on empirical investigation of the natural world. Nevertheless, the scientific outlook within Buddhism has contributed to its compatibility with scientific inquiry and the pursuit of knowledge about the nature of reality and the human mind.

8.3 Encouragement of Free Enquiry

According to Anagarika Dhammapala, "Buddhism may be called as the religion of analysis. It analyses every phase of cosmic phenomenon, the constituents that go to make up a human being and the differentiating states of mentality; it categorizes the differentiation of good, evil and neutral, it rejects every phase of superstitious belief and appeals to the purified heart to distinguish the good from the bad to free himself from covetousness, anger and lust. [68].

An individual waking on the path is always encountered with the situations which put his mind to complete perplexity, not able to understand the right and wrong. In such situations the directives of the Buddha to the people of Kalama becomes the charter of enquiry for a person. The reasonableness of the Dhamma, the Buddha's teaching, is chiefly evident in its welcoming careful examination at all stages of the path to enlightenment. The Kalama Sutta is a teaching given by the Buddha to the people of the Kalama town in ancient India is justly famous for its encouragement of free inquiry; the spirit of the sutta signifies a teaching that is exempt from fanaticism, bigotry, dogmatism, and intolerance.

The sutta addresses the issue of skepticism and encourages the Kalamas to use their own experience and judgment, rather than blindly following tradition or authority, in determining what is true and beneficial.

One of the main themes of the sutta is the importance of personal experience in the pursuit of truth. The Buddha advises the Kalamas to "know for themselves" and to "investigate" rather than accepting things on faith or authority. This emphasis on experiential knowledge is consistent with the Buddha's emphasis on the importance of personal practice and the cultivation of inner wisdom.

In the Kalama sutta, the Buddha advises the people of the Kalama village to rely on their own personal experience and judgment, rather than blindly following tradition or accepting the teachings of authority figures. He encourages them to use their own critical thinking skills and to test and evaluate the truth of any teaching or belief for themselves. This discourse of the Buddha refrain from criticizing the others' views but provides the wise advice to evaluate the truth themselves on the line of the following 10 points.

"It is proper for you, Kalamas, to doubt, to be uncertain; uncertainty has arisen in you about what is doubtful. Come, Kalamas. Do not go upon what has been acquired by (1) repeated hearing; (2) nor upon tradition; (3) nor upon rumor; (4) nor upon what is in a scripture; (5) nor upon surmise; (6) nor upon an axiom; (7) nor upon specious reasoning; (8) nor upon a bias towards a notion that has been pondered over; (9) nor upon another's seeming ability; (10) nor upon the consideration, 'The monk is our teacher.'

Kalamas, when you yourselves know: 'These things are bad; these things are blamable; these things are censured by the wise; undertaken and observed, these things lead to harm and ill,' abandon them.

In the above discourse the Buddha put forth the criteria for acceptance of the teachings on the basis of the absence of greed, hate and delusion. He advises the people of the Kalama not to accept the teachings on the basis of mere belief or reason but by following four steps in order to determine what is true:

1. Do not blindly accept any teaching or belief, but rather carefully evaluate and test it.

2. Do not follow any teaching or belief simply because it has been passed down through tradition or because it is held by a group of people.

3. Do not follow any teaching or belief simply because it is spoken by a respected or revered authority figure.

4. Do not follow any teaching or belief simply because it makes you feel good or brings you pleasure.

Instead, the Buddha advises the people of the Kalama village to rely on their own personal experience and judgment, and to use their own critical thinking skills to determine what is true and what is false. [1].

8.4 Path of Practice

Buddhism is often referred to as the path of practice, because it places a strong emphasis on the practical methods and actions that leads to personal transformation, spiritual development, and ultimately, liberation from suffering. It is not limited to specific belief system but can be followed by individuals from various cultural and religious backgrounds. Its practical and adaptable approach leads as a promoter of more mindful, compassionate and fulfilling life.

Suffering is the nature of this material world, and whatever enjoyment we are trying to achieve is simply illusion. After all, we all have to suffer the miseries of birth, old age, disease and death. Pure happiness and peace is not the domain of the material world. However, this domain of true happiness and peace is achievable through the practice of meditation and experienced within the framework of this very body and mind. The practice of meditation is open to all without any discrimination and the advantages of the attainment is not just limited to only happiness and peace but beyond the limits of the material world. The only condition for the being is that "You yourself must earnestly practice".

"The Buddha has acknowledged the four developments of concentration. Firstly, there is the development of concentration that, when developed and pursued, leads to a pleasant abiding in the here and now. Secondly, there is the development of concentration that, when developed and pursued, leads to the attainment of knowledge and vision. Thirdly, there is the development of concentration that, when developed and pursued, leads to mindfulness and alertness. Fourthly, there is the development of concentration that, when developed and pursued, leads to the ending of the effluents.

1. "And what is the development of concentration that, when developed and pursued, leads to a pleasant abiding in the here and now? There is the case where a monk-quite withdrawn from sensuality, withdrawn from unskillful qualities-enters and remains in the first jhana: rapture and pleasure born from withdrawal, accompanied by directed thought and evaluation. With the stilling of directed thoughts and evaluations, he enters and remains in the second jhana: rapture and pleasure born of composure, unification of awareness free from directed thought and evaluation-internal assurance. With the fading of rapture, he remains equanimous, mindful, and alert, and senses pleasure with the body. He enters and remains in the third jhana, of which the Noble Ones declare, 'Equanimous and mindful, he has a pleasant abiding.' With the abandoning of pleasure and pain-as with the earlier disappearance of elation and distress-he enters and remains in the fourth jhana: purity of equanimity and mindfulness, neither pleasure nor pain. This is the development of concentration that... leads to a pleasant abiding in the here and now.

2. "And what is the development of concentration that... leads to the attainment of knowledge and vision? There is the case where a monk attends to the perception of light and is resolved on the perception of daytime [at any hour of the day]. Day [for him] is the same as night, night is the same as day. By means of an awareness open and unhampered, he develops a brightened mind. This is the development of concentration that, when developed and pursued, leads to the attainment of knowledge and vision.

3. "And what is the development of concentration that... leads to mindfulness and alertness? There is the case where feelings are known to the monk as they arise, known as they persist, known as they subside. Perceptions are known to him as they arise, known as they persist, known as they subside. Thoughts are known to him as they arise, known as they persist, known as they subside.

This is the development of concentration that, when developed and pursued, leads to mindfulness and alertness.

4. "And what is the development of concentration that... leads to the ending of the effluents? There is the case where a monk remains focused on arising and falling away with reference to the five clinging- aggregates: 'Such is form, such its origination, such its passing away. Such is feeling... Such is perception... Such are fabrications... Such is consciousness, such its origination, such its disappearance.' This is the development of concentration that, when developed and pursued, leads to the ending of the effluents.

8.5 Root Cause-Ignorance (Avijja)

In Buddhism, ignorance (avijja), plays a central role in the understanding of human suffering and the path to liberation. It is one of the fundamental concepts in Buddhist philosophy and is considered one of the Three Poisons, along with greed (lobha) and hatred (dosa). Understanding the role of ignorance is crucial to comprehending the four Noble truths and the concept of dependent origination (paticcasamuppada).

Ignorance affects human life in many ways. Some of them may be elaborated as follows:

1. Root cause of suffering: Ignorance is considered the root cause of suffering (dukkha) in Buddhism. It is the fundamental ignorance about the true nature of reality, especially the Three Marks of Existence: impermanence (anicca), suffering (dukkha), and non-self (anatta). Ignorance blinds individuals to these truths and leads them to cling to what is impermanent, ultimately causing suffering.

2. Four Noble truths: Ignorance is directly linked to the four Noble truths, which form the foundation of Buddhist teaching. The first Noble Truth acknowledges the existence of suffering, and

ignorance is the primary reason for not recognizing the nature and causes of this suffering.

3. Dependent origination: Ignorance is a crucial link in the chain of dependent origination, a central concept in Buddhist thought that explains how suffering arises. The twelve links of dependent origination describe how ignorance leads to actions (karma), which in turn lead to rebirth and suffering. Breaking the cycle begins with dispelling ignorance,

4. Role of Kamma: Ignorance is responsible for the creation of karmic actions. When individuals act out of ignorance, they generate karma that binds them to the cycle of birth, death, and rebirth (samsara). Only by dispelling ignorance can one stop generating negative karma.

5. Cessation of Suffering (nibbana): The ultimate goal of Buddhism is the cessation of suffering and the attainment of Nirvana (enlightenment). Ignorance is the obstacle that keeps individuals trapped in the cycle of suffering, and overcoming it is a necessary step toward achieving Nirvana.

6. Role in Meditative practices and cultivation of Insight: Buddhist practices, including mindfulness meditation and insight (Vipassana) meditation, aim to dispel ignorance. By cultivating awareness and understanding the true nature of reality, practitioners can overcome ignorance and gain insight into the impermanent and selfless nature of existence.

7. Gradual Elimination: In Buddhist practice, ignorance is gradually eliminated through the development of wisdom (paññā) and insight. This involves a deepening understanding of the Three marks of existence, the Four noble truths, and the workings of the mind.

8. Transformative Knowledge: In Buddhism, the opposite of ignorance is transformative knowledge or wisdom (paññā). This wisdom arises from direct insight into the nature of reality and leads to liberation from suffering.

Ignorance (avijja) represents a fundamental misunderstanding of reality, which leads to suffering and perpetuates the cycle of birth and death (samsara). Overcoming ignorance through wisdom and insight is essential for liberation from suffering and the attainment of Nibbana. Recognizing the role of ignorance and actively seeking to dispel it is a central aspect of Buddhist practice and philosophy.

8.6   Three Marks of Existence-Anicca, Dukkha and Anatta

The three marks of existence, also known as the three universal characteristics, are fundamental concepts in Buddhist philosophy and practice. They provide insight into the nature of reality and form the basis for understanding the core teachings of Buddhism. These three marks apply to all conditioned things-that is, everything except for nibbana. According to the Buddha, fully understanding and appreciating the three marks of existence is essential to realizing enlightenment. These three characteristics are impermanence (anicca), suffering (dukkha), and not-self (anatta).

Impermanance (Anicca): Anicca is the first of the three marks of existence and underscores the idea that all things, without exception, are impermanent. Nothing in the world, whether material or mental, remains fixed or unchanging. This realization is central to Buddhist practice and is often illustrated through the metaphor of the ever- changing nature of a river's flow.

The understanding of impermanence challenges attachment and clinging to things in life. It encourages individuals to let go of their desire for permanence and to accept the transient nature of existence. In meditation and mindfulness practice, individuals observe the impermanence of their thoughts, emotions, and bodily sensations. This observation helps them detach from these fleeting experiences and cultivate equanimity.

Suffering (Dukkha): Dukkha is the second mark and refers to the unsatisfactory and inherently suffering nature of existence. It includes not only physical pain and emotional distress but also the general sense of dissatisfaction and unease that pervades human life. According to Buddhist teachings, dukkha arises from attachment and craving (tanha) for things to be different from the way they are. The relentless pursuit of pleasure and avoidance of pain only perpetuate suffering.

Recognizing dukkha is the first of the Four Noble Truths, and it serves as a wake-up call to acknowledge the existence of suffering and seek its cessation through the Noble Eightfold Path and other practices.

Not-Self (Anatta): Anatta is the third mark, which challenges the concept of a permanent, unchanging self or soul (atman). Instead, it asserts that there is no enduring, unchanging self in any aspect of human existence, whether it be the body, mind, or consciousness.

This teaching is often misunderstood as denying the existence of the self entirely. Instead, it emphasizes that what we typically consider as "self" is a composite of ever-changing components. Our identities and experiences are interdependent and conditioned by various factors, but they lack a fixed and independent essence.

Understanding anatta is essential for reducing ego-centered thinking and developing a more profound sense of interconnectedness and compassion. It encourages individuals to let go of the delusion of a separate, permanent self and to see themselves as part of the greater web of existence.

Three marks of existence are foundational concepts in Buddhist practice and philosophy that provide a deep insight into the nature of reality. Recognizing impermanence, suffering, and the absence of a permanent self helps individuals develop wisdom, compassion, and a clearer understanding of the human condition. These teachings are central to the path of liberation from suffering and the attainment of enlightenment.

8.7   Self (Atta): Virtuous Friend and Dreadful Enemy

A person living in the world as an individual is responsible for his fate, for his actions and reactions and for his achievements and failures. Buddha explain, "I walked over this path and benefitted to free myself from the sufferings of sansara. If you want to come along, then you also walk. Start taking steps." As many steps as you take, you will get that much benefit. If you take all the steps on the path, then you will reach the final goal. In delivering the Dhamma as an ideal teacher, the Buddha's declaration and appeal is very loud and clear, *"Tumhe hi kiccam atappam, akkhataro Tathagata."* "You yourself must earnestly practise; the Enlightened ones only proclaim the path." Tathagata, will only show the path; he won't carry you on his shoulders to the final goal. Someone can guide you because he has walked over the path, step by step.

Whole Tipitika is full with many discourses of the Buddha which shows each individual's potential and right to liberation from suffering. Many Dhammapada gatha or verses are so empowering and motivating to the seeker of the truth. One entire chapter on "Atta" has been dedicated to the role and importance of an individual self on the path of liberation. Some of these gathas have been presented here as an example:

> *Attánañ ce tathá kayirá yath'aññam anusásati,*
> *sudanto vata dammetha attá hi kira duddamo.*

(Dhammapada Verse-159)

"One should do what one teaches others to do; if one would train others, one should be well-controlled oneself. Difficult, indeed, is self-control."

> *Attá hi attano nátho; ko hi nátho paro siyá?*
> *Attaná va suddantena náthaí labhati dullabhaí.*

(Dhammapada Verse-160)

"One is truly one's protector. Who else could the protector be? With oneself fully controlled one gains a protector which is hard to gain."

Sukaráni asádhúni attano ahitáni ca,
yai ve hitañ ca sádhuñ ca, taí ve paramadukkaraí.

(Dhammapada Verse-163)

"Easy to do are things that are bad and harmful to oneself, but exceedingly difficult to do are things that are good and beneficial."

Attaná va kataí pápaí attaná saòkilissati;
attaná akataí pápaí attaná va visujjhati;
suddhi asuddhi paccattaí nánño aññaí visodhaye.

(Dhammapada Verse-165)

"By oneself is evil done, by oneself is one defiled. By oneself is evil left undone, by oneself is one purified. Purity and impurity depend on oneself-no one can purify another [69]."

While writing about the role of the self for the cultivation of insight, Edwin Arnold writes in his book, "The light of Asia" as follow [70]:

Pray not! The darkness will not brighten! Ask

Nought from the Silence, for it cannot speak!

Vex not your mournful minds with pious pain!

Ah! Brothers, Sisters! Seek.

Nought from the helpless gods by gift and hymn,

Nor bribe with blood, nor feed with fruits and cakes;

Within yourselves deliverance must be sought;

Each man his prison makes.

Sakkāyadiṭṭhi: Concept of the self would be incomplete without the consideration of the Sakkāyadiṭṭhi. An usual meaning of Sakkāyadiṭṭhi is taken as the physical body. However, its essence goes beyond to understand it as 'embodiment', 'identity' or personality. It involves the conversion of the instinctive sense of an 'I' at the core of subjective experience into a 'personification' yielding a notion of self and from this notion evolving into a full-fledged 'Personality view'. The genesis of such a full-fledged "Personality view' operates based on one other of altogether twenty possible modes in correspondence with the aggregates.

According to Sakkāya sutta (S.N. III, 159), the five aggregates of craving are what makes up Sakkāya. Such Sakkāya arises due to craving and will cease if craving is overcome. Hence the path leading to the cessation of Sakkāya is none other than the Noble eightfold path [71].

8.8 Law of Kammā

Kammā which includes our all our bodily, verbal and mental actions is a fundamental concept in Buddhism that is closely aligned with the teachings of all Buddhist traditions. In human life, kamma plays a central and significant role in all the activities and their consequences. It is intrinsically associated with almost all the aspects of human life. Some of them may be enumerated as follows:

1. Law of cause and effect: All Buddhist traditions, teaches that kamma is essentially the law of cause and effect. It means that every intentional action, whether mental, verbal, or physical, has consequences. These consequences are not only felt in this life but also in future lives, as Buddhists believe in the cycle of birth and rebirth.

2. Moral precepts: In Theravada practice, ethical conduct is of utmost importance. Lay practitioners are encouraged to observe the five precepts referred to as Panchasila, while Monastics (bhikkhus and bhikkhunis) adhere to a more extensive set of precepts. Observing these precepts helps individuals avoid unwholesome actions and generate positive kamma.

3. Generosity and Compassion: In addition to the five precepts, Buddhists are encouraged to practice generosity (dana), friendliness (Metta), compassion (Karuna) and equanimity (Upekkha) as part of their ethical conduct. These virtues not only generate positive karma but also cultivate a compassionate and altruistic mind-set.

4. Intention matters: Like in other Buddhist traditions, Theravada emphasizes that the intention behind an action is crucial. Kamma is not solely based on the external action but is intimately tied to one's mental state and motivation. Actions driven by wholesome intentions lead to positive kamma, while unwholesome intentions result in negative kamma.

5. Three types of Kamma: Buddhism classifies kamma into three main types depending on their consequences:

   Unwholesoms (akusala) kamma: These are unwholesome actions driven by greed, hatred, or delusion, leading to negative consequences.

   Wholesome (kusala) kamma: These are wholesome actions driven by generosity, compassion, wisdom, and other virtuous qualities, resulting in positive consequences.

   Inoperative (aviva) kamma: Actions performed without intention or consciousness, such as involuntary bodily functions, do not generate kamma.

6. Accumulation of kamma: Kamma accumulates over time as a result of one's actions. Positive actions lead to the accumulation of positive kamma, while negative actions accumulate negative kamma. These kammic imprints are believed to persist beyond death and influence one's future rebirths.

7. Spiritual progress: Practicing ethical conduct is seen as a means to purify the mind and create the conditions necessary for spiritual progress. When one refrains from harmful actions and

cultivates virtuous behaviour, the mind becomes more focused and tranquil, making it easier to engage in meditation and gain insight into the nature of reality.

8. Kamma and Rebirth: Buddhists believe that kamma is a determining factor in the cycle of birth and rebirth. One's kamma from past lives influences their present circumstances and future rebirths. Positive kamma leads to a favorable rebirth, while negative kamma results in an unfavorable one.

9. Personal Responsibility: Buddhism places a strong emphasis on individual responsibility. Each person is seen as the architect of their own destiny through their kamma. This perspective encourages practitioners to take ownership of their actions and make choices that lead to positive kamma and spiritual progress. The Buddha describe kamma as the fore runner of almost everything in life. In this context a following verse of Abhiṇhapaccavekkhitabbaṭhāna Sutta of the Anguttara Nikaya (AN 5.57) is self-explanatory [72].

Kammassakomhi, kamma dāyādo kamma yoni
kamma bandhu kamma patisarano
Yaṃ kammaṃ karissāma,
kalyāṇaṃ vā pāpakaṃ vā, tassa dāyādo bhavissami ti.

"I am my own kamma, I am an heir to my kamma, I am born from my kamma, I am the kinsman of my kamma, I am protected by my kamma. Whatever kamma I shall do, meritorious or sinful, I shall become their heir."

Dhammapada verse 127th quotes the consequences of the sinful deeds as follows:

Na antalikkhe na samuddamajihe, na pabbatanam vivaram
pavissa na vijjati so jagatippadeso, yatthatthito mucceyya
papakamma.

"Not in the sky, nor in the middle of the ocean, nor in the cave of a mountain, nor anywhere else, is there a place, where one may escape from the consequences of an evil deed. [69]"

The poet Edwin Arnold quotes about kamma in "The Light of Asia" as follows [70]:

Who toiled a slave may come anew a prince

For gentle worthiness and merit won;

Who ruled a king may wonder earth in rags

For things done and undone.

Thus, kamma supported by ethical conduct is a foundational concept in Buddhism that emphasizes the importance of mindful, virtuous living. Ethical conduct, guided by moral precepts and driven by wholesome intentions, shapes one's kamma, influences the cycle of rebirth, and paves the way for spiritual progress and the eventual liberation from suffering. It is a central component of the Buddhist path to enlightenment.

8.9 Faith in Three Jewels: Buddha, Dhamma and Sangha

One of the oldest ways of expressing faith in Buddhism is by taking refuge in the three Jewels. There are rare, precious and supreme three Jewels known as the triple gem and the three treasures in the world, Sansara. These three Jewels are the Buddha (the exemplar), the Dhamma (the teachings), and the Sangha (the community of practitioners). Journey of an individual starts on the path of wisdom and liberation with the refuge in three jewels:

I take refuge in the Buddha.
I take refuge in the dhamma.
I take refuge in the sangha.

Why take refuge in the three Jewels instead of something worldly? His Highness, the Dalai Lama explains: "… it would be like falling into a ditch and asking another who is in it to help you out. You need to ask someone who is standing outside the ditch for help; it is senseless to ask another who is in the same predicament. A refuge capable of protecting from the frights of manifold sufferings cannot also be bound in this suffering but must be free and unflawed." [73] "Doubt" (vicikiccha) is uncertainty with regard to the Buddha, Dhamma and Sangha, and the training; it is eliminated when the disciple sees for himself the truth of the Dhamma. The first step of declaring refuge in the three Jewels open the gates of the right view along with taking the percepts guidelines for an ethical life.

8.10   Diligence, Clear comprehension and Mindfulness

Throughout the Mahasatipatthānā sutta, the great discourse on the establishing of awareness, the triad of diligence (ātāpī), clear comprehension (sampajāno) and mindfulness (satimā), appears at the end of every section and subsection as an instruction to the disciples in the following form.

> *Kāye Kāyānupassī viharati **ātāpī sampajāno satimā**, vineyya loke abhijjhādomanassam.*
> *Vedanāsu Vedanānupassī viharati **ātāpī sampajāno satimā**, vineyya loke abhijjhādomanassam.*
> *Citte Cittānupassī viharati **ātāpī sampajāno satimā**, vineyya loke abhijjhādomanassam.*
> *Dhammesu Dhammānupassī viharati **ātāpī sampajāno satimā**, vineyya loke abhijjhādomanassam.*

"Monk dwells with diligence, clear understanding and mindfulness of impermanence, perceiving body as just the body, keeping away from craving and aversion towards the world;

he dwells with diligence, clear understanding and mindfulness of impermanence, perceiving feelings as just the feelings, keeping away from craving and aversion towards the world;

he dwells with diligence, clear understanding and mindfulness of impermanence, perceiving mind as just the mind, keeping away from craving and aversion towards the world; he dwells with diligence, clear understanding and mindfulness of impermanence, perceiving mental contents as just the mind contents, keeping away from craving and aversion towards the world [32]."

The Buddha frequently stressed that his disciple should not lose the thorough understanding of the phenomena and asked them to be diligent with clear comprehension and mindfulness at all times of wakeful moments of life. The meditators who exercise these three elements of awareness often speedily make a progress on the path of the cultivation of insight and wisdom. It is very important for a meditator to clearly understand the meaning of this triad at this point.

Atapi: The meaning of 'atapi' is taken here as 'diligent' or 'ardent'. When the meditator experiences a stressful condition, he feel a 'fire' in the mind and diligence (atäpi) is to remove that 'fire' and the stress from the mind, and calm the mind. When it is used along with 'Sampajañña' means remove the fire or heat from one's mind by being aware of the real nature of the things.

Sampajañña: "Sampajañña" is usually translated as "clear comprehension." Superficially this translation appears to be correct. One may take this to mean that one must merely have clear comprehension of body, feelings, mind and mental contents. The Buddha clearly emphasized the thorough understanding of impermanence (anicca) in all bodily and mental activities. Therefore, to understand the term "sampajañña" it can be better translated as: "The constant thorough understanding of impermanence." Mindfulness with clear comprehension (sati-sampajāna) means that the practitioner should note all the phenomena of the body, feelings, mind and mind contents without attraction of aversion towards them.

Satima: Mindfulness (sati) is one of the five spiritual faculties of power (balā), one of the seven factors of enlightenment (bojjaṅga) and the seventh link of the Noble eightfold path (magga). Mindfulness is said to have "non-superficiality" as its salient characteristic, the "absence of confusion" as its function, and the "state of being turned towards the object" as its manifestation. It is also called the "non- negligence" (appamāda) which indicates the state of unremitting alertness of the mind, the proficient in spiritual endeavor. Clear and strong mindfulness is conjoined with wisdom and is called the "prudence of mindfulness" (sati nepakkam). It is then pure cognition, the cognition which is free, from discrimination that proceeds from delusion [35].

This "objective" way of looking towards things, free from considerations of the personal reactions to any of them, is the pith of the method and constitutes what is called "knowing as it is" (yathabhuta ñanadassana). Also, by its quality of reckoning just what is present, mindfulness cuts down discursive thought and prepares the mind to take in the actual characteristics of the cognized objects. In this sense, mindfulness lets the objects speak for themselves and unfold their nature.

8.11 Four Noble Truths

The doctrine of the four Noble truths deals entirely with the problem of suffering. The first Noble truth expose the forms and the entire range of suffering. In the remaining three, the Buddha points out the cause of suffering, its cessation and the way to its cessation. This way to end the suffering is the middle way of ethical and mental training that avoid all extremes of conduct and view. This Noble eightfold path which is made up of right view, right intention, right speech, right action, right livelihood, right efforts, right mindfulness, and right concentration is the working area for an individual person in his entire internal and external world. The law of moderation, or Majjhima Patipada, is a central teaching in Buddhist practice, emphasizing the middle way between extremes. This principle, as taught by the Buddha, advocates for a balanced approach to life, avoiding both indulgence in sensory pleasures and the harshness of self-mortification. According to the Majjhima Patipada, the path to enlightenment lies not in excess or asceticism, but in finding a harmonious and sustainable way of living.

As the Dhamma is to be realized by the wise within themselves, this middle way directs and governs the entire development of the ethical conduct, mind training, and wisdom (sīla-samādhi-paññā).

The Eightfold path breaks open into three major divisions of ethical conduct (sila), concentration (samādhi), and wisdom (paññā). The basket of Ethical conduct contents right speech, right action, right livelihood. Samādhi's basket for mind training contains right effort, right concentration and right mindfulness. The Paññā's basket of wisdom contains right view and right intention. Sīla-samādhi-paññā, ethical conduct, mind training, and wisdom, are not three separate activities, they are part of the same fruit.

Ethical Conduct: Sila is the foundation of Buddhist practice. Ethical conduct (sila) is that embraces a commitment to harmony and self-restraint with the principal motivation being nonviolence, or freedom from causing harm. It has been variously described as virtue, moral discipline and precept. Each precept is said to develop its opposite positive virtue. There are only first five precepts for the households. However, there is also a stricter set of eight precepts which are taken by households at specific religious days or religious retreats. The eight precepts encourage further discipline and are modelled on the monastic code. The third precept on sexual misconduct is made stricter and becomes a precept of celibacy.

1. I undertake the training rule to abstain from taking life;

2. I undertake the training rule to abstain from taking what is not given;

3. I undertake the training rule to abstain from sexual misconduct;

4. I undertake the training rule to abstain from false speech;

5. I undertake the training rule to abstain from liquors, wines, and other intoxicants, which are the basis for heedlessness.

6. "I accept the training rule to abstain from food at improper times." (e.g. no solid foods after noon, and not until dawn the following day)

7. "I accept the training rule (a) to abstain from dancing, singing, instrumental music, and shows, and (b) from the use of jewellery, cosmetics, and beauty lotions."

8. "I accept the training rule to abstain from the use of high and luxurious beds and seats."

Novice-monk use the ten precepts while fully ordained Buddhist monks also have a larger set of monastic precepts, called the Pātimokkha consisting 227 rules for monks. In contrast to the 227 rules for monks, there are 311 rules for nuns in the Vinaya pitaka.

Practice of Concentration: Samādhi is the practice of concentration. It involves developing a focused mind that is free from distractions. This can be achieved through meditation. In Buddhism, the samadhi has been described in three parts. "Parikamma samadhi," "Upachara samādhi," and "Appaṇa samādhi" are used to describe different stages of concentration or meditative absorption. These stages represent the progression of meditative states on the path to deep absorption and insight. Let's briefly explore each of them: Parikamma samadhi (Preparatory concentration) is the initial or preparatory stage of jhana. It involves directing one's attention to a chosen object of meditation, such as the breath or a visualized image. The practitioner learns to focus the mind and gather it around the selected object. However, the mind may still be susceptible to distractions and wandering thoughts. Parikamma samadhi sets the foundation for deeper concentration. It's like preparing the soil before planting seeds; it's the beginning of the meditative journey.

Upacarā samādhi (Access concentration) is a deeper stage of concentration where the meditator's attention becomes more stable and less prone to distractions. During access concentration, the practitioner is close to achieving one-pointedness of mind but has not yet fully entered a state of deep meditative absorption (jhana). They are on the threshold of absorption. This stage is characterized by heightened awareness and a sense of calm and tranquility. It's often considered a bridge between the initial stages of concentration and the deeper absorption states.

Appaṇā samādhi (Attainment concentration) represents a state of deep meditative absorption or Jhana. In this stage, the meditator achieves a high degree of one-pointedness and is fully absorbed in the chosen object of meditation [66].

The mind is exceptionally still, and distractions are virtually non- existent. The meditator experiences profound inner peace, equanimity, and a sense of unity with the object of meditation. Appaṇā samadhi can be further divided into four Jhanas, each characterized by increasing levels of absorption and refinement of consciousness. This concentration is used as a basis for insight meditation (Vipassana) in Theravada Buddhism.

These stages of concentration are essential for the development of mindfulness and insight. They provide a stable platform from which practitioners can investigate the true nature of reality and gain deep insights into the Three marks of existence (anicca, dukkha, anatta). Ultimately, the goal of these practices is to achieve liberation, nibbana from suffering and the cycle of rebirth.

Cultivation of Wisdom: Pañña is the practice of wisdom. Pañña, plays a crucial role in understanding the nature of reality and achieving liberation from suffering. There are several aspects or types of pañña in Buddhism. Paññā is basically described in three categories as Sutamaya pañña, Chintamaya pañña and Bhavanamaya pañña.

Sutamaya pañña is the wisdom acquired through learning and hearing the teachings of the Buddha. It involves gaining knowledge of the Buddha's teachings, the four Noble truths, the Noble eightfold path, and other fundamental Buddhist concepts through study and listening to wise teachers.

Chintamaya pañña is developed through contemplation and reflection. It involves deep thinking and analysis of the teachings to gain a deeper understanding of their meaning and relevance to one's life.

Bhavanamaya pañña is the wisdom that arises through the practice of meditation. Bhavana means meditation or mental cultivation.

By observing the mind and its processes during meditation, practitioners gain insight into the impermanent, unsatisfactory, and selfless nature of all phenomena [66].

There are also other terminologies used for the above three types i.e. Pariyatti pañña acquired through the study of scriptures and texts. It involves understanding the Buddha's teachings intellectually. Patipatti pañña is practical wisdom, which is developed through the actual practice of the teachings in daily life and meditation to gain direct experiential insight. Pativedha pañña is the wisdom of realization or penetration. It is the highest level of wisdom characterized by the direct and profound insight into the true nature of reality. It leads to the experience of Nibbana, the ultimate goal of the Buddhist practice.

Pañña is the practice of wisdom. It involves developing insight into the nature of reality. This can be achieved through meditation and contemplation.

8.12   Army of the Mara

The person on the path of liberation and release is always distracted by number of inner and outer worldly conditions. Mara is supposed to be a great obstacle to spiritual practice. Mara is often personified in buddhist teachings but the term can best be defined as the internal negative forces present in all sentient beings. Concept of Ichinen sanzen believe that living being always possess all ten world states. It is believed that after your initial grace period Mara will attack relentlessly and if you do not cope with the challenges presented you will fail. If you fail and give up and walk away from your practice, the effects of taking that action will be grim. It is considered as the failure of monumental proportions because the effect will carry over into numerous future lives until that negative energy is irradicated. To be successful in these circumstances, one must determine to move forward ardently. As one advances, the challenges become greater but while going ahead one is really training one's own mind for developing and mastering the skills to handle these tests.

Several accounts in various suttas describe Buddha's defeat of Mara. In the Padhana Sutta (Suttanipāta, v. 426b–428), Mara comes to Bodhisatva engaged in ascetic practices, and says, "You are so thin and pale. Don't seek liberation and release - which would mean leaving the world - but stay in the world and do good." Mara sends an army to defeat Gautama. The Buddha enumerates the armies of Mara as: sensual desires, discontent, hunger and thrust, craving, laziness, fear, indecisive wavering (doubt), restlessness, longing for the transitory things in life (gain, praise, honor, and fame), and praising oneself and belittling others. Buddha saw that to overcome all of these, he must stop identifying with thoughts of these things [74].

8.13   Seating Posture for Jhana

Seating posture of the meditator is very important assistant for the concentration and meditation. A free and uninterrupted experience of sensation of the feelings (vedana) and its further clear perception is a very important milestone during meditation. In fact, different types of seating postures are exercised in different sects of Buddhism for meditation. However, the Buddha specifically appeals his disciples to sit cross legged with particular conditioning of the mind for meditation. The Buddha instructs, "Here a monk, having gone into the wilderness, or to the base of a tree, or to a solitary room, sits down cross-legged, keeping his body upright and fixing his mindfulness set forward, with this clear awareness, the disciple shall prepare for meditation and progression of mindfulness on contemplation of the body, feelings, mind and mental contents.

No doubt, one can select a seating posture in which a person is more comfortable for a longer period of time during the meditation retreats. However, it has been experienced by many that seating cross-legged in a lotus position is best suited for the meditation as it gives a very balanced and strong base to the body to keep it upright for longer time without exhaustion. The habit pattern of seating position once mastered becomes a very good support to a meditator during the progressive meditation at the various stages of the rūpa jhana and arūpa jhana.

8.14   Subject for Meditation (Kammaṭṭhāna)

Truly, a very positive support is necessary for an individual meditator for the successful trading through various stages of the meditation. A little wrong step on the path or a wrong thought may spoil the exercise. For this purpose, the Buddha has very compassionately explored and proposed forty subjects of practicing meditation referred to as kammaṭṭhāna. Its most basic meaning is as a word for meditation which may also means the place of work. Ven. Buddhaghosha in the Visuddhimaga, referred kammṭṭhāna as "occupations" in the sense of "things to occupy the mind" or "workplaces" in the sense of "places to focus the mind on during the meditation." Any one of these forty subjects of meditation may be recommended to the meditator on the basis of the temperament and state of the mind [66].

I. Ten Kasina: These are a class of basic visual objects-(1) earth, water, (3) fire, (4) air, (5) blue, (6) yellow, (7) red, (8) white, (9) bright light (ālok), (10) consciousness (viññāna) .

II. Ten Asubha: The ten objects of repulsion (asubha) - (1) swollen corpse, (2) discolored, bluish, corpse, (3) festering corpse, (4) fissured corpse, (5) gnawed corpse, (6) dismembered or hacked corpse, (7) scattered corpse, (8) bleeding corpse, (9) worm-eaten corpse, (10) skeleton.

III. Ten recollections (anussati): First three recollections are of the virtues of the three Jewels - (1) Buddha, (2) Dhamma and Sangha. Next three in this group are recollections of the virtues of (4) morality (sīla), (5) liberality (cāga), (6) the wholesome attributes of gods (devata). Further next four are associated with the recollections of (7) the body (kāyagata), (8) death (Marana), (9) the breath or breathing (ānāpāna) and (10) enlightenment (nibbana).

IV. Four "abodes of Brahma" (brahmaviharā)- (1) loving- kindness or goodwill (mettā), (2), compassion (karuna), (3) sympathetic joy over another's success (mudita), and (4) equanimity (upekkha).

V. Four formless states (arūpajhānas)-(1) sphere of infinite space (ākāśānantyāyatana), (2) sphere of infinite consciousness (viññānantyāyatana), (3) sphere of nothingness (akiñcanyayatāna) and (4) sphere of neither perception nor non-perception (naivasaññānasaññāyatana).

VI. One kammaṭṭhāna of the perception of disgust of food (aharapatikulasanna).

8.15 Five Mental Faculties (Indriya) and Five Powers (Bala)

Initiators on the path of the cultivation of wisdom and enlightenment needs a great support. A support from the internal and external world. There are some wonderful mental faculties, human beings are endowed with and it can provide great support to make steadfast progress on the path. Faculties means leaders. When skillfully cultivated the five faculties they become the powers of the mind. The five mental faculties are faith (saddhā), efforts (viriya), mindfulness (sati), concentration (samādhi) and wisdom (pañña). These five well cultivated and strengthened faculties becomes the five corresponding powers of the meditator. These two sets of five factors are very important in following the Noble eightfold path. The Buddha gave a simile to understand how mental faculties (indriya) can become power (bala) to overcome difficulties: When a river runs into an obstacle like a large boulder, it splits and goes around it, and merge together after the obstacle.

Faith (saddhā) is foremost without which one does not have the conviction to follow the path. However, the faith has to be based on wisdom. Faith and wisdom (paññā) need to progress together. It should be built upon the base of the truth of dhamma. Blind faith becomes the hindrance to progress since one will be setting on the wrong path and shaky foundation. The faith of the sotāpaññā is unshakable and will never be lost or even reduced. When saddhā and paññā are developed to a certain extent (before the sotāpaññā stage), one realizes the fruitlessness and the dangers of the sansaric journey. Thus, one is motivated to make an effort (viriya). Furthermore, one realizes that one needs to be mindful in one's actions, and thus mindfulness (sati) starts to build. One realizes that one has to act with righteous and thoughtful consideration (yonisomanasikāra). At the same time, one realizes that when the mind is not calm, one can make bad decisions; thus, one starts working on calming the mind and to attain a level of concentration (samādhi) by absorbtion in jhana.

8.16 Unwholesome Attitudes (Akusala)

A journey of a seeker of truth on the path of middle way is not all that easy. Every moment a practitioner has to walk over the sharp sword. A little heedlessness on the part of the seeker and the craving of something is ready to take over. The incessant flow of the craving for the samsara keeps on flowing and maintaining its supremacy by keeping a check with the unwholesome attitudes necessary for the purpose. The mind keeps on relishing and replenishing on the 14 unwholesome conducts (akusala) such as delusion (moha), shamelessness (ahiri), remorseless (anottappa), restlessness (uddhacca), greed (lobha), wrong views (ditthi), conceit (mana), anger (dosa), envy (issa), stinginess (maccariya), worry (kukkucca), sloth (thina), torpor (middha) and doubts (vicikiccha). These 14 unwholsome factors hold back the meditator and keep him engaged in the natural stream of hindrances. These factors shall be taken as the adversaries on the path of insight and wisdom [75].

8.17 Wholesome Attitudes (Kusala)

However, the seeker of truth on the path of enlightenment is supported by all the positive and wholesome forces of nature. In this regards, practitioner's own mind becomes the righteous friend (kalyanmitra) by developing 25 wholesome qualities (kusala) which work as the perfect antidotes to counter the unwholesome attitudes. It supports, inspires, guards and drives ahead a practitioner steadfastly on the path of liberation. In Abhidhamma, these 25 universal beautiful factors (sobhansadharana) of the mind are also referred to as sobhana cetasikas or beautiful mental factors which can be categorized in four groups as per their qualities. in Abhidhamma. They are:

1. Faith (saddha)

2. Mindfulness (sati)

3. Sense of shame (hiri)

4. Sense of guilt (ottappa)

5. Mind without greed (alobha)

6. Mind without anger (adosa)

7. Equanimity (tattamajjhattata)

And, 6 pairs of cetasikas altogether 19 in total. The 6 pairs are:

1. Serenity (passddhi): kayapassaddi and cittapassaddhi

2. Lightness (lahuta): kayalahuta and cittalahuta

3. Pliancy (muduta) kayamuduta and cittamudita

4. Adaptability or wieldiness (kammannata) kayakammannata and cittakammannata

5. Proficiency (pagunnata): kayapagunnata and cittapagunnata

6. Uprightness (ujukata) kayujjukata and cittujjukata

Thus, by cultivating 25 sobhana cetasikas the practitioner's mind open ups on the middle way for the steadfast practice of Dhamma.

1. Confidence-faith (saddha) makes citta believes in the Buddha, the Dhamma, the Sangha, Dependent origination (paticcasamuppada), the Noble eightfold path and the practice. This belief is not a blind faith but there is a strong reason for this. There is evidence for total belief. It is like confidence. When unwavering faith arise; citta and all other cetasikas become clean, active, alert and calm.

2. Mindfulness (sati) makes citta watch things actively and makes mindful. So citta remembers to do things in due course. In the presence of sati, citta can work according to its will as sati reminds him to remember things to do. It serves as a reminder. Sati also helps other cetasikas to remember to do their jobs.

3. Moral shame (hiri) hinders citta not to do bad things as doing so probably will face with disgraceful situations. In the presence of hiri, as it reminds to consider the consequences of the actions, citta will not do bad things due to this inhibition. It always arises with its friend ottappa cetasika as a companion.

4. Moral dread (ottappa) makes citta unwilling to do bad things as doing so will have negative effect and citta is fearful of that result. This cetasika like hiri looks the possible consequences of actions. And it is frightened by the possible result. So, in its presence, citta will not do bad things. This is also kind of inhibition. But character wise it is more in favour of fear than shame.

5. Together with hiri, these two cetasikas guard the world in the favourable social conditions. Men and women are attracted to each other and this finally leads to sex. But hiri and ottappa hinder unnecessary events. These two cetasikas are called the guardians of the world (lokapala dhamma). They work not only in avoiding sex matter in inappropriate relationship but also in avoiding all akusala dhamma.

6. Non-attachment (alobha) makes citta willing to offer things to sattas as citta becomes unattached to those things when alobha advises him. Alobha is more than unattachment or detachment.

It looks directly at receivers as satta and directs to him. At the same time it has no more likeness to its assumed own properties as his properties. Detach to properties and bend toward to receivers and there is unperceivable flow of energy to the receiver. It works with other 18 cetasikas including saddha especially.

7. Goodwill (adosa) has nondestructive effect. It urges citta to have a good mood and kindness. In the presence of adosa others wellbeing is always considered. This comprises physical, mental, emotional, psychological, social and any aspect of others. Its character is unhurting in nature. It is true friendship. It is loving kindness.

8. Equanimity (Tattamajjattata) is balancer. It is equalizer. It equalises the strength of all accompanying cetasikas and so it advises citta as well to work in a state of equillibrium that means it works without extremeness. This cetasika is like a charioteer. When two horses draw the cart, they have to draw equally in terms of strength. To do so, the charioteer does the job. Without the charioteer the desired direction will never be reached.

In the other six sets of duets or other 12 beautiful mental factors namely body calmness (kaya passaddhi), mind tranquillity (chitta passaddhi), body lightness (kayalahuta), mental buoyancy (chitta lahuta), body plasticity (kayamuduta), mental plasiticity (chitta muduta), body workableness (kayakammannata), mental workableness (chittakammannata), body competence (kaya pagunnata), mental cleverness (chittapagunnata), bodily straightness (kaya ujukata) and mental uprightness (chittaujukata) always arise with wholesome consciousness.

The first set is serenity of the mind (cittapassaddhi) and serenity of the body (kayapassaddhi) cetasikas. Cittapassaddhi is a cetasika which is coolness or calmness or tranquility of citta. It has soothing effect on citta. It calms down mind as well and causes citta free from all worries. When cittapassaddhi arises kayapassaddhi also arises. These two cetasikas always arise together and work together with the same citta.

The second set is lightness (lahuta). They are cittalahuta and kayalahuta. Cittalahuta is lightness of citta and kayalahuta is lightness of cetasikas. They also arise together and work together with the same citta. This pair of cetasikas helps mind ready to function well. These two cetasikas can be noticed in mind when in the state of good mood like kusala actions.

Third set is plasticity (muduta). They are cittamuduta and kayamuduta. Muduta is pliancy or tenderness. Cittamuduta is tenderness of citta and kayamuduta is pliancy of cetasikas. They arise at the same time with the same citta and they work together.

Fourth set is workableness (kammannata). They are cittakammannata and kayakammannata. Cittakammannata is adaptability or wieldiness of citta and kayakammannata is for cetasikas. They arise together and work together in the same citta with the same arammana (sense objects). They help citta and cetasikas to agree with other cetasikas and adapt to all.

Fifth set is competence (pagunnata). They are cittapagunnata and kayapagunnata. Cittapagunnata is proficiency of citta and kayapagunnata is proficiency of cetasikas. They also arise together and work together. Cittapagunnata helps citta to function properly and kayapagunnata helps all cetasikas to function appropriately.

Sixth set is uprightness (ujukata). They are cittujjukata and kayujjukata cetasikas. They arise together and they work together in the same citta taking the same arammana. cittujjukata is uprightness of citta or rectitude of citta and kayujjukata is for cetasikas. They make citta and cetasikas sincere and all will work straight forward in the presence of these two cetasikas.

There are three virati cetasikas which are the parts of the noble eightfold path that governs the ethical part (Sila) of the middle way. Virati means avoidance. They are:

1. Samma vaca (Right speech),

2. Samma kammanta (Right action), and

3. Samma ajiva (right livlihood).

Samma vaca is right speech. It helps citta not to indulge in bad speech like telling lies, saying bad words or rough words or rude words, telling non sense tales, telling divisive speech. It is a kind of inhibition. It focuses on verbal actions or speech.

Samma kammanta is right action. This cetasika helps citta not to do unwholesome things but to do righteous actions. It inhibits doing bad thing by abstinence. It is like hiri and ottappa. But its inhibition is at kaya kamma dvara or bodily actions while hiri and ottappa acts by considering the possible consequences. Samma kammanta considers the wickedness, unwholesomely actions as the bodily actions.

Samma ajiva is right livelihood which again is living on livelihood that is the result of samma kammanta or samma vaca or both. It is also a kind of inhibition. Unlike other two virati cetasikas, samma ajiva is related to livelihood. In the setting of livelihoods, it arises and helps citta not to do unwholesome bodily actions or speech in connection with livelihood.

There are 2 boundless (appamanna) cetasikas, namely:

1. Compassion (karuna): Karuna arises when poor sattas are encountered. Boundless compassion is putting a good will on worldly entities like sattas, men, woman, deva, devi, brahma etc.

2. Sympathy in others' welfare (mudita): Mudita arises when fulfilled sattas are encountered. Mudita is sympathetic joy.

In the 25 sobhana cetasikas or beautiful mental factors, the last to be mentioned but the most important is insight (paññā) or pannindriya cetasika. This cetasika is the Prime Minister for the king citta. It helps citta to see and to realize things in depth. It has a power of realization. It has a power of analysis and penetration. It has a good insight into the matter in question. If this cetasika is present and functioning well all other accompanying cetasikas work well and all are well organized. This cetasika is like a wise man or a wise minister that work. It presents the pros and cons of everything to the king citta. This paññā cetasika is the chief of all cetasikas in rupa and arupa jhana cittas, magga cittas, and phala cittas. Without this paññā cetasika there will not be any of jhana or magga or phala citta [75].

8.18   Noble Friendship (Kālyaṇmitta)

In the Pali Canon, Upaddha sutta (SN 45.2), there is a conversation between the Buddha and his disciple Ananda in which Ananda enthusiastically declares, 'This is half of the holy life, Lord: admirable friendship, admirable companionship, admirable camaraderie.' The Buddha replies: 'Don't say so, Ananda. Don't say so. Admirable friendship, admirable companionship, admirable camaraderie is actually the whole of the holy life. When a monk has admirable people as friends, companions, & comrades, he can be expected to develop and pursue the Noble eightfold path [76].

The Buddha points out nine main conditions that fuels and provides the proliferative conditions for the ignorance to widen its circle of craving. The Buddha puts forth ignorance as the first and foremost cause of the sufferings of the life. However, in his further analysis, he explains that there is a chain of the ten factors connected with and fueled by its immediate precursor for the sustenance of its descendant or successor. The Buddha explains in Avijjā sutta (AN-10:61) that ignorance is fueled by the five hindrances [77]. The five hindrances (nivāraṇa) are fueled by the three kinds of misconduct i.e. mental, verbal and behavioral actions (thrividha duscarita). The three kinds of misconduct are fueled by lack of sense restraint (indriya asayyam). Lack of sense restraint is fueled by lack of mindfulness and clear comprehension (asatisampajanna). Lack of mindfulness and clear comprehension is fueled by lack of wise investigation (yonisa manasikāra). Lack of wise investigation is fueled by lack of faith or lack of confidence in Dhamma (saddha). Lack of faith is fueled by not listening to Buddha's teachings, the Dhamma (saddhamma-savana). Not listening to the Buddha's teachings is fueled by not associating with Noble friends who explains the Buddha's real message. That is the fuel for ignorance, and that is how the circle of ignorance (avijjā) is fulfilled (Fig. 8.1).

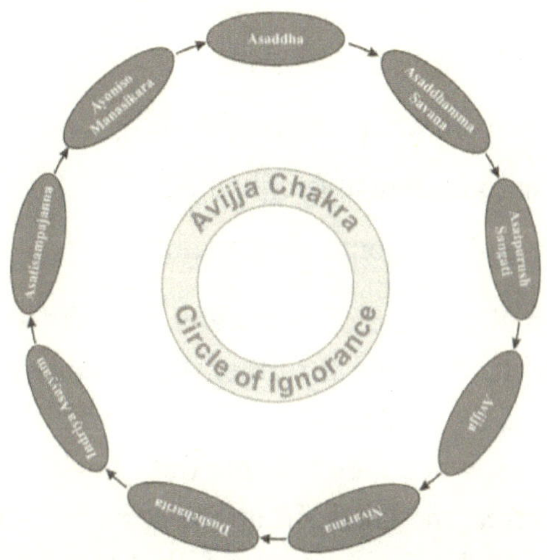

Fig. 8.1: The circle of ignorance (Avijjā)

In this way, when the factor of associating with Noble friends is fulfilled, it fulfills the factor of listening to the true teaching. When the factor of listening to the true teaching is fulfilled, it fulfills the factor of faith (saddha) ... wise investigation (ayoniso manasikāra) ... mindfulness and situational awareness (satisampajañña)... sense restraint (indriya saṃvara) ...the three kinds of good conduct (thrividha sucarita) ... the four kinds of mindfulness meditation (satipaṭṭhānā) ... the seven awakening factors (bojjhanga). When the seven awakening factors are fulfilled, they fulfill knowledge and freedom. That is the fuel for knowledge and freedom, and that is how it is fulfilled. The circle of knowledge and freedom (Vijjā-vimutti) is illustrated in fig. 8.2.

Thus, the Buddha points out nine main conditions that promotes the conditions supportive for the cultivation of the wisdom, insight and liberation from suffering.

1. Noble friends (Kalyāṇmitta)

2. Listening to the true teaching. faith (saddha)

3. Wise investigation (ayoniso manasikāra)

4. Mindfulness and situational awareness (satisampajañña)

5. Sense restraint (indriya saṃvara)

6. Good conduct (thrividha sucarita)

7. Mindfulness meditation (satipaṭṭhānā)

8. Factors of enlightenment (bojjhaṅga)

9. Knowledge and freedom (Vijjā-vimutti)

The Buddha gives the simile of rain water to make a description more emphatic or vivid to describe it further. It is like when the rain pours down on a mountain top, and the water flows downhill to fill the hollows, crevices, and creeks, when they become full, they fill up the pools. The pools fill up the lakes, the lakes fill up the streams, and the streams fill up the rivers. And as the rivers become full, they fill up the ocean. That is the fuel for the ocean, and that is how it is filled up.

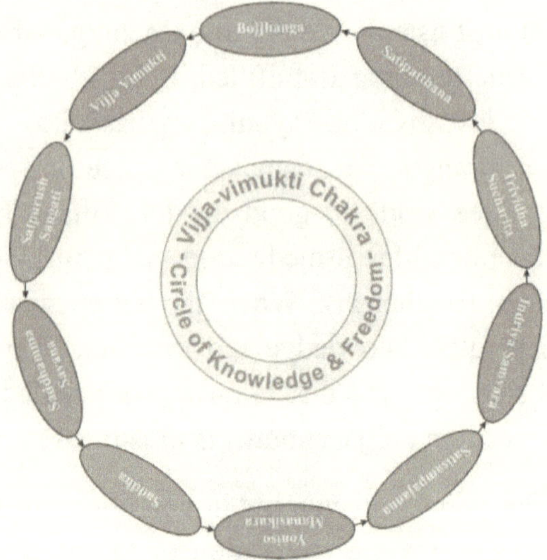

Fig. 8.2: The circle of knowledge and freedom (Vijjā-vimutti)

The strongest emphasis has been put by the Buddha on the supreme importance of having an unprejudiced mind before we start on the road of the truth. Prejudice, passion, fear of expression of one's convictions and the ignorance are the four biases that have to be sacrificed at the threshold.

8.19   Causal Genesis: Nothing Without Reason

Meditator and the seeker of the truth should always strive to see the conditioned origination of all the worldly things. When this becomes an attitude, a faculty of critical analysis (Dhammavicaya), second factor for insight attains the consummation. It uproots all the doubts (vicikicchaya) about the training on the noble eightfold path.

Key word of the Paticca-samuppada, 'Paccaya'- *Avidhya paccaya sankhara- Sankahara paccaya vinnanan*...and so on, runs the formula of causal genesis. Observation of the causal genesis is very important in the process of perception and clear understanding of reality. We have acknowledged it in the previous chapters. However, we are trying to explore the causal genesis here for looking into the immensity of the causal conditions. One can imagine now, in how many ways can there exist pacchayo between any two given phenomena or states. The great vision of the Buddha revealed to his age, a word of causal order, that so seeing man might get a grip on the inexorable truth that this kind of action or deed brought that kind of result, that in his own hands it lay to make or mar his destiny. This causal order continued again and again to breed or the cast out sorrow and suffering. This historic revelation by the Buddha before 2550 years, was the biggest blow to the established dogma and blind faith of the social traditions, that every person has an inherent ability to master his or her own destiny. The Buddha established the right view and a clear path of middle way among the people setting his own example as the enlightened personality by walking over the middle path.

The Buddha strengthened the doctrine of causal genesis by giving twenty-four means or requisites for clarifying the complexities of dependence origination. In Abhidhamma, the entire Patthana is devoted to an enquiry to illustrate how all the material and mental phenomena occur with dependence origination through these twenty-four conditions as illustrated in Table 4.9. These causal conditions of the worldly phenomena help the seeker to enquire and evaluate the causal genesis to develop the insight and wisdom [78].

Table 4.9: Twenty-four causal conditions of material and mental phenomena.

1	Root cause conditions (Hetupaccayo)	13	Kamma conditions (Kammapaccayo)
2	Object conditions (Arrammanapaccaho)	14	Resultant conditions (Vipakpaccayo)
3	Predominance conditions (Adhipatipaccayo)	15	Nutriment conditions (Aharapaccayo)
4	Proximity conditions (Anantarapaccayo)	16	Faculty conditions (Indriyapaccayo)
5	Contiguity conditions (Samanantarapaccayo)	17	Jhana conditions (Jhanapaccayo)
6	Conascence conditions (Sahajatapaccayo)	18	Path conditions (Maggapaccayo)
7	Mutuality conditions (Annamannapaccayo)	19	Association conditions (Sampayuttapaccayo)
8	Dependence conditions (Nissayapaccayo)	20	Dissociation conditions (Vippayuttapaccayo)
9	Strong dependence conditions (Upanissayapaccayo)	21	Presence conditions (Atthipaccayo)
10	Prenascence conditions (Purejatapaccayo)	22	Absence conditions (Natthipaccayo)
11	Postnascence conditions (Pacchajatapaccayo)	23	Disappearance conditions (Vigatapaccayo)
12	Repetition recurrence (Asevanāpaccayo)	24	Nondisappearance conditions (Avigatapaccayo)

8.20 The Factors of Enlightenment (Bojjhaṅga)

The Factors of Enlightenment, are essential components of Buddhist meditation and practice aimed at cultivating wisdom and enlightenment. These factors, when developed and balanced, play a crucial role in one's spiritual journey. These seven factors of enlightenment namely, Mindfulness (sati), Investigation of Dhamma (dhammavicaya), Energy (viriya), Delight (pīti), Tranquility (passaddhi), Concentration (Samādhi), and Equanimity (Upekkhā). We have discussed the factors of enlightenment in detail in the previous chapter. Here, we would like to see the role of the bojjhaṅga as the promoter in the spiritual journey.

The cultivation of wisdom and enlightenment is intricately linked to these factors in the following ways:

Clarity and Insight: Mindfulness, investigation of Dhamma, and concentration help individuals develop a clear and focused mind. This clarity enables them to see the true nature of reality, including the impermanence and interconnectedness of all things, which is a central aspect of wisdom in Buddhism.

Emotional Balance: The development of joy, tranquility, and equanimity helps practitioners cultivate emotional balance. This balance allows them to observe their emotions and thoughts without being overwhelmed by them, leading to greater self-awareness and wisdom.

Effort and Diligence: Energy is essential for maintaining a consistent meditation practice and for overcoming the hindrances that can impede progress on the path to enlightenment. Effort and diligence are crucial for making sustained progress.

Deepening Insight: The Factors of Enlightenment work together to deepen one's insight into the Four Noble Truths, the nature of suffering, and the path to liberation. As practitioners develop these factors, they gain a deeper understanding of the causes of suffering and how to transcend it.

The factors of enlightenment have a very specific characteristic of arising, developing and reaching to perfection. These characteristics are integral to the cultivation of wisdom and enlightenment in Buddhism. They provide a systematic framework for developing the mental and emotional qualities necessary for gaining insight into the true nature of reality and attaining spiritual liberation. By nurturing and balancing these factors, individuals can progress on the path toward enlightenment and a deeper understanding of the Dhamma.

8.21   Pāramītās against Hindrances

Human birth and life is very crucial juncture in the entire universe of consciousness. At this juncture, the living entity can work as its own architect for the spiritual evolution as an enlightened being. Indeed! the birth as a human being is a rarest of the rare opportunity to work out our own liberation from the clutches of ignorance and craving. Path of enlightenment is the path of perfection that passes through the four stages of realization. The ten perfections (pāramīs of pāramītās) have been described in Theravada Buddhism. These ten pāramīs are presented several times in the Jataka Tales as well as Sutta Pitaka of the Pali canon. However, some other sects of Buddhism such as Mahayana include eight and Sarvastivada includes six perfections.

Before the consideration of the ten perfections, let us see the objectives and relevance with which the ten perfections are highly valued and endorsed in Buddhism. There are many fetters on the path which we have seen in the army of the Mara. There are major ten hindrances to enlightenment and based on how many of them have been eliminated and / or the degree to which they have been eliminated, the stages of realizations comes to fruition (Anguttara Nikaya 10.13). These ten hindrances are:

1.   The belief in a permanent personality, ego (sakkāya-diṭṭhi)
2.   Doubt, extreme skepticism (vicikicchā)

3. Attachment to rites, rituals, and ceremonies (sīlabbata- parāmāso)

4. Attachment to sense desires (kāmacchando)

5. Ill-will, anger (vyāpādo)

6. Craving for existence in the Form world [heavenly realms] (rūparāgo)

7. Craving for existence in the Formless world [heavenly realms] (arūparāgo)

8. Conceit (māna)

9. Restlessness (uddhacca)

10. Ignorance (avijjā)

The Buddha and Arahats are the Noble Ones who has eradicated their all ten hindrances to enlightenment. An anāgāmī (non-returner) has completely eradicated the first five hindrances and never returns to earth or any other world system. Such a person is reborn to a heavenly realm and attains enlightenment from there. A sakadāgāmī (once-returner) has eradicated the first three hindrances and greatly weakened the fourth and fifth; attachment to sense desires and ill-will. Such a person will be reborn to either the human or heavenly realm and will attain enlightenment there. A sotāpaññā (stream-entrant) has eradicated the first three hindrances and will be re-born no more than seven more times and rebirth will either be as a human or a deva in a heavenly realm.

To counter the ten hindrances, ten Pāramī are the perfections of the heart to cultivate in one's practice of the Dhamma. These ten perfections are as follows:

1. Perfection of giving-Generosity (dana)

2. Perfection of morality-Moral conduct (sila)

3. Perfection of renunciation (nekkhamma)

4. Perfection of discerning wisdom (paññā)

5. Perfection of energy (viriya)

6. Perfection of patience (khanti)

7. Perfection of truthfulness (sacca)

8. Perfection of determination (adhitthana)

9. Perfection of loving-kindness (metta)

10. Perfection of equanimity (upekkha)

The ten hindrances to enlightenment show us what we need to get rid of, to assist us in the eradication of the hindrances and cultivation of ten virtues. In the ten perfections you can see elements of the five precepts and the Noble eightfold path and brahmaviharas. The Buddha spent many past lives as an ascetic monastic perfecting each of the ten perfections. He could not be reborn in his last and final life as the Buddha until all ten perfections were fully developed. Enlightenment is not something so simple as just sitting one day and all of a sudden feeling at "one with nature" and very "awake." Some practitioners and teachers say that they are enlightened when they have one momentary glimpse of jhanic pleasure in their meditation. Enlightenment is attainable, but no easy task and has the prerequisite of the ten pāramītās [79].

Dhamma is just like an ocean, full with many adversaries that work as the negative force. Yet there are many virtuous mental abilities that help one as the promoters. A long list may be made of all such virtuous mental abilities that extend support to the wayfarer on the path of enlightenment.

The Buddha's four Noble truths, which are the basic foundation of his teaching, display a rational analysis of the universal truth of suffering. This unprecedented discovery of the Buddha further unravels the root causes of the suffering which is craving (taṇhā); and, based on the principle of cause and effect, ultimate solution to this universal problem, the Noble eightfold path. This disciplinary approach and methodology of the Buddha is sometimes compared with medical diagnosis and treatment. What, however, began as a spiritual science of happiness, peace and enlightenment, common in ancient times, was transformed over time to a religion replete with myths, legends, a complex symbol system and monastic discipline where the followers revered the monks and rituals encouraged popular devotion. For many, Buddhism became a belief system rather than a way to understand and deal with life issues.

As much as we read or listen to the Buddha's words in the discourses, our wisdom gradually increases. Our delusions and ignorance about all the worldly phenomena of Sansara falls down. With this clear understanding of the Buddha's teaching if we practice in our day to day life, we are bound to move forward on the path of purification and liberation.

8.22 Brahmavihāra: Four Immeasurables

The Buddha has described four wholesome and positive virtues called Brahmavihāras inherent in the human mind which can give rise to positive emotional health, happiness, rewarding social relationships and contribute to spiritual development when they are developed and maintained. Vihāra is a noun from the verb "viharati" meaning to reside, abide or dwell. So, brahma viharas mean excellent dwelling places which means these four wholesome qualities should become constant dwelling places of the mind states. The four Brahmavihāra are also referred to as four aparimana or immeasurables:

1. Goodwill (*mettā*)

2. Compassion (*karuṇā*)

3. Empathetic joy (*mudita*)

4. Equanimity (*upekkhā*)

Through regular practice of jhana, it is possible to develop these great virtues of unlimited love-that is, love which is not withheld from anyone.

In deep meditation practice with the Brahmavihāras, the experience of mettā, karuṇā, mudita, and upekkhā can become, as described by the Buddha, "extensive, expanded, limitless, free from hatred and ill-will." When they radiate outward in all directions of the compass without limit [66].

8.23 Enlightenment within Everybody's Reach

The concept of enlightenment in various spiritual and philosophical traditions, including Buddhism, often carries the idea that it is attainable by anyone who earnestly seeks it. While the paths and practices may vary, the fundamental belief is that enlightenment is within everybody's reach. Here are some key points supporting this idea:

1. Innate potential: Many spiritual traditions teach that all individuals possess the innate potential for enlightenment. It is not reserved for a select few but is a natural state of being that can be uncovered or realized through specific practices and understanding.

2. Equality: Enlightenment teachings often emphasize the equality of all beings. Enlightenment does not discriminate based on race, gender, social status, or any other external factor. It is a matter of inner transformation and realization.

3. Accessible teachings: Spiritual and philosophical teachings on enlightenment are often made accessible to the general public through scriptures, books, and oral traditions. These teachings offer guidance and practices for individuals who seek to progress on their spiritual journey.

4. Meditation and Mindfulness: Practices such as meditation and mindfulness, which are central to many paths to enlightenment, can be learned and practiced by anyone willing to put in the effort. These practices are not exclusive to a particular group but can be adopted by anyone seeking inner transformation.

5. Diverse paths: There are various paths to enlightenment within different spiritual traditions. For example, Buddhism offers multiple vehicles (Theravada, Mahayana, Vajrayana) with different approaches to enlightenment, catering to a wide range of individuals with varying capacities and inclinations.

6. Efforts and Dedication: While enlightenment may be within reach for everyone, it still requires effort, dedication, and sincere practice. It is not something that can be achieved easily or without commitment. However, the potential to reach it is open to all.

7. Cultural variation: Different cultures and spiritual traditions may have their own interpretations of enlightenment, but the underlying principle that it is attainable by individuals who sincerely seek it remains a common thread.

8. Historical examples: There are historical and contemporary examples of individuals from diverse backgrounds and life circumstances who have attained high levels of spiritual realization or enlightenment. These examples serve as inspiration and proof that it is possible for anyone.

It is important to note that the path to enlightenment is highly personal and may vary from person to person. What works for one individual may not work for another. Additionally, the journey towards enlightenment often involves overcoming obstacles, doubts, and setbacks. Nevertheless, the belief that enlightenment is within everybody's reach underscores the idea that the potential for spiritual growth and realization is a universal aspect of the human experience.

8.24 Greatest Blessings

The discourse recorded in Sutta Nipata (SN-2.4), and popularly known as the Mahāmangala sutta was preached by the Buddha at Jetavana vihara as an answer to a question asked by Deva as to which things in this world could truly be considered blessings. In this discourse, the

Buddha describes 'Blessings' that are wholesome personal pursuits or attainments, identified in a progressive manner from the mundane to the ultimate spiritual goal [80]. The views expressed by the Buddha in Mahamangal sutta are the masterpiece of practical wisdom. It is the rewarding text for the wholesome shaping of complex human civilization. It is true to say that the appeal of the sutta is universal. It is just as valuable to non-Buddhists, valuable in fact for all people at all times. The sutta describes thirty-eight blessings in ten sections as below:

Section-1: (1) Not associating with fools, (2) Associating with the wise, (3) Expressing respect to those worthy of respect;

Section-2: (4) Living in an amenable location, (5) Having meritorious deeds in one's past, (6) One's self directed well;

Section-3: (7) Learnedness, (8) Artfulness, (9) Self-discipline (10) Well-spoken words;

Section-4: (11) Support father & mother, (12) Cherishing one's children, (13) Cherishing one's spouse, (14) Peaceful occupations;

Section-5: (15) Generosity, (16) Dhamma practice, (17) Caring for extended family, (18) Blameless action;

Section-6: (19) Avoiding evil and abstaining, (20) Not drinking intoxicants, (21) Non-recklessness in the Dhamma;

Section-7: (22) Right reverence, (23) Humility, (24) Contentment, (25) Gratitude, (26) Listening regularly to Dhamma;

Section-8: (27) Patience, (28) Be easily admonished, (29) sight of the monk (Bhikkhu), (30) Regular discussion of the Dhamma;

Section-9: (31) Practising Austerities, (32) Practising the Brahma-faring, (33) Seeing the four Noble truths, (34) Attainment of Nibbana;

Section-10: (35) Mind free of worldly vicissitudes, (36) Sorrowlessness, (37) Free of subtle defilements, and (38) Blissful mind.

These are the greatest blessings and those who thus abide, ever remain invincible and establish themselves in happiness.

In a nutshell, a single verse of Dhammapada records that all the Buddhas of past, present and future, preach the suffering humanity to "Discard all that is immoral, what should not be done; Take in what is moral by sorting out and achieve this by controlling one's thoughts, that is the doctrine [69].

"Sabbapāpassa akaraṇaṃ, kusalassa upasampadā; Sacitta pariyo dapanaṃ, etaṃ Buddhāna sānsanaṃ."

Chapter 9
Conclusion

"I like the religion that teaches Liberty, Equality and Fraternity."

– Dr. B. R. Ambedkar

The mindfulness meditation based on the Satipaṭṭhāna and Ichinen sanzen are two different teachings from different spiritual traditions that is Theravada and Mahayana Buddhism respectively. It is difficult to make a direct comparison in between these two practices. However, practically achievable objectives of both of the teachings can be discussed with reference to the meditative practices and the outcome of the meditative practice. This book has envisaged to critically analyze this aspect. Initially general aspects of both the practices have been discussed in introduction.

The Mahāsatipaṭṭhānā sutta is a core teaching of Buddhism that focuses on mindfulness meditation. It presents a framework for developing awareness of the body, feelings, mind, and phenomena. Within this framework, there are 84,000 Dhammakkhandha or "mental factors" that can be observed and analyzed through the practice of Dhammanupassana or "mindfulness of phenomena." These factors are categorized into four main groups: feeling, perception, mental formations, and consciousness. The goal of this practice is to develop insight into the nature of reality and to cultivate wisdom and compassion. Mahāsatipaṭṭhānā sutta is a foundational teaching that provides instructions on how to practice mindfulness meditation. The practical objectives of the Mahāsatipaṭṭhānā sutta include:

1. Developing awareness and concentration: Through the practice of mindfulness meditation, practitioners can develop greater awareness of their thoughts, emotions, and physical sensations. This can lead to greater concentration and focus in daily life.

2. Overcoming negative mental states: Through the practice of mindfulness meditation, practitioners can learn to observe and overcome negative mental states such as anger, greed, and delusion. This can lead to greater inner peace and happiness.

3. Cultivating insight and wisdom: The Mahāsatipaṭṭhāna sutta emphasizes the importance of developing insight into the true nature of reality. By observing the impermanence, unsatisfactoriness, and non-self nature of all phenomena, practitioners can develop wisdom and insight into the true causes of suffering.

4. Bringing the mind to the experience of exuberant joy, delight (pīti), happiness (sukha), one pointedness (ekaggatā) and equanimity (upekkhā) as the sequential rewards of the first four material jhana.

5. Evolution of mindfulness further for the four supermundane, immaterial jhana for the experience of the infinite space, consciousness, nothingness and the state of neither perception nor nonperception which ultimately merge with the cessation of the suffering.

Achieving the practical objectives of cultivation of transcendental wisdom through the step-wise directions of the Buddha in the Mahāsatipaṭṭhāna sutta requires dedication and practice. However, many practitioners have found that these teachings provide practical tools and techniques for overcoming suffering and achieving greater peace and happiness in life. Ultimately, the achievability of these objectives depends on the individual's commitment to their practice and their willingness to cultivate the qualities necessary for spiritual growth.

On the other hand, Ichinen sanzen is a teaching from the Nichiren school of Buddhism that emphasizes the interconnectedness of all things. It describes the universe as consisting of 3,000 realms or "realms of existence," which are divided into the ten worlds of hell, hunger, animality, anger, humanity, heaven, learning, realization, bodhisattva, and Buddhahood. Each of these worlds represents a different state of consciousness or level of spiritual development. The practice of Ichinen sanzen involves chanting the phrase "Nam- myoho-renge-kyo," which is believed to connect the practitioner with the fundamental law of the universe and to enable them to manifest their highest potential. It has practical objectives that are intended to help practitioners achieve a state of enlightenment and lead a fulfilling life. Some of the practical objectives of Ichinen sanzen:

1. Cultivating self-awareness: By understanding that everything is a reflection of our mind, we can become more self-aware and identify our own negative tendencies and attachments. This self-awareness can help us to overcome our limitations and achieve our goals.

2. Developing positive attitudes: The concept of Ichinen sanzen emphasizes the importance of developing positive attitudes, such as compassion, gratitude, and wisdom. By cultivating these attitudes, we can create a positive outlook on life and attract positive experiences.

3. Overcoming obstacles: The concept of Ichinen sanzen teaches that all obstacles and challenges are ultimately rooted in our own minds. By acknowledging this and working to overcome our own limitations, we can overcome any obstacle that comes our way.

4. Achieving inner peace: By understanding that our mind is the source of our suffering, we can work to eliminate negative thoughts and emotions and achieve a state of inner peace. This can lead to greater happiness, fulfilment, and a deeper sense of purpose in life.

Overall, the practical objectives of Ichinen sanzen are centered around the idea that we have the power to create our own reality through our thoughts and actions. By cultivating positive attitudes, overcoming obstacles, and achieving inner peace, we can live a more fulfilling and meaningful life. However, the practice of the Ichinen sanzen is not actuating the process of the purification of the mind to establish the bliss of wisdom and enlightenment.

To understand both the practices in profile this book discusses the details of the fundamental factors of Ichinen sanzen that construct 3,000 realms. The factors of the ten worlds, extended ten worlds, ten factors and three realms of existence were routed through the critical analysis as per the directives of the Buddha as a test of the truth. For this purpose, the conceptual design was questioned for the soundness and credibility of the concept. It was also discussed towards achievement of the objectives visa-vis the practical limitations of the human mind to fulfil the goals of the practice.

Satipaṭṭhānā practice of meditation was also subjected to the critical analysis and subjected to the similar scrutiny of the conceptual design of 84,000 Dhammakkhandha. Five divisions of Dhammanupassana that is Nivaraṇā dhamma, Khandha, Āyatana dhamma were analysed in details to explore the soundness and credibility of the concept. Detailed breakdown of the Āyatana to 120 worlds of six sense bases and the calculations of 3,000 Dhammakkhandha. To make it easier to handle the concept of the 3,000 realms and 3,000 dhammakkhandha, discussion of 84,000 Dhammakkhandha has also been segregated in two parts. In the second part of the 3,000 dhammakkhandha were further amalgamated with the two integral divisions of the foundation of mindfulness that is bojjhaṅga and saccha to reach the final calculation of 84,000 Dhammakkhandha.

Setting the foundation in the first five chapters of the book then the author tried to correlate the concept of 3,000 realms with 3,000 Dhammakkhandha visa-vis 84,000 Dhammakkhandha in the practice of the cultivation of insight and wisdom.

This book has specific objective to explore the science behind the process of cultivation of the happiness, peace, insight, and enlightenment. Hence a separate chapter on the Science of Happiness, Peace and Enlightenment has been designed and presented. The interplay of all the factors of the Dhamma aggregates reveals the interconnectedness of all the phenomena and its psycho- cosmic topography on the path and in the process of enlightenment. On the path of mindfulness and insight there are great obstacles, challenges that obstruct the seeker. However, there are many supporting mental attitudes which motivates and promote the seeker of truth on the path. Some of these adversaries and promoting attitudes have been enlisted.

The author wished to talk his heart out by putting his thought process forefront to his readers. Though he had a clear idea in his mind to put forth his revelation and analysis of '3,000 realms with respect to 84,000 Dhammakkhandha', he was a bit reluctant to do so thinking that it would be an act of hurting the sentiments of the Buddhist people by taking up such issue for scrutiny and analysis. While entering in the depth of the realization of the satipaṭṭhānā, it was more and more convincing for him that the clustering of the khandha and the various Dhamma makes the Dhammakkhandha or Dhamma aggregates which are expressed on the body and mind. It was not just talk the talk, but walks the walk in true sense. While exploring the 84,000 dhammakkhandha, my thoughts were exploring the, "3,000 realms in a single moment of life". Both the philosophies have the same goal of attainment of enlightenment. However, the means have been drastically deviated to achieve the objective of enlightenment. It was then planned to address the whole issue of the 84,000 Dhammakkhandha in a systematic way by evaluation of the idea with the review of the available literature and associating and assessing the analysis in the light of the present-day information.

84,000 in the form of dhamma, dhammakkhandha or the dhamma hooks have been projected in the legend of King Ashoka, where much more boldly reiterated records have been given. Writers of the legend of

Ashoka even go further in mentioning that this act of construction of the 84,000 stupa and viharas by Ashoka, based on the available information of the Dhammakkhandha, the emperors got the sovereign recognition as the 'Dhammasoka'. The author wished to expand and delineate the view of all these historical records with more satisfactory analysis. The matter shall now be seen through the four important records that we came across in the review.

1. Theravada record of Theragatha and Attakatha,

2. Mahayana record of the 84,000 Hooks,

3. Sarvastivada record of Dharmaskandha and Arahat's progress and

4. The 84,000 iterations in Buddhist Meditation.

5. 3,000 realms in a single moment of life.

Theravada Record: Ven. Ananda's statement in Theragatha, would be perfectly true to have total 84,000 discourses of the Buddha and other monks. However, the Theravada records put to rigorous scrutiny and analysis by many Buddhists thinkers and writers, the outcome of the scrutiny could not resolve the issue with full proof. It is also a matter of debate, whether all the discourses of the Buddha given in his preachings for 45 long years have really been recorded in its completeness or there had been additions and deletions in them during the period of time. It is also an issue whether the total discourses of the Buddha could be referred to as Dhammakkhandha.

Mahayana Record: Mahayana in Zen Buddhism described the 84,000, as a mind of 84,000 sharp hooks, walking through a very tight corridor of the individual person's present consciousness field. These hooks, all in number more than you can ever keep count of at any given moment, and all created by your every desire since beginning less time of countless births you cannot recall in your ordinary state of mind. This explanation seems to go hand in hand with the progressive realization of Satipaṭṭhāna meditator. Having now become aware of the 84,000 Dhammakkhandha of Buddhism through the scrutiny and analysis of Mahasatipaṭṭhāna

Sutta, one can rightly fit the 84,000 Dhammakkhandha as the sharp hooks passing through the field of consciousness. So, the Zen Buddhism's way of looking towards the figure 84,000 as the mind of 84,000 sharp hooks seems to be plausible and progressive for the realization of the goal of enlightenment. It does not demand the knowledge of the whole canon for the achievement of the goal.

Sarvastivada Record: A brief but a substantial and clear reference of the Dharmaskandha, "Aggregate of Dhamma" in the Sarvastivadin Abhidharma in the second text of Sarvastivada doctrine shows the concern of the Dharmaskandha with the stages of the Arahat's progress. Unshakable deliverance of the mind is the highest goal in the Buddha's doctrine. Here, deliverance means the freeing of the mind from all aggregates through a steadfast practice of meditation on the four foundations of mindfulness and the comprehensive structure of the Mahāsatipaṭṭhānā sutta seems to be remarkably true to its capacity.

In all the above three references, the examples are only associated with the meditation practice, may it be 84,000 dhamma hooks in Zen meditation or the progressive stages of Arahat ideal as per Sarvastivada 84,000 Dhammakkhandha or the process of the repetition of a sequence of 84,000 iterations in meditation practice. If we refer the Tharagatha and Therigatha statements of the enlightened venerable monks and venerable nuns in the form of verses, we would come across ample examples of the realization of the Nibbana, more through the meditative practices and much less through the knowledge of entire Tipitaka.

Ven. Ananda who through his narration of 84,000 dhamma in Theragatha, opens the issue of the 84,000 total Dhamma. The brief story of the Ven. Ananda, cousin brother and the personal attendant of the Buddha shall be quoted here. Ven. Ananda joined the Sangha when he was a child. Among the disciples of the Buddha, he had the most retentive memory. However, despite his long association with and close proximity to the Buddha, Ven. Ananda was only a stream-winner prior to the Buddha's Mahaparinibbāna. When Ven. Mahakassapa, as a leader, chose five hundred Arahat bhikkhus to participate in the first Buddhist council, held soon after the Mahaparinibbana of the Buddha, Ven. Ananda was not selected though Ven. Mahakassapa was aware of his strong point, especially his memory of the discourses given by the Buddha. That was a great blow to Ven. Ananda, but he was not discouraged. At night before the conclave, he practiced hard, pondered deeply, let down everything for one entire night. He practiced four foundations of mindfulness. As his mindfulness was pure, sharp and powerful, he perceived that each part of his body, each tiny physical movement, feeling, perception, thought and even consciousness itself is impermanent, unsatisfactory and without self. At dawn, as he was beginning to lie down, he lifted his foot. In that instant he reached enlightenment. The story of Ven. Ananda does not necessitate the prerequisite of the knowledge of complete Tipitaka in the form of its 84,000 Dhamma for the attainment of enlightenment.

3,000 Realms: In these conclusive remarks, one of the most important parts is the 3,000 realms in a single moment of life. The author has been fascinated by this extraordinary feat of human mind to see the reality of the worldly phenomena in a single moment of a thought. However, he has been led to an impasse at this complex cross-road of realms verses dhamma aggregates conceptual framework. As he tried to delve in the depth of the conceptual framework, he found it more and more challenging to practically work on the perception of the phenomenal reality with the concept of 3,000 realms. The Buddha has emphasized the perception of sense organ-based framework of reality over the mystical framework. Hence, author is inclined towards the comprehensive structure of the Mahāsatipaṭṭhānā sutta based conceptual framework of 3,000 realms for the perception of the reality of the phenomenal world.

Author is quite aware that his critical enquiry and analysis of the 3,000 realms and its relativity with 84,000 dhamma aggregate will perhaps be strongly objected by many. His sincere efforts are only to put forth the conceptual design and framework of the wisdom and enlightenment as propounded by the Buddha in the one and only path, "Ekayano Maggo" of the four foundations of mindfulness which is well proved on the framework of the body and mind since the passage of centuries. However, the author is leaving it to the wise readers to contemplate and draw their own appropriate conclusions and all such conclusions are not intended by the author.

Final Analysis: Satipaṭṭānā is the one and only way leading to the correct path and final emancipation. Mindfulness or awareness is a non-physical or psychological capacity that forms a vital part in practice. The Buddha has primarily addressed the Mahāsatipaṭṭhānā sutta to the community of bhikkus, monks and nuns who have dedicated their lives to spiritual practice. However, Ven. Bhante Gunaratana, in his book-"A critical analysis of the Jhanas in Theravada Buddhist meditation," [64], writes that the practice of contemplation of the four foundations-mindfulness of the body, feelings, mind and Dhamma (mind contents) is recommended for people at every stage of the spiritual path. Buddha goes on to explain: everyone - trainee aspirants who have recently introduced to the way, monks and nuns, advanced meditators and even arahats who have already reached the goal of liberation from suffering, "should be exhorted, settled and established in the development of these four foundations of mindfulness.

An aspirant must wisely explore, examine and scrutinize all the Dhammas i.e. all the worldly phenomena with bare attention, mindfully applying 'sati', without application of conceptual ways to understand real nature of the phenomena without any distortions; without any prejudices; without any responses or feedbacks to what one perceives. All that we experience are events that arise and pass away in a moment, without a time lag. It is a mental condition attempting to disguise itself as a solid object or a thing that subsists independently, outside of the I, me and mine. Mindfulness is a straightforward authority, a defensive cover and refuge for the mind. The role it plays in the conversion from unawareness to awareness depends on the condition of mind.

The way is clear; "Ekayano Maggo", the One and only way or the direct path is open for us, and when we have turned out to be as calm, as pure, as sensible, as concerned, and as impeccably self-controlled as an Arhat, then shall we recognize, then shall we comprehend 'Nibbana'.

To conclude this book, it would be fitting to include a poem, 'Journey to Nibbana,' that highlights the significance of the eight jhānas, leading to the ultimate attainment of enlightenment.

Poem on Jhana and its Attainments

Journey to Nibbana

Unshakable trust in three worthy Jewels,
In secluded silence, noble path unveils.
Every breath, a labyrinth of reality unfolds;
Where rejoice and pleasure forever beholds.

A sense of separation from worldly strife
Fills with gladness, rapture-a peaceful life.
Causal law illuminates, irradicates doubts;
Extinguishing hindrances, insight sprouts.

Serene, calm heart, like still alpine lake,
Reflections clear, without any more shake.
Freedom from remorse sets joy, happiness;
Confidence, faith help deepen mindfulness.

Equanimity's balance, noble middle path,
Without aversion-attachment's aftermath.
One pointed mind in ever-happy state lives;
As wisdom's insight gently heart receives.

Beyond pleasure and pain, a tranquil mind,
Mindfulness shines like radiant sun's kind.
Neither joy nor sorrow in equanimous sight;
Observer, shadows' shade becomes the light.

Boundaries dissolve like a morning mist;
Mind freely expands into an endless bliss.
No beginning, no end-just vast expanse,
There freedom's essence takes its stance.

World within, without-just a mirror's gaze;
Consciousness shines, clears boundless haze.
Seamless nonduality flows in unity's stream;
Equanimity reigns, filling up mind to brim.

In depths of nothingness, a mystery lies,
Insight see-through, awakening the wise.
No form, no thought; voidness prevails;
Here essence of truth in stillness dwells.

Beyond inner duality, vast domain sublime,
Where mind transcends all space and time.
Unconditioned, unbecoming-ultimate goal;
Enlightenment burns I, me, mine, and soul.

Such is voidness and bliss of Nibbana,
Full-bloomed lotus in mud of Samsara.
Suffering ceases without fuel and fire,
Freeing mind from all bonds of desire.

In this sweet liberation, all bonds break;
Craving and nescience find no stakes.
Mind stainless, impartial in natural state
Reflects Dhamma through gateless gate.

In timeless silence, pure mind finds a home,
Eternal universe beyond this material dome.

Dr. Vinod D. Rangari alias **Suddhadhamma**

Selected Bibliography

1. Kalama Sutta: The Buddha's Charter of free Inquiry, translated from the pali by Soma Thera. Access to Insight (BCBS Edition), 30 Nov., 2013,

2. Gethin, R., *The Foundations of Buddhism*. Oxford University Press, 1998.

3. Melford, A. (2006). *Theravada Buddhism: Continuity, Diversity, and Identity*. Routledge.

4. Pali Tipitaka-Mahāsatipaṭṭhānā Sutta: The Great Discourse on the establishing of Awareness, Vipassana Research Institute, Dhamma Giri, Igatpuri. http://www.tipitaka.org/stp-pali-eng-parallel.

5. Lopez, D. S., *The Story of Buddhism: A Concise Guide to its History & Teachings*. HarperOne, 2004.

6. Williams, P., *Mahayana Buddhism: The Doctrinal Foundations*. Routledge, 2009.

7. Suzuki, D. T., *Zen Mind, Beginner's Mind*. Weatherhill, 1970.

8. Kapleau, P., *The Three Pillars of Zen*. Anchor Books, 1989.

9. Senzaki, N.' *The Zen Teaching of Bodhidharma*. New York: Numata Center for Buddhist Translation and Research, 1960.

10. The mind of 84,000 hooks|UnbornMind Zen (https://unbornmind.com/2015/03/14/the-mind-of-84,000-hooks/).

11. Bechert, H., *The Historical Buddha: The Times, Life, and Teachings of the Founder of Buddhism*. Motilal Banarsidass Publishers, 1996.

12. Strong, J. S., *The Experience of Buddhism: Sources and Interpretations*. Wadsworth Publishing, 2008.

13. Dalai Lama, *The Art of Happiness: A Handbook for Living.* Riverhead Books, 1997.

14. Gyatso, T., *The Essence of the Heart Sutra: The Dalai Lama's Heart Sutra Teachings.* Snow Lion Publications, 2002.

15. Chögyam Trungpa, *The Myth of Freedom and the Way of Meditation.* Boston: Shambhala, 2000.

16. Nichiren, *The Writings of Nichiren Daishonin.* Vol. 1 & 2. Translated by The Soka Gakkai. Tokyo: Soka Gakkai Publications, 1999.

17. Mochizuki, T., *Nichiren Buddhism and the Soka Gakkai: A Religion in Transition.* New York: Oxford University Press, 2009.

18. Soka Gakkai International, Buddhism in action for Peace. http://www.sgi.org/about-us/buddhism-in-daily-life/three-thousand-realms-in- a-single-moment-of-life.html.

19. The Lotus Sutra (Saddharma Pundarika Sutra). Translated by Hodous, L., *The Lotus Sutra: The Lotus of the Wonderful Law.* New York: The Buddhist Society, 1932.

20. Daisaku Ikeda, The Heart of the Lotus Sutra (Santa Monica, CA: World Tribune Press), 111, 2013.

21. Faith in Nichiren Buddhism: Guidance on Happiness and Relationship (Vol. 1, Book-1) Kindle Edition, Buddhahood Times, 2022.

22. Eugene Gallagher (Editor), Visioning New and Minority Religions: Projecting the future (Routledge Inform Series on Minority Religions and Spiritual Movements), Routledge; 1st edition 2016.

23. Susanne Matsudo-kiliani and Yukio Matsudo, Transform Your Energy - Change Your Life!: Nichiren Buddhism 3.0, Createspace Independent Pub., 2016.

24. Susanne Matsudo-kiliani and Yukio Matsudo, Change your Brainwaves, Change your Karma: Nichiren Buddhism 3.1, Createspace Independent Publishing Platform, 2017.

25. "The Object of Devotion for Observing the Mind," The Writings of Nichiren Daishonin, vol. 1, p. 356.

26. Writings of Nichiren Daishonin, Vol. 1, Sokka Gokkai, 1 Jan.,1999.

27. Buddhahood Times, Faith in Nichiren Buddhism: Guidance On Happiness & Relationship (Vol. 1, Book-1) Kindle Edition

28. Living Buddhism, May 2003 p. 24, 29.

29. The Wisdom of Buddhism, Christmas Humphreys (Editor), Michael Joseph Limited, London.

30. Three Thousand Realms in a Single Moment of Life | Soka Gakkai (global) (sokaglobal.org)

31. Skill in Questions-How Buddha Taught, Thanisaro Bhikkhu (Geoffrey DeGraff), Metta forest Monastery, Val L Ey Center, CA 92082-1409, USA.

32. Mahaparinibbana Sutta, Digha Nikaya-20.

33. Ryusho Jeffus Shonin, Ten Suchness: Equality Despite Differences: Vol. 2 (Ichinen Sanzen), Createspace Independent Pub (27 August 2018).

34. Mahāsatipaṭṭhānā Sutta: The Great Frames of Reference, translated from the Pali by Thanissaro Bhikkhu © 2000.

35. Vinod D. Rangari (Suddhadhamma), Encounter with Satipaṭṭhānā: 84,000 Dhammakkhandha of Buddhism, Embassy Books Distributors, Mumbai, 2019.

36. Ajahan Brahmavanso, Buddhist Society of Western Australia, News Letter, April, 1999.

37. Mahadukkhakkhandha Sutta, Majjhim Nikaya-141 (MN-141).

38. The Ten Soldiers of Māra, Vipassana Research Institute, Vol. 26, No. 4, 22 April, 2016.

39. Goenka, S.N., The Discourse Summaries, Vipassana Research Publications, 2000, 131.

40. Upacālā suttaṃ (Saṃyutta Nikāya, 1.168): Upacālā Sutta (SN 5:7).

41. Adittapariyaya Sutta: The Fire Sermon" (SN 35.28), translated from the Pali by Thanissaro Bhikkhu. Access to Insight (BCBS Edition), 30 Nov. 2023.

    http://www.accesstoinsight.org/tipitaka/sn/sn35/sn35.028.than.html

42. Dhammacakkappavattana Sutta (The Wheel of Law), Translation by Soma Thera, Buddhist Publication Society, Kandy, Sri Lanka.

43. Rhys Davids & Stede (1921-25), pp. 24-25, entry for Attha defines aṭṭhakathā.

44. Theragatha (1024-29), Khuddaka Nikaya, Sutta Pitaka.

45. Hazra, KL, Pali language and literature, Vol. II, D. K. Printworld Pvt. Ltd., New Delhi, 499, 1998.

46. King Asoka and Buddhism, Historical and literary studies, Edited by Anuradha Seneviratna, Buddhist Publication Society, Sri Lanka, First edition, 1998.

47. The Mind of 84,000 Hooks/Unborn mind/Zen

48. Sarah Shah, Buddhist Meditation: An Anthology of Texts from the Pali Canon, London: Routledge, 2006.

49. Diener, E. (2019). Happiness: the science of subjective well-being. In R. Biswas-Diener & E. Diener (Eds), Noba textbook series: Psychology. Champaign, IL: DEF publishers. Retrieved from http://noba.to/qnw7g32t

50. William James, The Energies of Men, Science, N.S. 25 (No. 635), 1907, 321-332.

51. Dariush Dfarhud, Maryam Malmir, and Mohammad Khanahmadi, Happiness & Health: The Biological Factors- Systematic Review Article, Iran J Public Health. 2014 Nov; 43(11): 1468-1477.

52. Robert Lustig, The Hacking of the American Mind: The Science Behind the Corporate Takeover of Our Bodies and Brains, Penguine Random House, 2017.

53. James Clear, Atomic Habits: Tiny Changes, Remarkable Results, Penguin random House, India, 2018.

54. Ashby, F.G., Issen and U. Turken, Neuropsychological theory of Positive affect and its influence on cognition, Psychol Rev., 1999.

55. Og Mandino, The Greatest Secret in the World, Bentham Books Inc, 1983.

56. *Journal of Personality and Social Psychology*, 39(6), 1161-1178, 1980.

57. Plutchik, R., *A General Psychoevolutionary Theory of Emotion.* In R. Plutchik & H. Kellerman (Eds.), Emotion: Theory, Research, and Experience (Vol. 1, pp. 3-33). New York: Academic Press, 1980.

58. Scherer, K. R., Appraisal considered as a process of multilevel sequential checking. *Appraisal Processes in Emotion: Theory, Methods, Research*, 92-120, 2001.

59. Watson, D., & Tellegen, A., Toward a consensual structure of mood. *Psychological Bulletin*, 98(2), 219-235, 1985.

60. Knuth, D. E., *The Art of Computer Programming, Volume 1: Fundamental Algorithms*. Boston: Addison-Wesley, 1997.

61. Zohar, D., & Marshall, I., *SQ: Connecting with Our Spiritual Intelligence*. New York: Bloomsbury, 2000.

62. Wilber, K., *A Theory of Everything: An Integral Vision for Business, Politics, Science, and Spirituality*. Boston: Shambhala, 2000.

63. Samaññaphala Sutta, Digha Nikaya, 2:131-32.

64. Henepola Gunaratana, A Critical Analysis of the Jhanas in Theravada Buddhist Meditation, Buddha Dharma Education Association Inc., 1980.

65. Piya Tan, Living Word of the Buddha SD, 26, 2, Buddhist Atomism, The theories of parmanu and kalāpa in post-canonical Buddhism. http://dharmafarer.googlepages.com

66. Visuddhi Magga, Part-1, Bhikkhu Dharmarakshta, Maha Bodhi Sabha, 1957.

67. Satipaṭṭhānā Sutta, Majjhim Nikaya-10 (MN-10).

68. Anagarika Dhammapala, The life and teachings of the Buddha. Gyan publishing House, 2021.

69. Dhammapada Verses-159, 160, 161, 165, 183.

70. Sir Edwin Arnold, Light of Asia, Interprint, New Delhi, 1995.

71. Encyclopedia of Buddhism (Vol.VII), W. G. Weeraratne (Ed.), The Department of Buddhist Affairs, Sri Lanka, 2006.

72. Abhiṇhapaccavekkhitabbaṭhāna Sutta, Anguttara Nikaya (AN 5.57).

73. Dalai Lama, quoted from Rigdzin Dharma.

74. Padhana Sutta, Khuddaka Nikaya, Sutta Nipāta, v. 426b–428).

75. Abhidhammattha Sangaha, A Comprehensive Manual of Abhidhamma, Editor, Bhikku Bodhi, eBook, www.pariyatti.org.

76. Thanissaro Bhikkhu (1997). '*Upaddhā Sutta*: (Half of the Holy Life) (SN 45.2),' Retrieved April 15, 2007.

77. Avijja Sutta, Anguttara Nikaya-10:61 (AN 10:61).

78. S.N. Goenka, Tikpatthana, Vipassana Vishodhan Vinyas, Dhammagiri, Nashik, India.

79. "A treatise on the Pāramīs: From the commentary to the Chariyapitaka" www.accesstoinsight.org., Retrieved 2023-09- 08.

80. Mahamangala Sutta, Khuddaka Nikaya, Sutta Nipata, 2.4 (SN-2.4).

Index

H

I